AFTER KARABAKH

After Karabakh: War, Peace, and the Forging of a New Caucasus
Copyright © 2025 by Svante E. Cornell and Damjan Krnjević Mišković

All rights reserved under the Pan-American and International Copyright Conventions. This book may not be reproduced in whole or in part, except for brief quotations embodied in critical articles or reviews, in any form or by any means, electronic or mechanical, including photocopying, recording, or by any information storage and retrieval system now known or hereinafter invented, without written permission of the publisher.

Library of Congress Control Number: 2024947161

ISBN (paperback): 978-1-963271-90-4
ISBN (Ebook): 978-1-963271-91-1

AFPC Press
American Foreign Policy Council
509 C Street NE
Washington, DC 20002

Published by Armin Lear Press, Inc.
215 W Riverside Drive, #4362
Estes Park, CO 80517

AFTER KARABAKH

War, Peace, and the Forging of a New Caucasus

Edited by
**SVANTE E. CORNELL &
DAMJAN KRNJEVIĆ MIŠKOVIĆ**

AFPC

CONTENTS

Foreword   1
    Michael Doran

Introduction: The Second Karabakh War and a
New Caucasus: The Regional Peace Dividend Playing
Out at the Card Table   9
    Damjan Krnjević Mišković and Svante E. Cornell

The Geopolitics of the Caucasus and the Road to War   23
    Svante E. Cornell

Perfect Timing and Statecraft: On the Onset of the
Second Karabakh War   53
    Damjan Krnjević Mišković

The Foreign and Security Policies of Armenia and
Azerbaijan, 1994-2020   71
    Robert M. Cutler

The Evolving Role of the West in the Armenia-
Azerbaijan Conflict   105
    Svante E. Cornell

Sitting on Two Chairs: Russia's Pragmatic, Transactional
Approach to the Karabakh Question   131
    Nikolas K. Gvosdev

Gradually, then Suddenly: The Evolution of
Türkiye's Role in the Armenia-Azerbaijan Conflict   167
    Michael A. Reynolds

Iran's Role in the Armenia-Azerbaijan Conflict   205
    Brenda Shaffer

Armenia's Pashinyan Conundrum: Implications of the
Second Karabakh War   239
    Onnik James Krikorian

No More War, Not Yet Peace: On the Second Karabakh
War and Its Aftermath   271
    Fariz Ismailzade

Military Lessons from the Second Karabakh War   295
    Niklas Nilsson

The Geopolitical Causes and Consequences of the
Second Karabakh War: Armenian Tragedy, Azerbaijani
Vindication, and Prospects for Peace   317
    Damjan Krnjević Mišković

About the Contributors   359

FOREWORD

Michael Doran

Congratulations are due to the editors and contributing authors of this book, which performs a great service to students of international politics. We now have in one volume a set of comprehensive analyses of the main dimensions of the Second Karabakh War. By producing sharp, judicious, and readable accounts, the authors, who are all internationally recognized experts in their fields, have ensured that this volume will become the standard account of the conflict.

Until now, the Second Karabakh War has attracted much less scholarly attention than it deserves. Together with the Syrian civil war, the withdrawal of the United States from Afghanistan in 2021, the Russian invasion of Ukraine in 2022, and the war that Hamas initiated against Israel, the war belongs on the list of key events and conflicts that have shaped the contours of the contemporary international system. But the other items on the above list have received far more attention, partially because regional experts are scarce, and partially because the impact of the war was not felt immediately, at least not in the United

States and Europe. Seen from Washington and EU capitals, the Second Karabakh War strikes the eye as a remote and localized conflict—one that is of little importance to the world beyond the South Caucasus.

In fact, the Second Karabakh War is a turning point in a long and complex process of great importance to the world, namely, the re-shaping of the post-Soviet world due to the decline of Russia. For almost two hundred years, Moscow has regarded the South Caucasus as its sole preserve. Since the Russo-Persian War of 1826-1828, which ended with the Treaty of Turkmenchay, Moscow has jealously guarded its primacy in the region. With the defeat of Armenia, Russia's longstanding ally, Azerbaijan announced its unambiguous rise, its arrival as a wholly independent actor strongly allied, in matters of defense, with Israel and, especially, Türkiye.

The consequences of that fact are significant. For example, the coercive techniques to which Moscow routinely resorts to force Ukraine, Georgia, and Moldova to its will are no longer available to it with respect to Azerbaijan. Under the leadership of President Ilham Aliyev, Baku has managed to raise its military to the standard of the North Atlantic Treaty Organization by developing military-to-military relationships with Türkiye and Israel. Save for the three Baltic states, how many other former Soviet states have developed their military power outside of the Collective Security Treaty Organization? How many have done so, moreover, on the watch of Russian President Vladimir Putin?

But even as he led Azerbaijan to a victory that weakened Moscow's grip on the South Caucasus, Aliyev succeeded (in sharp contrast, for example, to Georgia) in preserving cordial relations with the Russian leader. Indeed, in the Second Karabakh War, Aliyev maintained better relations with Putin than did Armenian Prime Minister Nikol Pashinyan—and this despite Yerevan's status as Moscow's treaty ally. Yerevan, the party to the conflict over Karabakh that has the most to gain from preserving Russian influence in the South Caucasus, has less influence over Putin than Baku. On this count, several insightful chapters shed great light on the complex crosscurrents in Armenian politics and Armenian-Russian (and Armenian-Iranian) relations that made Pashinyan's challenge all but impossible—and that, incidentally, convinced Armenian voters to reelect him instead of punishing him for the defeat.

When the Second Karabakh War ended in November 2020, Putin attempted to safeguard Russia's status as the holder of the balance between Baku and Yerevan. He cleverly focused his aspirations on retaining control of the Lachin Corridor. The Russian peacekeepers stationed there assured, it was thought, that Moscow would be indispensable in any future negotiation over the status of the ethnic Armenians of Karabakh. Yerevan and Baku both depended on Moscow for their territorial connection to Karabakh.

Or so it seemed. The Azerbaijani military retook Karabakh by force in a matter of hours on 19-20 September 2023, thereby erasing the rationale for stationing Russian peacekeepers on Azerbaijani soil. Thereafter, Putin had no realistic option but to withdraw the troops. If the rise of Azerbaijani military power alone was all that restrained Putin, he might have been tempted to demand, for example, that Russian forces remain in the Lachin Corridor as guarantors of a special status for the ethnic Armenians of Karabakh. If he even contemplated such a move, he no doubt dismissed the idea for fear of permanently alienating Azerbaijan—a country whose geostrategic importance in the past few years has further risen in the eyes of all the major powers with ambitions in the South Caucasus and Central Asia.

But behind Azerbaijan also stood the power of the Turkish military. Indeed, the Second Karabakh War announced the undeniable arrival of Türkiye as a major player in the South Caucasus. Nothing less than a tectonic shift in international politics—that is, the sudden rise of the Azerbaijani-Turkish alliance—makes it highly unlikely that Russia, regardless of its aspirations, will ever regain military primacy in the region. Seven months after the defeat of Armenia in 2020, Baku and Ankara signed the Shusha Declaration, a mutual defense treaty that implicitly warns Moscow to accord Baku a level of respect that it refuses to accord to any other post-Soviet state.

The implications of the Declaration extend well beyond the South Caucasus. Indeed, the text expresses, explicitly and implicitly, shared aspirations of Baku and Ankara that have the potential to alter the geopolitical landscape of Eurasia (alternatively, the Silk Road region). Five of them—three explicit and two implicit—deserve particular attention as we follow events.

First, the Shusha Declaration explicitly announces the intention of both Ankara and Baku to enlarge the Middle Corridor, the trade route between China and the European Union which runs through Central Asia, Azerbaijan, and on to Türkiye.

The impact of this aspiration on the states of Central Asia is profound. When viewed from Moscow, Azerbaijan is, in the words of Zbigniew Brzezinski, "the cork in the bottle of Central Asia." By forcing Moscow to recognize the rise of Azerbaijan, the Second Karabakh War has removed the cork. Azerbaijan now offers the Central Asian states a gateway to Europe that is controlled by neither Russia nor Iran, whose value as hosts of alternative trade routes has in any case been severely curtailed by Western sanctions. The Middle Corridor, if it indeed develops as Ankara and Baku hope, will offer Uzbekistan and Kazakhstan a lifeline to Europe that will help both to behave toward Moscow with something approaching the self-confidence and independence that now characterizes Azerbaijani policies. Indeed, as one of the book's co-editors put it in one of his contributions, Azerbaijan has become an "indispensable country for the advancement of the strategic energy and connectivity ambitions of all major outside powers in the Silk Road region—Western and non-Western alike."

Second, the Shusha Declaration also expresses the aspiration of Ankara and Baku to open what they call the Zangezur Corridor, a trade and transport passageway that, as a branch of the Middle Corridor, will connect Baku, through Armenia, to the Azerbaijani exclave of the Nakhchivan Autonomous Republic and, on from there, to Türkiye. The Turkish and Azerbaijani plans for the Zangezur Corridor alarm and provoke debates in Moscow, Yerevan, and Tehran, where the question is whether to try to block it or to shape it in ways that benefit all parties. Some Armenians and Iranians, in particular, fear that the free movement of people and goods across sovereign Armenian territory will become the first chapter in an Azerbaijani and Turkish plot to annex the southern part of Armenia to Azerbaijan. Alternatively, if Ankara and Baku succeed in assuaging these fears and completing the corridor, the resulting integration between Armenia and its neighbors could offer attractive economic benefits that hitherto would have been unthinkable. This will require agreements on customs and border control arrangements that are as efficient as possible.

Third, the Declaration applauds the intensification of pan-Turkic sentiment in Central Asia, represented, most notably, by the rise of the Organization of Turkic States. Throughout Central Asia, Turkic peoples are shedding their Soviet skins: discarding the Cyrillic alphabet, rediscovering their pre-Soviet cultural identities, and exploring the potential for some sort of heightened cooperation with their fellow Turkic peoples. The Second Karabakh War, not to mention the Azerbaijani-Turkish relationship that helped to win it, spurred on this process. Meanwhile, China, Russia, and Iran—all of whom rule over Turkic minorities who are excited by the growing bonds of affinity with their fellow Turks—are following this development with (varying degrees of) trepidation. Whether the Turkic bond will prove strong enough to shape the relations among the Central Asian states and between them and the Turkish-Azerbaijani alliance remains to be seen. But for the first time in over a century, pan-Turkism has once again emerged as a factor in the politics of the core Silk Road region.

Fourth, the Shusha Declaration lays some of the groundwork for normalization of relations between Armenia, on the one hand, and, on the other, Türkiye and Azerbaijan. To be sure, the Declaration does not call explicitly for normalized relations, but it does envision a future of "peace, friendship and good neighborliness through stability and prosperity on a regional and international scale." With Karabakh having been returned fully to Azerbaijanis sovereignty, the worst impediment to such a future has disappeared, and new vistas have emerged.

Finally, the Declaration also implicitly suggests that Türkiye, or, perhaps more accurately, the Turkish-Azerbaijani alliance, will be the main motor of the four aspirations enumerated above. Throughout the history of the Soviet Union, the suppression of pan-Turkism had been a major theme running through Moscow's policy like a bright red cord. The Kremlin saw the support of Armenian nationalism as a major tool in ensuring that Türkiye could not pursue closer political, economic, and security arrangements with its Eastern Turkic brethren. If we are asked to issue a preliminary judgment on the Second Karabakh War, we might say that it appears to be the moment when Russian policy decisively shifted. From now on, Russia, a declining power, will attempt to shape pan-Turkism rather than to fight it directly.

Russian policy may be less hostile, but it is by no means friendly to the worldview expressed in the Shusha Declaration. Nor will the Turks and the Azerbaijanis find strong support from the Chinese or the Iranians. The success of Ankara and Baku in turning their aspirations into reality, therefore, will hinge on the answers to three questions. First, will Ankara and Baku remain as strong, united, and diplomatically skillful in the coming decades as they have been over the last ten years? Second, will pan-Turkic sentiment in the relevant Central Asian states become a serious and lasting element in their international politics? And finally, whither the West? When examining American and European policy over the past decade, it is difficult if not impossible to discern a coherent Western vision of Eurasia's future and the place of the Turkish-Azerbaijani motor in it.

The success of the Turkish-Azerbaijani project, therefore, is by no means guaranteed. Many years will pass before we will be able to determine with any certainty the balance, in the Shusha Declaration, between pious aspiration and practical politics. Even as mere aspiration, however, this document, which nears the level of a formal treaty, is already influencing the direction of events. Anyone interested in understanding that direction has no place better to start their effort than by reading this book.

INTRODUCTION

The Second Karabakh War and a New Caucasus:
The Regional Peace Dividend Playing Out at
the Card Table

Damjan Krnjević Mišković and Svante E. Cornell

As editors of this volume—a post-mortem on the thirty-year territorial conflict between Armenia and Azerbaijan over Karabakh—we began planning for the book's publication about a year after the end of the 2020 war. However, the manuscript is only now going to press, more than four years later, just as an announcement was made that the text of the peace treaty had been agreed but was not yet able to be signed. Various reasons account for this interval, none of which warrant exposition—although we do wish to stress that the distinguished authors whom we commissioned to contribute individual chapters to this project are blameless for its deferment. Still, we do not believe that the delayed timing negatively affects the project's salience. Quite the contrary, in fact: subsequent events in this and neighboring theaters deepen our conviction that the outcome of the Second

Karabakh War was a watershed event in the modern history of the region. Indeed, we are even more persuaded that it represents the moment of conception of a new South Caucasus—the geopolitical and geoeconomic reverberations of which will continue to be felt far beyond this part of the world for decades to come. The ongoing fallout from the war in Gaza, including Assad's departure from Syria, and the increasing tensions between China and the United States, coupled with the onset of the present stage in the conflict over Ukraine in February 2022, has made the foregoing line of reasoning more straightforward. The imposition by the West of a sanctions and export regime against Russia in response to its renewed armed offensive deeper into Ukraine, coupled with the various sanctions regimes imposed by the UN and the West against Iran, means that the South Caucasus, in general, and Azerbaijan, in particular (for reasons of basic geography), has become indispensable in advancing—in a politically unimpeded manner—the strategic east-west (and north-south) Eurasian connectivity ambitions of all major neighboring and outside powers. This characterization is even more convincing given that Azerbaijan is now evidently the preeminent political and military power in the South Caucasus—a state of affairs that appears quite unlikely to change for a long time to come.

The historic document that ended the Second Karabakh War is, in terms of scope, more than a narrow ceasefire agreement but less than a general peace settlement. Strictly speaking, only its first article dealt with the cessation of hostilities in Karabakh. The others laid out various interconnected and concrete measures that, taken as a whole, aim towards a future predicated implicitly on the establishment of peaceful relations between two sovereign states, Armenia and Azerbaijan. Such an outcome, which subsequent events have demonstrated is not illusive yet remains elusive as of this writing (Spring 2025), is increasingly likely to serve as a catalyst for the instauration of a peace dividend—centered on optimizing the region's strategic connectivity potential—the ripened fruits of which this part of the world has not born in centuries.

The Card Table, Not the "Grand Chessboard"
Parts of the peace dividend already seem to be taking shape in ways in which at least some of the major neighboring and outside powers could find objectionable, for they appear to still cling to, or at least prefer, to envision the South Caucasus as separate from Central Asia. If they do emphasize conceptual cohesion, then they tend to view this part of the world—traditionally called Eurasia (or "core Eurasia") but better termed the "Silk Road region" or the "Trans-Caspian region"[1]—through Zbigniew Brzezinski's metaphor of the "grand chessboard."[2] We believe

---

1   See Damjan Krnjević Mišković, "On Some Conceptual Advantages of the Term 'Silk Road Region': Heralding Geopolitical and Geo-Economic Emancipation," *Baku Dialogues* 6, no. 4, Summer 2023, pp. 20-27. For an alternate moniker, see S. Frederick Starr, "In Defense of Greater Central Asia," Policy Paper, Central Asia-Caucasus Institute & Silk Road Studies Program Joint Center, September 2008.

2   Zbigniew Brzezinski, *The Grand Chessboard: American Primacy and Its Geostrategic Imperatives*, New York: Basic Books, 1997. He may have adapted the phrase from the comments of military historian Spencer Wilkinson, who was the formal respondent to Halford Mackinder's 1904 lecture: "Whereas only half a century ago statesmen played on a few squares of a chessboard of which the remainder remained empty, in the present day, the world is an enclosed chess-board, and every movement of the statesman must take account of all the squares in it. [...] Any movement which is made in one part of the world affects the whole of the international relations of the world." See Halford Mackinder, "The Geographical Pivot of History," *The Geographical Journal* 23, no. 4, April 1904, pp. 421-444 and Halford Mackinder, *Democratic Ideals and Reality: A Study in the Politics of Reconstruction*, Washington, DC: NDU Press, 1996 (1919). Cf. Hans J. Morgenthau, *Politics among Nations*, New York: Alfred A. Knopf, 1948, p. 272: "the extreme flexibility of the balance of power resulting from the utter unreliability of alliances made it imperative for all players to be cautious in their moves on the chessboard of international politics and, since risks were hard to calculate, to take as small risks as possible."

that this metaphor is outdated and misleading, for it presupposes that the Silk Road region was, is, and will remain an *object* of great power relations.

We disagree with Brzezinski's presupposition of a "chessboard," for it requires of its adherents to make an argument along the lines of "the Silk Road region is too important for the major neighboring and outside powers to allow its core states to be given the opportunity to build up and manage it on their own." In fact, the "grand chessboard" metaphor does not provide conceptual room for any substantive agency on the part of the states that actually belong to the core region, viewing them simply as pawns on the chessboard, to be moved around at will by the larger players.[3] However, we do subscribe to Brzezinski's offhand remark that the core Silk Road region has the prospect of becoming an "assertive single entity, the concrete beginnings of which are being set in motion."[4]

This last is neither to be feared nor is it likely to be stifled, for the balance of power in the Silk Road region is in the midst of a transformative shift that was at least in part sparked by the outcome of the Second Karabakh War. In making this assertion, we are hardly alone. And yet, relatively few observers of the region are today ready to admit to the possibility that this ongoing shift strategically favors the onset of home-grown integration—with both its main architects and core participants belonging to the region itself. Fewer still would suggest, as we do, that this could open the door for the region to become a fully-fledged, distinct,

---

[3] See Svante E. Cornell and S. Frederick Starr, "Chessboard No More: the Rise of Central Asia's International Agency," *Central Asia-Caucasus Analyst*, October 3, 2023.

[4] Brzezinski, *The Grand Chessboard*, p. 35.

and emancipated subject of an international order. In other words, we believe that regionally driven economic connectivity is on the way in, and that outside power agenda-setting is on the way out. While some major neighboring or outside powers are seeing their relative power decline in this part of the world, others are seeing an increase; but in the aggregate, the power of outsiders is on its way to being reduced overall. We do not see this happening in one fell swoop, and we are not suggesting that institutional arrangements akin to those of some existing regional fora are destined to be established. Rather, we envision the onset of a predominant reality in the Silk Road region consisting of a combination of formal documents and informal understandings in which no single power dominates, equilibrium (but not necessarily equidistance) is maintained, a general balance is kept, and cooperation in various fields increases with no negative impact on sovereign prerogatives.

Our alternative to the "grand chessboard" metaphor, which framed Western (and, to a lesser degree, non-Western) mainstream geopolitical thinking about the Silk Road region in the post-Cold War period (and to some extent continues to do so), is that of *a room at the center of which is a circular card table*.[5]

Think of it this way: Various players are opting to stay in their chairs; some are re-taking their seats after a break; others are coming through the door for the first time; a few just decided to get up from their chairs but seem to want to remain in the room;

---

5   The card table metaphor was first put forward publicly by one of us (Krnjević) during an online event hosted by the Central Asia-Caucasus Institute on 25 November 2021 to launch a study by Svante E. Cornell, S. Frederick Starr, and Albert Barro, "Political and Economic Reforms under President Tokayev," Silk Road Paper, November 2021, https://www.youtube.com/watch?v=EKWqRrMHrz8.

and all the while, the deck is being reshuffled and new cards will soon be dealt.

This is our mental snapshot of what the Silk Road region looks like at present.

Chess is a game played between two players, although Brzezinski imaginatively conceives of his grand chessboard as accommodating four players.[6] But at a card table, there is plenty of room for more chairs to be added smoothly, without disrupting the general flow of play. New players can join, old ones can fall by the wayside, and anyone can pretty much cash out at any time.

In addition, chess involves no hidden information. Calculating the odds and thinking ahead is important to both chess and cards; but at a card table, the ability to bluff effectively is an integral part of the game. So is making sure a player can conceal a tell while trying to uncover the respective tells of the other players.

In chess, moreover, moving is compulsory: no player may skip a turn, even when doing so is detrimental to his or her position. In contrast, some of the more complex card games, like poker, do not have this requirement. Players can check—they can choose not to make a move, draw a card, and so on. This adds layers of subtlety and complexity that correspond more closely to the reality of the way the geopolitical game is played in the Silk Road region.

Another useful layer of metaphorical complexity is the existence in some card games of what are called community cards—cards that are dealt face up and shared by all the players during the hand. Relatedly, each hand played at a card table also involves

---

[6] See Brzezinski, *The Grand Chessboard*, pp. 31-34: "Although geostrategy—the strategic management of geopolitical interests—may be compared to chess, the somewhat oval-shaped Eurasian chessboard engages not just two but several players, each possessing differing amounts of power. The key players are located on the chessboard's west, east, center, and south."

commonly agreed but potentially changing rules of the road that apply to all: minimum buy-in, ante and raising procedures, and so on. At the same time, all partnerships and alliances are temporary at a card table.

Furthermore, at a card table—depending on the game—other players and even spectators can stake fellow players. Furthermore, there are disparities in stack sizes amongst the players seated around a card table—and this can matter quite a bit. Players' stack sizes also change over time, with real consequences affecting their subsequent strategies.

In addition, starting hands are never even at a card table: we are all familiar with the expression "to play the hand you're dealt." So, in other words, equality of opportunity and notions of fairness and transparency are not concepts that can be effectively executed by players seated at the card table.

At the card table, the importance of oral declarations and announcements can also be important—decisive, even—as can be positional priority (that is, the position of players seated at the table in relation to the dealer), which also affects each player's strategy at the card table. For example, in the Texas Hold'em variant of poker, the rules dictate that some players, depending on their table position, must place compulsory bets at the start of each hand; others, again depending on table position, do not have this obligation.

In sum, the overall point of our card table metaphor is quite simple: essentially, if a player has what it takes—or if he *thinks* he does—he can pull up a chair, take a seat at the card table, and partake in the great game. And if he does not, he can pack it up—even walk out of the room. If his fortunes change and circumstances allow, he could be dealt back in. But regardless, the game goes on.

This is quite different from how the great game is played on the "grand chessboard," where, according to Brzezinski, four not precisely identified major neighboring and outside powers are the region's only truly independent players. They and they alone control the board: they and they alone are equipped with the independent agency needed to formulate strategies and tactically execute them by moving pieces on the board, including the choice to sacrifice. This is the inescapable logic of the metaphor.

Thus, while the principle of *exclusivity* lies at the heart of the grand chessboard metaphor, its opposite—*inclusivity*—lies at the heart of the card table metaphor. The game is not played just between Moscow and Washington. Astana, Baku, and Tashkent have also taken their seats, and they are being joined by their core Silk Road region neighbors, some of which play intermittently, while all remain in the room. Ankara, Beijing, Delhi, and Tehran each have chairs, alongside more obviously external players like Abu Dhabi, Athens, Baghdad, Brussels, Budapest, Berlin, Delhi, Doha, Islamabad, Jerusalem, Kabul, London, Riyadh, Rome, and Paris—on some days, at least, or for some rounds of play.

From our vantage point, we see that a new hand is presently being dealt—a clear indication that the next round of play is about to get underway. When it does, it seems increasingly likely to eventuate the autonomous geopolitical and geoeconomic development of the states that geographically belong to the core of the region itself.

The End of the Territorial Conflict Over Karabakh

Although various events that took place on either side of the Caspian and in neighboring theaters—both prior to and in the wake of the Second Karabakh War—have contributed to the latest reshuffling of the cards, we believe that the Second Karabakh War symbolizes the moment when this reshuffling began to be understood as being possible to undertake in practice: when the cards for a new hand to be dealt could be set in motion, as it were. The Second Karabakh War thus represents the moment of conception of a new South Caucasus and, indeed, of a new Silk Road region.

But the moment of conception is not the same as viability, much less birth—to speak nothing of growth, nurture, development, maturity, and so on. One of the questions this raises concerns the actual end of the territorial conflict over Karabakh between Armenia and Azerbaijan.

Strictly speaking, it has not yet ended. Formally, one can say that it will not come to an end until a legally binding peace agreement is signed and ratified by both Baku and Yerevan. But for all *political* intents and purposes, the territorial conflict over Karabakh seems pretty much over. Still, the question needs to be asked: when did the territorial conflict over Karabakh between Armenia and Azerbaijan end?

Was it when Azerbaijan won the war under the terms enshrined in a tripartite statement signed by Armenian Prime Minister Nikol Pashinyan, Azerbaijani President Ilham Aliyev, and Russian President Vladimir Putin on 10 November 2020—a document that, after all, makes no provision for any consideration of Karabakh outside Azerbaijan's constitutional framework?

Or did it end later? One can point to the Prague document, which was the written outcome of a meeting between Aliyev, Pashinyan, EU Council President Charles Michel, and French President Emmanuel Macron that took place on the margins of the inaugural meeting of the European Political Community (EPC) on 6 October 2022, which "confirmed" a commitment to "recognize each other's territorial integrity and sovereignty?"

Or was it the more explicit Grenada document, which was the outcome of a meeting between Pashinyan (again, on the margins of the EPC Summit) on 5 October 2023 with Michel, Macron, and German Chancellor Olaf Scholz that reaffirmed a "commit[ment] to all efforts directed towards the normalization of relations between Armenia and Azerbaijan, based on mutual recognition of sovereignty, inviolability of borders and territorial integrity of Armenia (29.800 km^2) and Azerbaijan (86.600 km^2)," as mentioned in President Michel's statements of 14 May and 15 July 2023?

Or was it the direct, un-mediated agreement between Armenia and Azerbaijan, made public on 7 December 2023, for the former to support the latter's bid to host COP29 in Baku in November 2024, signaling the onset of a "no Russia, no West" approach to the peace talks?

Or did the territorial conflict over Karabakh between Armenia and Azerbaijan come to an end with the text of the 22 February 2022 Declaration on Allied Interaction signed by Aliyev and Putin? After all, this document unambiguously commits Russia to respect—for the first time ever[7]—the "independence,

---

7   Heydar Isayev and Joshua Kucera, "Ahead of Ukraine Invasion, Azerbaijan and Russia Cement 'Alliance'," *Eurasianet*, February 24, 2022: "Russia has never, at the top level, officially and explicitly confirmed Azerbaijan's territorial integrity on any occasion, not even in multilateral contexts," Kamal Makili-Aliyev, an Azerbaijani expert on international law, told Eurasianet. "This is why the declaration is important."

state sovereignty, territorial integrity, and inviolability of the state borders of [Azerbaijan], as well as adhere […] to the principles of non-interference in [its] internal affairs, equality and mutual benefit, peaceful settlement of disputes, and non-use of force or threat of force." This formulation—the significance of which is generally underappreciated—may help to explain three crucial postwar developments that revolve around the role of Russian peacekeepers present in parts of the former Nagorno-Karabakh Autonomous Oblast since the end of the Second Karabakh War: one, their conduct during the Lachin Corridor crisis that began in December 2022; two, their bearing during and after Azerbaijan's 19-20 September 2023 "antiterrorist measure;" and three, the choice to withdraw completely from sovereign Azerbaijani lands as agreed by Baku and Moscow (with seemingly no involvement by Yerevan) and made public on 17 April 2024. The outcome of the withdrawal announcement—coupled with one made the next day indicating that the Russian-Turkish Joint Monitoring Center would cease to function—marks the first time that Baku "enjoys complete sovereignty over all its territories without any foreign troops present."[8]

On the basis of the foregoing, it seems to us that the safest date marking the end of the territorial conflict over Karabakh is this last one, for it allows one to state unequivocally that de jure and de facto realities have fully achieved *political* congruence, after having been in effectual opposition for more than three decades. The start of a border demarcation process between the two countries, complete with the agreed erection of the first border

---

8   Vasif Huseynov, "Opinion: Russian withdrawal from Karabakh allows Azerbaijan to strengthen its ties with its Turkic 'family,'" commonspace.eu, April 28, 2024. We can go further still: Azerbaijan is the only Eastern Partnership country that "enjoys complete sovereignty over all its territories without any foreign troops present."

markers in late April 2024, speaks to this point. The signing and ratification of a peace agreement between Armenia and Azerbaijan would formally enshrine this congruence whilst endowing it with a sense of permanence. This would, as noted above, serve as a catalyst for the instauration of a peace dividend, centered on optimizing the region's strategic connectivity potential (strictly speaking, this process seems already to be underway, albeit without the inclusion of one route that should traverse through a sliver of sovereign Armenian territory, which does not affect the overall viability of what is called, in one prevailing concept, the Middle Corridor). Such a peace agreement would also remove a critical prerequisite for Ankara and Yerevan to come to terms on normalizing their own bilateral relations. The foregoing would, moreover, go a long way toward ending Armenia's regional isolation. Perhaps it might mitigate the negative effects of the West's encouragement—spearheaded by France and the United States—of Pashinyan to diversify his country's political, economic, and security dependence on Russia and Iran, an encouragement that is unlikely to be backed with hard power and which could easily turn out to be too little, too late. Ending Armenia's regional isolation could even be accomplished with the active support of Azerbaijan, which would have an interest in limiting such fallout. This would be entirely consistent with how the game is now quite likely to be played at the card table.

Benefiting from the Future

Conceivably, then, the signing and ratification of a peace agreement between Armenia and Azerbaijan would provide the EU with one less reason to consider the South Caucasus as part of what the Union's now former chief diplomat called its "ring of fire" neighborhood, and what Brzezinski had characterized nearly 30 years earlier as the "global zone of percolating violence" and the "Eurasian Balkans."⁹

Unlike perhaps in earlier times, today such and similar views about this part of the world confuse a few nearby trees for the forest. Should these misperceptions linger for much longer, geopolitical and geoeconomic malpractice by those who hold them could be the result. No one with a stake in the success of the Silk Road region can afford to misdiagnose the overriding reality that, taken as a whole, this part of the world is on the cusp of becoming a relatively tranquil and predictable place—particularly when compared to neighboring regions. This assessment should not result in complacency, of course: like anywhere else, circumstances can change for the worse. But postures and policies that look to the entirety of the Silk Road region's future should be formulated with this prevailing trajectory in mind. Especially since the locals seem to have developed effective home-grown firefighting and rebuilding capabilities.

As we noted above, the principle of inclusivity lies at the heart of the card table metaphor, which means that all outside players remain more than welcome to stay in the room, take their seats, and participate in the next round of play—so long as they accept in both theory and practice that the rules of the game are not theirs to either set or revise anymore. For quite a few of these external actors, this would constitute a heretofore largely untried approach. To succeed, they will need to show a degree

---

9   Josep Borrell, "The World Confronted by Wars," speech at Oxford University, May 3, 2024; Brzezinski, *The Grand Chessboard*, pp. 53, 123.

of restraint, humility, and respect that has been traditionally exhibited in a limited manner towards the countries that make up the core Silk Road region. Perhaps this explains why the peace dividend has taken so long to begin bearing fruit.

As things now stand, local suspicions regarding the preferences and aspirations of the various outsiders remain very much alive. These can be mitigated, and perhaps even removed, in the time ahead largely in proportion to the extent that these same outsiders choose to temper their speeches and deeds in such a way as to harmonize them with those now prevalent in the Silk Road region itself. For most external, that is, foreign players, this will be easier said than done. Those for whom more interest-based, transactional approaches represent their diplomatic norm could be said to have an advantage over those habituated to pursue different ones. But this does not have to be a decisive hindrance. Coming to the card table in good faith would be a suitable beginning, especially when combined with a staunch commitment to abide by local conditions and consequent realities—to know and play by the rules consistently and reliably. This kind of conduct will largely determine how each foreign player will be received by those players who, by right of geography, are permanently seated around the card table. Surely, this will have a direct strategic impact on how each player—local and foreign alike—can benefit from the flagship east-west economic connectivity project that represents the backbone of the new Silk Road region in general, and the new Caucasus in particular, and which was brought to life due in no small measure to the outcome of the Second Karabakh War.

THE GEOPOLITICS OF THE CAUCASUS AND THE ROAD TO WAR

Svante E. Cornell

The escalation to war between Armenia and Azerbaijan in 2020 was in many ways a foregone conclusion. While many outside observers were comfortable in the understanding of the conflict as "frozen," to those who looked deeper momentous changes had taken place during the three decades after the May 1994 ceasefire. Changes on several levels—the global, regional, and domestic— indicated that the conflict would escalate to war sooner or later. These processes culminated in 2020, largely as a result of an ill-advised Armenian overreach that triggered Azerbaijan's decision to deal with the problem through military force.

The Origins of the Geopolitics of the Armenia-Azerbaijan Conflict

When the Soviet Union collapsed, the geopolitical importance of the South Caucasus was not immediately obvious to Western powers. Expertise on the region was weak; it appeared to be a hopeless quagmire of warring ethnic groups, and there was a strong tendency to consider the region a part of Russia's exclusive backyard. Moreover, the conflicts in the Caucasus took place at a time when issues considered to be much more pressing were on the Western agenda. These included the Gulf War, the wars in the Balkans (geographically much closer to the heart of Europe), and the management of Russia's transition (not least the fate of Russia's nuclear arsenal).

This was the context when the Armenia-Azerbaijan conflict reached a halt in 1994. The conflict had been the first territorial issue to emerge when Mikhail Gorbachev began to reform the Soviet Union in 1986-1987. This was a logical result of the complicated and in many ways illogical territorial settlement that Soviet leaders had imposed upon Armenians and Azerbaijanis in the 1920s. The Soviet Union was organized as an asymmetric ethnic-based federation: in other words, the Union was divided into ethnic-based national homelands. These had different levels of self-rule, ranging from full Union Republics like Armenia and Azerbaijan to Autonomous Republics and Regions within Union Republics like Nagorno-Karabakh (Azerbaijan) and Abkhazia (Georgia). In principle, Soviet nationality policy allowed only one national "homeland" per ethnic group. It did not allow any self-rule for national minorities that happened to be on the wrong side of an internal border—such as Russians in Kazakhstan or Tajiks in Uzbekistan. But in the Caucasus, the Soviet leadership departed from this principle in several instances. For example, the small Ossetian people was divided into two autonomous entities, one in Russia and one in Georgia.

The early Soviet policy concerning Armenia and Azerbaijan was even more complex. Armenia and Azerbaijan were made into Union Republics when the Transcaucasian Federative Soviet Republic was abolished in 1936. The contested area of Mountainous Karabakh—with an Armenian majority—was made an autonomous region under Azerbaijani jurisdiction, without any common border with Armenia. Thus, Soviet leaders created *two* Armenian homelands in the Soviet Union. Even more perplexingly, they created two *Azerbaijani* homelands as well: the second was the Nakhchivan Autonomous Republic, separated from Azerbaijan by Armenia and bordering Iran and Türkiye. It also was placed under Azerbaijani jurisdiction. The logic behind these decisions remains untraceable; the process involved little consultation with local leaders (or populations), leaving the legitimacy of the delimitation subject to question. What was clear was that it left Armenia the loser of the Soviet delimitation, as it handed most of the contentious territories to Azerbaijan. Only the third contested territory, the southern part of Armenia known in Azerbaijan as Zangezur, was given to Armenia, thus neatly inserting a wedge between Azerbaijan and Nakhchivan.

Armenians never truly made peace with this state of affairs, and successive Armenian leaders tried and failed to contest this delimitation in the Soviet era. In the 1980s, their fortunes seemed to take a turn for the better: while Azerbaijani Soviet leader Heydar Aliyev had been a close ally of Soviet leaders Leonid Brezhnev and Yuri Andropov, Gorbachev demoted Aliyev in October 1987 while Armenian Abel Aganbegyan rose to become one of his main advisors. This set in motion growing Armenian demands for change, as well as ethnic unrest on the ground.

Toward the end of 1987 and January 1988, the first Azerbaijanis were pressured to leave Armenia.[10] By February 1988, a petition drive to unify Armenia with Nagorno-Karabakh escalated to huge demonstrations in Yerevan, and the parliament of the Autonomous Oblast officially demanded to be transferred to Armenia. Six days later, resettled Azerbaijanis from Armenia went on a rampage against Armenians in the Azerbaijani coastal city of Sumgayit—with Soviet interior ministry troops garrisoned three miles away electing not to interfere.[11] Inter-ethnic violence intensified and militia groups on both sides worked to ethnically cleanse their respective republics, a process that was completed by late 1990 (with the exception of several thousand ethnic Armenians, mostly in mixed families, that continued to live in Baku.)

Armenia found that while Gorbachev was sympathetic to their demands, he decided to maintain the status quo in fear of the potential domino effect that could result from a change of internal boundaries.[12] Armenia therefore grew increasingly anti-Soviet. Azerbaijan, by contrast, relied on the Soviet central power to maintain its rule over Nagorno-Karabakh. This seemed a fine bet at first, but it meant that Armenia developed its own governing institutions while Azerbaijan did not. It also meant that Yerevan asserted control over the various irregular armed formations that had emerged, while Baku did not start the process of building its own national army. When Soviet power collapsed, Armenia was prepared to take advantage, while Azerbaijan proved essentially

---

10 Svante E. Cornell, *Small Nations and Great Powers: Ethnopolitical Conflict in the Caucasus*, New York: Routledge, 2001, pp. 65-66.
11 Igor Nolyain, "Moscow's Initiation of the Azeri-Armenian Conflict", *Central Asian Survey* 13 no. 4, 1994, pp. 541-563.
12 Mikhail Gorbachev, "The Karabakh Explosion," *Memoirs*, New York: Doubleday, 1996, p. 334-337.

helpless. Led by a determined nationalist leadership, Armenia moved on the offensive in early 1992, at a time when Azerbaijan was led by an inept Communist leadership led by apparatchik Ayaz Mutallibov. Without Soviet forces to prevent the belligerents from clashing, the conflict escalated to war in the spring of 1992.

The Armenian side benefited greatly from the domestic preoccupations of the Azerbaijani elite. Azerbaijan's Communist government fell in May 1992. But by then, Armenians had taken the citadel city of Shusha and formed a road corridor to Karabakh by taking the Lachin region. In early 1993, Armenia conquered the province of Kelbajar, which is sandwiched between Armenia and Nagorno-Karabakh, and began moving into territories to the southeast of the disputed region. In June, a renegade Azerbaijani commander—Surat Huseynov—fielded a military coup against the nationalist government of Abulfaz Elchibey, prompting its downfall. The Armenian side did not miss the opportunity to benefit from the power vacuum in Azerbaijan, moving to conquer and ethnically cleanse the southern Azerbaijani provinces of Fizuli, Jebrail, Qubatli, and Zangilan, as well as parts of Agdam province to the east of Nagorno-Karabakh. From exile in his native Nakhchivan, Heydar Aliyev emerged to take the reins of power in Baku and managed in short order to stabilize the Government and the country. But the damage had been done, and when a ceasefire was announced in May 1994, Azerbaijan had lost Nagorno-Karabakh as well as (in whole or in part) seven provinces surrounding it.

Thus far, the process was in many ways comparable to the conflicts in former Yugoslavia. The difference lies in what happened after major hostilities ended. The conflicts in Croatia,

Bosnia-Herzegovina, North Macedonia, and to a lesser extent Kosovo all came to a form of closure, which has proven more or less lasting. But in Karabakh (as in Abkhazia, South Ossetia, and Transnistria), the conflict ended by a ceasefire regime that left the territory in legal and political limbo, leading to the unfortunate term "frozen conflict." The key difference was that Western-led involvement in the former Yugoslav conflicts was much more decisive. Nothing akin to the NATO-led Implementation Force (IFOR) or Kosovo Force (KFOR) was deployed in Nagorno-Karabakh. Uniquely, for close to three decades a major unresolved conflict prevailed where two armies were eyeball-to-eyeball across a ceasefire line not separated by a peacekeeping force.

There being no peacekeeping force and only a largely inept international effort toward conflict resolution, the notion of a frozen conflict was always erroneous because the *status quo* was not sustainable. Armenia continued to hold the occupied territories as a bargaining chip to achieve recognition of their control over Nagorno-Karabakh. But while Armenia enjoyed considerable international sympathy in the early days of the conflict, this evaporated because of its ethnic cleansing of several hundred thousand Azerbaijanis from territories that had never been disputed by Soviet or post-Soviet Armenian leaders. Furthermore, this occupation ensured that Azerbaijan saw itself as the victim of aggression, and thus never came to terms with the outcome of the war. In sum, the way the First Karabakh War ended all but guaranteed a new bout of fighting at some point in the future.

Over the years, the economic and strategic disparity between the two nations only grew, an indication that the situation that allowed Armenia to claim victory in 1994 had been truly exceptional. Armenia won the war in 1993-94 largely because Azerbaijan was collapsing into a failing state. Armenia's pre-war population was roughly three million but has shrunk precipitously as a result of mass emigration. Azerbaijan's population, by contrast, stood at close to ten million. And while Azerbaijan's GDP was only double that of Armenia in 1995, oil and gas led it at one point to be six times larger. Furthermore, the unresolved conflict resulted in the strategic isolation of Armenia from the large infrastructural projects of the region, in accordance with Azerbaijani and Turkish preferences. The reason is obvious: in pure geostrategic terms, the value of the South Caucasus is its role as a conduit between Europe and Central Asia. Armenia can be circumvented by transiting through Georgia, but Azerbaijan—bordering both Russia and Iran—is irreplaceable in the corridor. And in geo-economic terms, Azerbaijan's control over large hydrocarbon resources meant that it held a veto over the determination of export routes of Caspian oil and gas to the West, and thus essentially over the routes of energy, road, rail, and trade corridors more broadly. As a result, in the past two decades the balance of power between Armenia and Azerbaijan shifted dramatically in Azerbaijan's favor. In parallel, revanchist sentiments in Azerbaijan were growing stronger by the year; and since 2010, the incidence of violence along the ceasefire line grew in an almost linear fashion.

As the 1994 ceasefire took hold, it was clear that the conflict existed on several levels simultaneously. It was, on one hand, an intra-state conflict, pitting the ethnic-Armenian population of Nagorno-Karabakh against the government of Azerbaijan. But the conflict was never *only* about this territory: most of the protagonists as well as victims of the conflict were not residents of Mountainous Karabakh. From the beginning, it was also a conflict between two states—Armenia and Azerbaijan—with the former having a territorial claim on the latter. And finally, it was also from the start a conflict with a geopolitical dimension—at first a result of Moscow's involvement in it, something gradually complemented by Iranian, Turkish, and Western interests in it and the region.

Shifting Geopolitics of the Caucasus

Already in the early 1990s, it was clear that Russia's leadership—particularly the defense and security services—paid an inordinate amount of attention to reasserting Russian power in the South Caucasus, including through the manipulation of ethnic conflicts.[13] This effort had no parallel even in other parts of the former Soviet Union, indicating that Russian leaders saw the region as exceptionally important. Moreover, it took place at a time when Russia itself was not only weak, but dealing with serious internal problems. Between 1991 and 1994, Chechnya and Tatarstan had both declared independence, and it would have seemed natural for Russia's leadership to focus on putting its own house in order before attempting to secure its influence in the South Caucasus. But instead, Russia's leadership spent scarce resources on subduing the newly independent states of the South Caucasus. Russia quickly secured its influence over Arme-

---

13 Cornell, *Small Nations and Great Powers*, pp. 334-343, See Fiona Hill and Pamela Jewett, 'Back in the USSR': Russia's Intervention in the Internal Affairs of the Former Soviet Republics and the Implications for United States Policy Toward Russia, Cambridge, Mass: Harvard University JKF School of Government, Strengthening Democratic Institutions Project, January 1994; Thomas Goltz, "Eurasia Letter: The Hidden Russian Hand," in *Foreign Policy*, no. 92, Fall 1993.

nia through military agreements in May 1992, and in May 1993 deployed subversive efforts to topple the nationalist government of Azerbaijan. But nowhere were Russia's intentions more obvious than in Georgia, where Russia both trained North Caucasian volunteers and deployed its air force and other assets in Georgia's conflicts with South Ossetian and Abkhaz rebels.[14] Moscow also worked hard to subdue the independent-minded leadership of Eduard Shevardnadze through various subversive efforts, which succeeded in forcing Georgia to accept Russian control over its border with Türkiye and the deployment of four Russian military bases on its territory. In Azerbaijan, Russia attempted similar tactics to gain influence—among others by half-heartedly backing fringe Lezgin and Talysh separatist groups and playing favorites in Azerbaijan's domestic affairs. However, it quickly became clear that Heydar Aliyev's Azerbaijan was not easily affected by such tactics, as a result of the country's greater homogeneity, its more assertive leadership, and its hydrocarbon resources.[15]

This reflects the longstanding geopolitical importance Russia has attached to the Caucasus, which it identified in the late eighteenth century as its buffer to the Middle East. For millennia, the Caucasus has been a link—or buffer—between the Black and Caspian Sea, and thus between Europe and Asia as well as between Russia and the Middle East. In the post-Cold War era, its key value has been its location at the mouth of the east-west corridor connecting Europe with Central Asia; and simultaneously, at the intersection of Russia, Iran, and Türkiye. As a result,

---

14   Tornike Gordadze, "Russian-Georgian Relations in the 1990s", in Svante E. Cornell and S. Frederick Starr, eds., *The Guns of August 2008: Russia's War in Georgia*, Armonk: M.E. Sharpe, 2009.

15   Cornell, *Azerbaijan since Independence*, pp. 338-358 on Russian influence in Azerbaijan. See also *Small Nations and Great Powers*, pp. 343-348.

the Caucasus emerged as a key factor shaping the intersection of Europe and the Middle East. This has taken place in three related areas: in the realms of energy resources, military logistics, and civilian trade.

The contemporary development of the Caspian Sea basin's energy resources began in earnest in the mid-1990s. The successful projects, involving Western multinational companies, to develop the oil and gas resources of Azerbaijan, Kazakhstan, and Turkmenistan have proven crucial to the economic and political independence of the states of the Caucasus and Central Asia. Indeed, they were the only independent income stream that enabled these countries to consolidate their sovereignty. Specifically, the creation of the pipeline system connecting Azerbaijan's energy resources via Georgia to Türkiye and beyond provided an opportunity to develop these resources while avoiding the control of the former colonial overlord. While this primarily benefited Azerbaijani resources, it held great importance for Central Asian states as well. This infrastructure broke the Russian monopoly over the transportation of energy resources, and only after this was accomplished was China able to further shatter that monopoly through inroads into Central Asia, particularly through the Turkmenistan-China gas pipeline. The bulk of Kazakhstan's oil and Turkmenistan's gas resources have yet to come online, but the further potential of the South Caucasus to serve as a key corridor for these energy resources is very significant, in particular in the aftermath of the February 2022 onset of the Russian war in Ukraine, which has forced Kazakhstan to seek to diversify its exports through transportation routes that traverse the Caspian Sea and the Caucasus.

Secondly, the role of the South Caucasus for international security was proven in the aftermath of the 9/11 terrorist attacks. Waging a war in the heart of the Eurasian continent, thousands of miles from the closest U.S. military bases, posed enormous logistical challenges to the United States. The rapid American response, which led to the crippling of the Taliban and Al Qaeda in Afghanistan, was possible only through the introduction of U.S. military power into Afghanistan via the Caucasus and Central Asia. Because Iran was not an option and Russia provided highly restricted terms for the use of its airspace, the overwhelming majority of the overflights that supplied the U.S. forces in Central Asia transited the airspace of Georgia and Azerbaijan. A decade later, when the U.S. expanded its troop levels in Afghanistan, the Caucasus corridor ensured that America was not solely dependent upon Northern Distribution Network (NDN) land transportation routes across Russia. At least 30 percent of the overall land transit was conducted through the territories of Georgia and Azerbaijan.[16] Following the deterioration of U.S.-Russian relations since 2014, and the growing isolation of Russia since 2022, the Caucasus corridor (specifically: Georgia and Azerbaijan) will certainly be crucial to any future Western presence in Afghanistan or Central Asia—including the EU's Global Gateway initiative.

Thirdly, the Caucasus has also emerged as a crucial artery and the most efficient component of an emerging system of continental trade by land. Most east-west trade between China, India, and Europe at present is by sea and air. But land routes across Eurasia provide a third option, which is far cheaper than air travel

---

[16] Zaur Shiriyev, "NATO and the South Caucasus: The Impact of the Northern Distribution Network," in Andris Spruds and Diana Potjomkina, *Northern Distribution Network, Redefining Partnerships within NATO and Beyond*, Riga: Latvian Institute of International Affairs, 2012.

and much faster than sea routes.[17] As in the case of the NDN, the Caucasus is far from the only route, but it is the best means of assuring that neither Russia nor Iran has a monopoly on these emerging transportation and connectivity corridors. Considerable investments have already been made in port facilities in Georgia, Azerbaijan, Kazakhstan, and Turkmenistan, as well as railroads across the region. In the longer term, the stability of the South Caucasus will be a concern not just for major Western oil and gas firms, but also for Chinese and Indian interests in uninterrupted trade between Asia and Europe. Since February 2022, there has been a surge in demand for shipping along this corridor due to the West-led sanctions regime against Russia; but because of a lack of investments, a number of bottlenecks restrict the volume of trade it can carry—although strategic plans have been set in motion to overcome this sort of limitation in the years ahead.

The geopolitical role of the Caucasus has been somewhat impeded by the unresolved conflicts of the region, which as a consequence has kept some borders closed. In the past two decades, the Armenia-Azerbaijan, Armenia-Türkiye, and Russia-Georgia border have all been closed either permanently or for years at a time, while the Iran-Azerbaijan border has remained open for trade but remains dependent on the Iranian regime's caprices. Not staying at that, the unresolved conflicts of the region have served as a considerable inhibitor to economic development and foreign investment. The OSCE-led negotiations over the conflict gradually declined in intensity and frequency, it being clear to all parties that the process was leading nowhere. The outside world

---

17   S. Frederick Starr, *The New Silk Roads*, Washington: Central Asia-Caucasus Institute, 2008, https://www.silkroadstudies.org/publications/silkroad-papers-and-monographs/item/13125-the-new-silk-roads-transport-and-trade-in-greater-central-asia.html.

appeared resigned to a situation where the Armenia-Azerbaijan conflict was and would remain unresolved—akin to the Israel-Palestinian conflict or the conflict over Kashmir between India and Pakistan. But this would prove a mistaken assumption: changes on the global, regional, and domestic level would combine to lead to the renewal of war in 2020.

Global Changes

On the global level, the main shift that took place in the past decade was the erosion of the West-led "rules-based" international order. In a sense, this order did not apply to the Armenia-Azerbaijan conflict, since the Armenian occupation of Azerbaijani territory continued in violation of UN Security Council resolutions. Still, it was one of the "frozen" conflicts that came out of the dissolution of the Soviet Union, alongside those in Moldova's Transnistria and Georgia's Abkhazia and South Ossetia. The point is that in the international order set up in the wake of the end of the Cold War, the emphasis was on the primacy of multilateral institutions, diplomacy, and negotiations to resolve conflicts.

This emerging order was not devoid of challenges: Iraq's invasion of Kuwait and the wars in former Yugoslavia were important setbacks. But these landmarks ultimately reinforced the emerging order. The U.S. Operation Enduring Freedom rolled back the Iraqi invasion of Kuwait and contained Saddam Hussein's Iraq until the 2003 U.S.-led invasion that toppled the regime. As for the wars in former Yugoslavia, the civil war in Bosnia-Herzegovina at first showed the weakness of European institutions. Still, by 1995 the U.S. took a more active role in the conflict, with NATO's intervention leading to the Dayton Accords of November 1995, which brought that war to an end. In 1998, an armed conflict broke out in Kosovo, but here too, a NATO air war brought the fighting to an end and left Kosovo under a UN Security Council-backed international administration.

Armenia and Azerbaijan adapted to this order and sought to appeal to great powers and multilateral institutions to support their understanding of the conflict. Armenia sought to emphasize any indication that the West-led "rules-based" international order promoted the right of self-determination of ethnic minorities; while Azerbaijan emphasized the principle of sovereignty and territorial integrity, and the inviolability of borders of UN member states. As a doctrine of "humanitarian intervention" began to build, both similarly adapted to this: Armenia sought to emphasize the historic suffering of the Armenian people and allegations of Azerbaijani violations against Armenians before the Soviet collapse; meanwhile, Azerbaijan made a much stronger case built on the ethnic cleansing of Azerbaijanis from the territories occupied by Armenia. These dueling narratives were at their height during the Kosovo conflict, when both sides drew such parallels. The point, however, is that they adapted and related to the "rules-based" international order, upheld by Western powers and multilateral institutions.

The global order, however, began to shift at some point in the 2000s. When exactly the shift occurred is open for debate. Some will undoubtedly point to the 2003 U.S. invasion of Iraq as a key to subsequent changes: it split both NATO and the EU into two camps, and it undermined the authority of the United States when no weapons of mass destruction were found, and the invasion did not go as planned. While Iraq was indeed important, a perhaps more important turning point for this region occurred a few years later. President Putin's speech to the Munich Security Forum in February 2007 signaled Russia's break with the West. It was followed by the Western recognition of Kosovo the next year, another landmark event with global significance. It solidified the rift between Russia and the West, while also indicating a departure from key international norms. Under the doctrine of "humanitarian intervention" or "remedial secession,"[18] Western powers departed from the principle of inviolability of borders to support the declaration of independence of Kosovo from Serbia. This served as a direct trigger less than six months later for Russia's invasion of Georgia, a country that had long irked the Kremlin through its independent-minded politics, leading to a long series of efforts to undermine Georgia ever since Putin came to power in 2000.[19] Following the Western recognition of Kosovo, Russia clearly stated this would have consequences in the Caucasus. Putin told Georgian President Mikheil Saakashvili that "as for the disputed territories of Abkhazia and South Ossetia, we shall respond to [...] America and NATO, and in connection to Kosovo. What we will do will be [...] our response to them."[20] In August, Russia launched its war on Georgia at least in part as a retribution against Western actions in the Balkans.

In retrospect, this was the starting point for a new trend that would spread to other parts of the world: a great power unilater-

---

18 Jure Vidmar, "Remedial Secession in International Law," *St Antony's International Review* 6, no. 1, 2010, pp. 37-56.
19 See Svante E. Cornell and S. Frederick Starr, eds., *The Guns of August 2008: Russia's War in Georgia*, Armonk: M.E. Sharpe, 2009.
20 "Georgian Pundits Comment on Results of Putin-Saakashvili Meeting," *24 Saati*, February 28, 2008, via BBC Monitoring.

ally altering the boundaries of a UN member state—effectively, ignoring the norms and rules of international law and politics, and instead doing what it thought it could get away with. Had Western powers either tempered their ambitions with regard to Kosovo or mustered a strong response to Moscow, it is possible that what occurred in Georgia would have remained an isolated event. But Russia was successful in deflecting part of the blame on Georgia, and soon after the invasion, the Western financial crisis of Fall 2008 occurred, which must in retrospect be seen as the most significant driver of the shift that took place. The immediate effect was regional: Western sanctions on Russia proved short-lived, and by March 2009, the Obama Administration had launched its "Reset" with Russia, essentially turning the page and "agreeing to disagree" on Russia's occupation of Georgia. This provided Moscow with a sense that it had a green light to step up its pressure on Ukraine. But in parallel, the effects of the financial crisis reduced the power and influence of the West, which in turn provided new impetus for emerging or expansionist powers to challenge the West-led order.

These powers took note. For instance, Iran and China soon identified the opportunity of rekindling their imperial designs on their respective neighborhoods. Starting in 2006, Tehran took an increasingly direct role in internal Lebanese affairs, building up its proxy Hizballah as a state within a state in that country. In subsequent years, Iran also methodically built a network of militias in Iraq, as well as in Gaza, and following the Arab upheavals of 2011, ramped up its role in Syria and Yemen, supporting the Assad regime in the former and the Houthi militias in the latter, and used these proxies to wage war on Israel in October 2023.

In a similar manner, China gradually abandoned its cautious and lower-profile approach and switched to a more assertive stance following the 2008 financial crisis.[21] This could be seen in its stance toward the U.S. in bilateral affairs, but also in the attitude China adopted towards states in east and southeast Asia. The rise of Xi Jinping in 2013 saw the acceleration of this process, with China largely abandoning its cooperative approach to foreign partners, and adopting an aggressive, nationalist approach first and foremost in the South China Sea, but also in relations with other Asian and Western powers.

This shift, which led to a decline of Western influence and a rise of non-Western powers, changed the calculus for both Armenia and Azerbaijan. Before 2008, their main audience was West-led institutions, and the language they adopted was designed accordingly. After 2008, they gradually came to realize that this was increasingly irrelevant to the outcome of their conflict. Armenia visibly lost interest in the process of negotiations, instead betting on its alliance with Russia to extend its *de facto* control over Mountainous Karabakh and the other occupied territories indefinitely. Azerbaijan, for its part, shifted its foreign policy to adapt to the new reality. It lowered its emphasis on relations with the West and adopted a position of non-alignment or multi-vectoralism. Events also strengthened the growing sense in Azerbaijan that the conflict would not be resolved through negotiations and the work of multilateral organizations. If this was now a world where the threshold to use military force was being lowered, Azerbaijan would have to look to a military option to resolve the conflict. But

---

21 Michael D. Swaine, "Perceptions of an Assertive China," *China Leadership Monitor*, May 3, 2010.

this, in turn, would not be possible unless events at the regional and domestic level permitted it.

Regional Changes

The shifts at the global level were accompanied by shifts on the regional level as well. Key among these were Russia's growing ambivalence between Azerbaijan and Armenia, and Türkiye's growing role in the South Caucasus.

Moscow's ambivalence may seem surprising at first glance. Armenia has been a loyal ally of Russia ever since it joined the CIS Collective Security Treaty and provided Russia with bases in the country in May 1992.[22] It subsequently joined the CSTO and the Eurasian Economic Union and reneged on an attempt to sign an Association Agreement with the EU in 2013 following Russian pressure. Azerbaijan, on the other hand, left the Collective Security Treaty in 1997, beginning instead to pursue an independent foreign policy while maintaining a refusal to join Russian-led structures. But as Pavel Baev explains in a previous book edited by this author, Russia had increasingly become a "counter-change" force in the South Caucasus.[23] The Kremlin viewed with growing suspicion the Armenian government's unwillingness to establish a Russian-style "power vertical" in the country, and this suspicion was exacerbated by the Armenian government's flirtation with European integration in the early 2010s, during the premiership of Tigran Sargsyan. By contrast, Moscow harbored no such

---

22   Svante E. Cornell, *Small Nations and Great Powers*, Richmond, Surrey: Curzon Press, 2001, p. 344.
23   Pavel Baev, "Russia: A Declining Counter-Change Force," in Svante E. Cornell, *The International Politics of the Armenia-Azerbaijan Conflict*, New York: Palgrave, 2017.

suspicion concerning Azerbaijan, whose domestic governance model ensured its relationship with the West remained tense. The personal relationship between Vladimir Putin and Ilham Aliyev also played an important role. While Aliyev frequently refused to acquiesce to Russian demands, he also proved reliable and predictable in his pronouncements. In other words, Armenia became an unreliable vassal that Moscow did not trust, whereas Azerbaijan appears to have impressed Putin as an independent force that was willing to work with Moscow while refusing to submit to its wishes. This, of course, only confirms the old adage that Russia respects strength and despises weakness.

More important than these considerations was the pure geopolitical and geo-economic logic that Azerbaijan is much more important than Armenia. While Armenia is small, poor, and landlocked, Azerbaijan borders both Russia and Iran, has energy resources that make it influential on the international scene, and can thus make or break the east-west corridor linking Europe to Central Asia. Since Moscow already effectively exercised an influence bordering on control in Armenia, it was only logical that Moscow would seek to build on that to develop influence also in Azerbaijan. In so doing, Moscow shamelessly brandished both carrot and stick—propping up Armenia with military bases and low-cost weapons deliveries, while offering Azerbaijan the same weapons systems at world market prices. Crucially, Moscow over time understood that it could not gain influence in Azerbaijan only by wielding a stick: it actually had more success with carrots, realizing that it may prove unable to achieve the same level of control over Azerbaijan as it had over Armenia. In fact, Moscow appears to have understood that it may have to settle for an independent Azerbaijan that was not anti-Russian. This Russian thinking would be exacerbated by Armenia's Velvet Revolution of 2018, which alarmed the Kremlin, and drastically decreased Moscow's interest in supporting Armenia in its confrontation with Azerbaijan. In fact, the Kremlin's distaste for independent-minded neighbors is far surpassed by its revulsion of popular revolts unseating authoritarian or semi-authoritarian regimes.

While Moscow's approach was changing throughout the 2010s, Türkiye's approach to the South Caucasus went through even more dramatic shifts. While Türkiye had long sided with Azerbaijan in the conflict over Karabakh, it briefly dallied with the notion of normalizing relations with Armenia in 2009-10. At this time, the Turkish leadership appeared to ignore Azerbaijan's interests, but this soon changed after Baku mobilized nationalist support in Türkiye for its cause.[24] Prime Minister Recep Tayyip Erdoğan soon brought the Turkish approach back in line with the traditional Turkish stance, and from 2015 onward, Türkiye's endorsement of Azerbaijan's position strengthened considerably. This was largely a result of two factors: first, Türkiye's misadventure in the Middle East, and second, a reshuffling of Erdoğan's ruling coalition at home. Ankara had focused increasingly on an embrace of Islamist forces in regional politics following the 2011 Arab Upheavals, but this endorsement of the Muslim Brotherhood and similar forces failed to make Türkiye the "manager of change" in the Middle East, as then-Foreign Minister Ahmet Davutoğlu would have had it. Instead, it brought Turkish rela-

---

24 A senior Turkish diplomat at an event organized by this author in Washington, DC in 2010 spoke openly about his irritation at "third countries" seeking to influence Ankara's normalization process with Yerevan. See discussion in Svante E. Cornell, "Balancing the Armenia-Azerbaijan Conflict and Turkish-Armenian Relations," in Cornell, ed., *The International Politics of the Armenia-Azerbaijan Conflict* (New York: Palgrave, 2017), pp. 89-106.

tions with almost every Middle East power to a low point, and locked Türkiye out of most of the region. This forced Türkiye to focus its attention elsewhere.

Meanwhile, the Islamist approach of the Turkish leadership moderated as the ruling coalition shifted in a nationalist direction from 2013 onward, a process cemented with the 2015 elections and the aborted 2016 coup attempt against Erdoğan. The Turkish president had previously relied largely on the forces in the bureaucracy loyal to the self-exiled preacher Fethullah Gülen, but the fallout between the two men forced Erdoğan to look elsewhere for support. In so doing, he had few options but to align with the old-fashioned Turkish nationalist forces both in Turkish politics and within the bureaucracy. As it happened, these nationalists were adamant supporters of Azerbaijan, and of a greater Turkish engagement with Central Asia.[25] Thus, from 2015 onward, the relationship between Ankara and Baku intensified, not least in the military realm. Not staying at that, this more nationalist Türkiye ended up confronting Russian interests first in Syria and then in Libya, acquitting itself very well in the process and displaying the quality of Turkish-made weaponry (particularly unmanned aerial vehicles) against Russian-made arms systems.

Azerbaijan had thus improved its regional standing considerably toward the end of the 2010s. Its non-alignment or multi-vectorial policy had enabled it to challenge Armenia's position in Moscow; meanwhile, Türkiye had emerged as a true challenger to Russian interests in the Mediterranean and Black Sea regions and made relations with Azerbaijan a priority in its foreign policy. This dramatically shifted the balance of forces in the region in

---

25 Svante E. Cornell, "Turkey's Hour of Nationalism: The Deeper Sources of Political Realignment," *The American Interest*, June 18, 2019.

Azerbaijan's favor. The only missing ingredient now was the domestic situation in both countries.

Domestic Changes

On the domestic level, Armenia and Azerbaijan went through significant convulsions from 2015 onward. Those in Azerbaijan had the effect of strengthening the leadership of Ilham Aliyev; those in Armenia had the effect of weakening Russian support for Yerevan and triggering Turkish action.

Azerbaijan's political system was, prior to 2015, a paradox. On paper, Aliyev stood at the top of a super-presidential system of power characterized by few checks and balances on his power. Reality, however, was very different: his power was checked by a coterie of "barons" that held key government posts and controlled large sectors of the economy. This formed a sort of "checks and balances" on the President, but not the classical form of checks and balances first envisaged by Montesquieu and later enshrined in the U.S. Constitution. These "barons" were often deeply corrupt, had linkages to foreign powers that made their loyalty to the country questionable, and the President was aware of the need to consolidate power sufficiently before moving decisively against them. In other words, the informal political makeup of Azerbaijan affected the President's freedom of movement with regard to the conflict with Armenia. Simply put, Aliyev made sure he had consolidated control over the powerbrokers in the country before taking decisive steps in the conflict.

Unsurprisingly, the most retrograde forces were those that also had close connections to Russian state organs and were most opposed to Azerbaijan's ties with the West. These operated relatively independently from the President, and pursued policy goals that did not always coincide with his foreign and security policy. In years past, Aliyev had removed figures known to be loyal to Moscow—such as former Minister of State Security Namik Abbasov in 2004. For a variety of reasons, Aliyev did not clean house until after the 2014 collapse of the oil price and the ensuing economic crisis in the country, which necessitated rapid action to reform the administration and economy. Aliyev instituted the position of First Vice President, to which his wife Mehriban was appointed. Her office would emerge as the primary locus of the reform-minded government officials in the country. In 2019, Aliyev dismissed recalcitrant "oligarchs," and it is not a coincidence that the decision to finally liberate the occupied territories was taken shortly after he completed his consolidation of power.

In Armenia, momentous changes took place as well. These related both to the conflict and to the country's internal governance. The path to confrontation was paved soon after the Velvet Revolution of 2018, which brought a new, populist government to power led by Nikol Pashinyan. As will be seen, after having initially signaled a willingness to reach an accommodation on the occupied territories, Pashinyan soon took a hardline approach to the conflict that departed from the previous government's positions. But the shift had begun earlier.

In April 2016, an escalation of tensions led to a "four-day" war in which Azerbaijan, for the first time since 1994, regained control of some occupied territories. To Armenia's great chagrin, Moscow did not immediately intervene to stop Azerbaijan's advances. This should have led alarm bells to ring loudly in

Yerevan. But strangely, Armenia did not sue for peace—instead, particularly after the 2018 change of government, it doubled down on its intransigent approach.

A first step was semantic: around the time of Russia's Crimea operation, Armenians began to refer to the occupied territories around Nagorno-Karabakh as "liberated territories"—a major shift, since they had previously been held as a security buffer and negotiating chip to secure Azerbaijani concessions on Karabakh's status. No longer: Armenia now indicated it might not be willing to return those territories at all, ignoring the four UN Security Council resolutions that called for their "immediate and unconditional" return to Azerbaijan.[26]

When Pashinyan took power in late 2018, he first appeared willing to restart the peace process, and Baku could hardly hide its pleasure that the ethnic-Armenian Karabakhi elite (which had been in power since 1997) had been removed from power in Yerevan. But then, something changed. In 2019, Pashinyan repudiated the OSCE's "Madrid Principles," which had served as the basis for negotiations since 2007.[27] He also sought to change the very format of negotiations, demanding the involvement of the local "Artsakh" leadership in the talks.[28] But he also stated, in the administrative center of Karabakh, that "Karabakh is Armenia, and that's that."[29] These two statements were not only contradictory: they appeared to remove any space for negotiations on the territory's status.

---

26   Thomas De Waal, "Prisoners of the Caucasus: Resolving the Karabakh Security Dilemma," Carnegie Europe, June 16, 2015.
27   "Newspaper: Armenia's Pashinyan rejects Madrid Principles for resolving Karabakh conflict?" News.am, May 10, 2019.
28   Karlen Asanyan, "Yerevan Insists On Karabakh's Involvement In Peace Talks," Azatutyun.am, April 2, 2018.
29   "'Artsakh is Armenia,' Says Pashinyan during Stepanakert Rally," *Asbarez*, August 5, 2019.

In parallel, Armenia's military strategy also changed. In 2019, Defense Minister David Tonoyan stated that Armenia rebuked the land-for-peace idea that had served as the logic of negotiations, and adopted instead a strategy pursuing "new wars for new territories."[30] This was coupled with assertive moves that changed the situation on the ground: Armenia openly began to resettle ethnic Armenians from Syria and Lebanon into the occupied territories, creating new facts on the ground.[31]

As if this was not enough, Armenian leaders in the summer of 2020 took steps to draw Türkiye into the dispute. When fighting erupted in July on the undisputed Armenia-Azerbaijan border way north of the conflict zone, it triggered fears in Türkiye that Armenia was threatening the energy infrastructure carrying Azerbaijani oil and gas in the very vicinity of the flareup. Then, in early August, Armenia's President and Prime Minister each made a point of commemorating the hundredth anniversary of the Treaty of Sèvres, which would have carved out an Armenian state out of eastern Türkiye—claiming that while it was not ratified, this treaty was still "alive."[32] This Treaty has been a *bête noire* for Türkiye for much of the last century and seemed to confirm Turkish fears that Armenia does, indeed, harbor territorial ambitions against Türkiye. The Turkish response was swift and unprecedented: Defense Minister Hulusi Akar declared Türkiye henceforth to be a party to the Armenia-Azerbaijan conflict,

---

30 Eduard Abrahamyan, "Rationalizing the Tonoyan Doctrine: Armenia's Active Deterrence Strategy," *Eurasia Daily Monitor*, May 2, 2019.

31 Vasif Huseynov, "Armenian Resettlement From Lebanon to the Occupied Territories of Azerbaijan Endangers Peace Process," *Eurasia Daily Monitor*, September 23, 2020.

32 "President Armen Sarkissian: Treaty of Sèvres Remains an Essential Document for the Right of the Armenian People," *Massis Post*, August 10, 2020.

and Ankara immediately ordered joint military exercises with Azerbaijan.

In sum, Armenian leaders committed several grave miscalculations.

Armenia's Miscalculations

First, the rhetoric of "liberated territories" suggested that Armenia appeared to take advantage of the weakening of international law and institutions. Azerbaijan's efforts had largely centered on diplomatic means to undo Armenia's attempt to change international borders through military force. A weakening international order appeared to give Armenia a free hand to maintain its control over these lands indefinitely. What the Armenian leadership neglected to see is that it this weakening international order had also deterred Azerbaijan from abandoning diplomacy and pursuing a military solution. In 2019, Aliyev noted that a world was emerging where "might is right," and that Azerbaijan would act accordingly if it could not achieve its goals through diplomacy.[33] Armenia did not realize the grave danger that ensued. It also appears to have failed to comprehend the implications of its failure to achieve international recognition for its occupation of Azerbaijani territory. As long as the fighting remained centered on Azerbaijani territory, there was little that Western or other powers would do aside from their habitual calls for restraint and negotiations.

Second, Armenia failed to act on the increasingly apparent fact that it could not take Russian support for granted. Russian

---

33 "President Ilham Aliyev: Today, 'might is right' principle prevails in the world," MENAFN, February 15, 2019.

influence over Armenia was so strong that Putin saw no risk in also courting Aliyev and seeking to draw Azerbaijan into the Russian orbit. It is not an exaggeration to state that the Kremlin viewed Armenia mainly as a lever to achieve influence over Georgia and Azerbaijan, both of which carry much greater geopolitical significance. Moscow began selling large amounts of weaponry to Azerbaijan—certainly at higher prices than what Yerevan paid, but still a move that should have caused Armenian leaders to fundamentally question their strategy of dependence on Russia. But nothing of the sort happened. Even after Armenians expressed their frustration with Moscow for not taking their side in 2016, Yerevan did not alter course.

Like a poker player with a bad hand, Yerevan instead raised the stakes in a rather transparent bluff that Baku now decided to call. Putin deeply distrusted Pashinyan and the way he came to power, and appeared content to see him slapped in the face—perhaps in the hope that the *ancien régime* would return to power in Yerevan. Armenian leaders, perhaps, failed to see that Russia is, for all its bluster, a declining power—both globally and in the Caucasus.

Third, Armenian leaders failed to correctly analyze the shifting geopolitics of the region. The South Caucasus was no longer a post-Soviet backwater: for the past decade, it has been intimately tied into the geopolitics of the Middle East, as Russia, Türkiye, and Iran uneasily jockey for influence in both theaters. In particular, Armenia failed to comprehend the shift in Turkish domestic politics. Since 2015, a powerful nationalist force has been ascendant within the Turkish state and increasingly set the parameters of Turkish foreign policy. President Erdoğan—himself an Islamist rather than a nationalist—has been forced in a more nationalist direction, as became visible in, among other issues, Türkiye's approach to the Eastern Mediterranean. This nationalist turn led Ankara to challenge Moscow both in Syria and in Libya. For Armenia, the fact that Turkish drones appeared to have outsmarted Russian-built air defenses in Libya should have led to considerable alarm and signaled the need for great caution.[34] Against this background, Yerevan's embrace of the Treaty of Sèvres in 2020 appeared to constitute serious diplomatic malpractice that, without any visible upside, triggered a lethal Turkish reaction.

Fourth, Armenian leaders failed to grasp the recent internal transformation of Azerbaijan. While Ilham Aliyev had been hamstrung by the presence of various "barons" around him, for several years he had embarked on a far-reaching purge seeking to make the Azerbaijani state more effective. To a keen observer, it should have been clear that Aliyev was consolidating power and now free to move according to his own priorities. Armenian leaders appear not to have understood that this enabled Aliyev to focus on Azerbaijan's most pressing problem, over which he had so many times signaled his great frustration.

Conclusions

Subsequent chapters in this book will delve into greater detail into the implications of the war. But a few preliminary conclusions are in order.

---

[34] "From Syria to Libya, Turkish Drones Outsmarting Russian Air Defence Systems?" *Eurasian Times*, May 23, 2020.

The aftermath of the Second Karabakh War was rapidly compounded by the Russian escalation on Ukraine's borders, and since early 2022 the bloody war between these two states. In parallel, a new geopolitical map is being drawn in the Caucasus well, even though the uncertainties remain significant.

It is clear that both events have diminished Russia's influence in the South Caucasus. In the immediate aftermath of the end of the 2020 war, many observers deemed Russia a winner, having been able to deploy a peacekeeping mission that Moscow could use to pressure both the Armenian and Azerbaijani sides, as required.[35] But as will be seen in subsequent chapters, Aliyev and Erdoğan in summer 2021 signed the Shusha Declaration on Allied Relations, establishing a defense treaty between the two countries—a dramatic and underreported development, which for the first time provided a post-Soviet state outside the Baltics with a non-Russian security and defense guarantee that was unambiguously binding.

Whatever influence Moscow stood to gain from its peacekeeping operation was thus checked by this Turkish move, and further negated by Moscow's spectacular inability to achieve its military objectives in Ukraine. Indeed, Moscow's political grasp over the two protagonists appears to have waned. By early 2022 it became clear that the EU, led by European Council President Charles Michel, was stepping into the void left by the demise of the OSCE Minsk Group. Michel led a series of trilateral talks that appeared to advance the agenda of a negotiated end to the

---

[35] See e.g., "Analysts: Russia Comes Out on Top in Nagorno-Karabakh Conflict Between Armenia, Azerbaijan," *Current Time*, November 10, 2020, "Russian President Putin Wins Upset Victory in Nagorno-Karabakh," Institute for the Study of War, November 13, 2020, and Jack Losch, "Russian Troops in Nagorno-Karabakh 'Clearly a Win for Moscow'" *Foreign Policy*, November 25, 2020.

conflict. Moreover, by fall 2022, this process was supported also by the U.S. State Department. It is doubtful that both Baku and Yerevan would have been willing and able to shift the locus of negotiations to the West so decisively had the war in Ukraine not occurred. It was thus only logical that Russia's peacekeeping mission discreetly left the region in April 2024.

Other important developments took place in Iran, where a protest movement that started following the regime's killing of a young woman in September 2022. As these protests spread to over 100 Iranian towns and cities, they proved to be the most daunting challenge to the Islamic Republic since its establishment over three decades ago. While the regime survived these protests, it is already clear that Iran's leverage in the South Caucasus has declined. This is significant as Tehran had taken a more overtly pro-Armenian stance between the Second Karabakh War and the September 2023 events, indicating its displeasure at any moves to compromise Iran's connection with Armenia through the southern Armenian lands through which a corridor linking Azerbaijan and Türkiye would be constructed, and which Azerbaijan targeted in the late summer of 2022.

As this book went to print, thus, the situation in the region was very much in flux. Russia and Iran were in decline, while Türkiye was on the ascendant. But the future of the Caucasus remained in the hands of the regional states themselves. Armenia and Azerbaijan appeared on the verge of concluding a peace agreement that would once and for all close this unfortunate chapter in the region's history and allow the two countries to move toward a more cooperative future.

PERFECT TIMING AND STATECRAFT

On the Onset of the Second Karabakh War

Damjan Krnjević Mišković

As a companion to this author's other contribution to these pages, the present chapter examines what can be considered Azerbaijan's perfect timing regarding the onset of the Second Karabakh War, which began on 27 September 2020 and ended victoriously 44 days later, on 10 November 2020. It does not examine the epilogue to the war, which brought the conflict over Karabakh to an end: the 19-20 September 2023 "antiterrorist measure" during which most of the remaining ethnic-Armenian population departed the territory instead of heeding Baku's call to stay and to reintegrate into the constitutional fabric of Azerbaijan (this was followed by the complete withdrawal of Russian peacekeeping troops from the territory between April and June 2024).

This examination begins in earnest in the next section, and some readers may prefer to proceed directly to it. Others may be interested in our explanation for not entering here into the debate that goes all the way back to the Thucydidean distinction between (a) the "grounds of accusation [*aitia*] and difference" made in public by various Athenian and Spartans prior to the onset of the Peloponnesian War, and (b) the Greek thinker's own view of the "truest" reason or cause (*prophasis*) of its onset (Thuc. I.23.5-6). This is not simply a practical matter of wanting to limit the scope of our inquiry for reasons of space. Rather, it speaks to a broader purpose of this chapter: to contribute to a "coherent and comprehensive understanding of what is frequently called the common-sense view of political things"—that is to say, a "fully conscious" understanding of "the political things as they are experienced by the citizen or statesman."[36]

This "common-sense view" suggests to us that the "effectual truth" (NM, *P.* 15) of "the political things" is that history never ends, geography matters, the future is uncertain, one's friends are always imperfect, power politics never go away, and no political cause is ever truly just. This view is illustrated with particular clarity by a thread woven into the original Thucydidean narrative, namely the antithesis between a nation's dreams and the reality of its power (Thuc. VI:31.5-6; VII:75.6-7; VII:87). No specialized knowledge of foundational texts is needed, however, to take seriously the argument that the aforementioned antithesis has been around for as long as human beings have lived together in political communities advancing claims to justice, set down laws in accordance with these claims, and witnessed the perversion of these same claims by those who advanced their particular or private interests to the detriment of the common good of their political community in the name of advancing those same claims.

---

36   Leo Strauss, *The City and Man*, Chicago: University of Chicago Press, 1964, pp. 12, 11.

It is quite enough, for starters, to know something of the history and geopolitical circumstances of the South Caucasus.

Closely related to the foregoing is another Thucydidean antithesis: that of the burdens and responsibilities of statecraft and the necessary acknowledgment of even an accomplished statesman's inefficacy in the face of grave disadvantage (Thuc. V:85-116); this is, of course, even more applicable in cases involving political communities led by run-of-the-mill politicians. Again, even a cursory examination of the history and geopolitical circumstances of the South Caucasus speaks to the veracity of this mode of reasoning.

In this context, it may be useful to reproduce a passage written by someone with firsthand experience in proper statecraft, who also bore witness to the consequences of the onset of its tragic degeneration:

> While the politician merrily plays his game from one short-lived smartness to another, trusting that he will find a way out of every mess in which he gets entangled, the real statesman is not allowed to be, like ordinary man, a short-range planner and a long-range dreamer. He is bent on shaping the future. He does not take it for granted. If he fails—there may be no future for his nation [...]. He knows his ends, he has a goal, a hierarchy of purposes, long-term and short-term; he subordinates one to the other; he has a vision of both the possible and the desirable and looks at the one under the aspect of the other; he thinks the possibilities through to their end; he follows up his actions, keeping ready a possible answer for whatever their

foreseeable consequence—trying to keep his hand on the events and their interaction, flexible at short range, rigid at long range, passionately reasonable, a knower of human nature, suspicious even of his own love and hate and of the many passions that blind the children of man. His eyes are cold and hard yet the flame burns in his heart as he opposes his specific virtue to the play that necessity and chance [or fortune] play with each other.[37]

Preoccupations and Distractions: Major Powers and Other External Actors

It is with this in mind that we can inquire into what the world looked like in late September 2020 from the point of view of Azerbaijan's statecraft.

Most obviously, humanity was in the midst of what appeared to be an uncontrollably lethal global pandemic, with no vaccine having yet come to market (although three were, by that point, in the final stage of clinical trials). Pretty much all UN member states were preoccupied with what was in many ways an unprecedented public policy emergency, including all the major powers. Notwithstanding the universality of the challenge, the level of practical inter-state coordination was far below the standard one would have expected from those who champion the "rules-based international liberal order"—as no major power had brought under control the pandemic within its own borders, it thus competed with others for prime and privileged access to most any resource having to do with mitigating its domestic socio-economic

---

37 Kurt Riezler, "The Philosopher of History and the Modern Statesman," *Social Research* 13, no. 3, September 1946, p. 375.

effects, including masks and other pieces of personal protective equipment, ventilators, respirators, and COVID-19 tests. By and large, professions of solidarity, assistance, and cooperation towards the developing world were failing to meet expectations encouraged by liberal international rhetoric, producing what later came to be called "vaccine nationalism." At that time, there was no coherent and effective planet-wide response.

The universal preoccupation with dealing with the pandemic within one's own state borders applied also to the EU (with an emphasis, in this context, on France), Russia, and the United States—the three most relevant power centers from Baku's standpoint, because they were the Co-Chairs of the Minsk Group, that is, they were the countries that had been put in charge by the OSCE to (unsuccessfully) mediate a just end to the conflict over Karabakh.

Aside from dealing with the pandemic, what else was going on in Washington, Moscow, and Paris immediately prior to and during the Second Karabakh War?

The presidential campaign in the United States was in full swing, and, in terms of foreign policy priorities, the attention of the incumbent officeholder, Donald Trump, was largely focused on escalating tensions with China and Mexico, finalizing the historic Abraham Accords, and brokering the so-called "economic normalization agreements" between Serbia and the ethnic-Albanian authorities of its breakaway province of Kosovo and Metohija. The fact that the Armenian-American community leans heavily, in terms of both political and campaign finance support, towards the Democrat Party also likely played a role in the Trump Administration's calculus. So did its evident disdain for multilateralism (including Trans-Atlanticism), with Trump and his senior officials seeing it as impeding America's ability to maintain global primacy. The doctrine of "America First"—the pursuit of which Trump had consistently advocated throughout his presidential term—limited the degree of American engagement with other states, including treaty allies, and produced a reneging on multilateral commitments, like the Paris Climate Agreement, even prior to the onset of the pandemic.

Halfway across the world, in Russia, the foreign policy focus was on dealing with major political crises in two of its neighboring countries, the outcomes of which was seen in the Kremlin as integral to the perpetuation of its ability to project power and influence in its self-designated sphere of influence. The first was Belarus, where mass demonstrations before, during, and after the presidential election that took place on 9 August 2020 could have led to the overthrow of longtime ally Aleksandr Lukashenko through a "color revolution." The second was Kyrgyzstan, whose internal crisis was triggered by the cascading response to an announcement in early August 2020 that parliamentary elections on 4 October 2020 would not be postponed, notwithstanding the effects of the pandemic: Moscow's focus was informed by the lessons of two successful "color revolutions" in that country (in 2005 and 2010). Ongoing brinksmanship with the West regarding the conflict over Ukraine was also part of the geopolitical background, as was Vladimir Putin's ambiguous relationship with Nikol Pashinyan, who had after all come to power in a "color revolution" in 2018 (the details of which are discussed in several chapters in this book). Moscow's public (and, presumably, private) messaging to Yerevan, especially in the wake of Armenian attacks in mid-July 2020 on undisputed Azerbaijani territory involving artillery and mortar attacks quite near oil and gas pipelines, effectually constituted a warning to the Armenian prime minister. This warning could be understood in the following way: do not provide Baku with any sort of casus belli that could produce a resumption of large-scale armed hostilities in the conflict over Karabakh, since Russia will not intervene militarily in defense of Armenia on lands that Armenia itself does not consider to be its own sovereign territory.

Aside from intra-EU bickering regarding the response to the pandemic, France was preoccupied by two other internecine political struggles. The first was an ongoing acrimonious debate about EU reform—everything from new enlargement criteria to the championing of the EU's "strategic autonomy" from the United States (in October 2019, Emmanuel Macron had given an interview to *The Economist* in which he had spoken of a "strategic agenda of sovereignty" and the "brain death of NATO"). The second was, of course, the ongoing Brexit talks, which were led by a Frenchman.

What then of the postures of other relevant foreign actors with perceived stakes in the conflict over Karabakh in September 2020?

Like the major powers, Iran was also primarily focusing inward because of its particularly evident mismanagement of the COVID-19 pandemic, which resulted in further economic freefall. To the extent that it could attend to developments beyond its borders, Tehran's gaze was directed towards Iraq, Lebanon, and Syria; keeping relations with Türkiye on an even keel; and also on making sure its nuclear ambitions would not get thwarted by Trumpian unilateralism and the possibility of an "October surprise." The assassination by the United States of Qasem Soleimani in Baghdad in January 2020 was still a fresh wound.

Also, the two most active Arab states belonging to the Gulf Cooperation Council (i.e., Saudi Arabia and the UAE) were both preoccupied with supporting various factions in various civil wars in various other Arab countries, particularly in Yemen. Neither had any stomach (or, for that matter, interest) to cross Türkiye in any part of the Silk Road region, particularly in the context of the conflict over Karabakh. In this context, ongoing talks with Qatar on ending the diplomatic crisis and economic blockade of neighboring Qatar also occupied much diplomatic attention.

As other chapters in this book detail, Türkiye was, of course, completely on board with the possibility of a war to liberate its ally's occupied lands. What amounted to unconditional support for Baku served as a firm guarantee that neither Moscow nor Tehran could intervene militarily in the conflict over Karabakh without risking direct military confrontation with Ankara. Neither Russia nor Iran wanted such a confrontation (and neither could have won it easily), in part because of the strategic interest of each to maintain a complex "frenemy" relationship with Türkiye.

Preoccupations and Distractions: Inter-State Organizations

By September 2020, all relevant inter-state organizations were also well-covered, so to speak, thanks to Baku's concerted outreach and engagement efforts. This reinforces the argument regarding the impeccable geopolitical timing of the onset of the Second Karabakh War from the perspective of Azerbaijan.

The OSCE Minsk Group had faded into irrelevance through a combination of factors, some of which have been discussed above. To this can be added what amounted to Pashinyan having effectually pulled out of the negotiations process led by the Co-Chairs.

Much evidence in support of this argument has been provided in other chapters to this volume; we will briefly focus on one aspect that has not been made sufficiently explicit in these pages, namely Pashinyan's demand that the ethnic-Armenian secessionist entity ("Artsakh") should be included in the talks as a full negotiating party. Admittedly, this had been the case for the first four years after the end of the First Karabakh War and had been widely considered a major diplomatic coup at the time, since it legitimized the Armenian argument that the conflict over Karabakh was not simply a territorial one between Armenia and Azerbaijan, but rather an ethnic conflict. This enabled Armenia and its supporters, for a time, to contest the primacy of the cornerstone right of UN member states to defend their sovereignty and territorial integrity, which in turn enabled Yerevan to deny the subordinate right to self-determination of minority groups by invoking it and then by falsely equating it with an avowed right of secession (remedial or otherwise). In the context of the conflict over Karabakh, this Armenian negotiating advantage came to an end in 1998, when Yerevan itself insisted on exclusively representing Artsakh in the OSCE-brokered talks. At the time and subsequently, this Armenian position was readily accepted by the three Co-Chairs as well as by Azerbaijan. Pashinyan's demand two decades later to return to the status quo ante format was rejected not only by Baku, but by Moscow, Paris, and Washington, as well. His indication (for instance, at a press conference on 25 January 2020 in the Armenian town of Kapan[38]) that the continuation of negotiations without an Artsakh presence was a waste of Armenia's time and that all previous Co-Chair proposals needed to be set aside effectually put an end to the OSCE negotiation format and made its Minsk Group irrelevant in the eyes of Baku. Aside from ignoring all the relevant global and regional geopolitical developments since 1998, none of which favored Armenia, Pashinyan's demand failed to take into consideration the legal consequences of the European Court of Human Rights' holding in the landmark *Chiragov and Others v. Armenia* (2015) decision that Armenia is the occupying power in Karabakh in that it "exercises effective control over Nagorno Karabakh and the surrounding territories."[39]

Moreover, as an institution, the OSCE was a particular mess in the run-up to and during the Second Karabakh War. The crisis with electing its new Secretary General meant that it was literally leaderless: Thomas Greminger's term had expired in July 2020 without the participating states having come to a consensus on his successor (Helga Schmid commenced her term only in December 2020). This failure had something to do with a response by Azerbaijan to earlier backroom diplomatic actions undertaken by France and the United States. At the same time, Albania held

---

38 See https://www.youtube.com/watch?v=BqFM3UnVbMs and Kristine Khanumian, "How Pashinyan in Effect Pulled Out of Negotiations on Live Television," *iLur.am, 18 August 2022.*

39 *Chiragov and Others v. Armenia*, Grand Chamber Judgement App. no. 13216/05, ECHR 186 (2015). On this entire question, see Javid Gadirov, "International Law and the Karabakh Question," in Fariz Ismailzade and Damjan Krnjević Mišković (eds.), *Liberated Karabakh: Policy Perspectives by the ADA University Community,* Baku: ADA University Press, 2021, pp. 33-49.

the Chairmanship-in-Office, which ensured for various political and diplomatic reasons that no proactive leadership would be forthcoming from Tirana.

Other relevant regional organizations were largely supportive of Azerbaijan, some for reasons that do not need to be elaborated here—the two most obvious examples being the Organization of Islamic Cooperation and the Organization of Turkic States. Another was the Non-Aligned Movement (NAM): Azerbaijan's chairmanship of NAM (2019-2023) was fortuitous in this regard, especially when put alongside Baku's various initiatives that provided institutional leadership in drawing attention to the plight of the developing world in the context of the pandemic. For example, Azerbaijan initiated an online NAM leaders' summit (4 May 2020) that directly led to the calling of a rare Special Session of the UN General Assembly in response to the COVID-19 pandemic (it took place on 3-4 December 2020). The decision taken at the summit generated significant diplomatic goodwill for Baku in the developing world and ensured either outright support or mitigated criticism of Azerbaijan's position on the war among NAM member states.

In addition, the two most relevant organs of the UN system were also taken care of, as it were. A seasoned Turkish diplomat (Volkan Bozkır) had been elected President of the UN General Assembly in June 2020 and had taken up his duties on 16 September 2020. Accordingly, he was more than able to handle attempts by Armenia or its allies to submit condemnatory resolutions or initiate debates in that organ, which anyway was operating at less than usual efficiency due to restrictions imposed by the pandemic.

In the UN Security Council, meanwhile, two closed debates took place: on 29 September and 19 October 2020 (prior to this, the last debate in this UN organ on the conflict over Karabakh had taken place in 1995). During this second debate, several NAM member states (the Dominican Republic, Indonesia, Niger, Saint Vincent and the Grenadines, South Africa, Tunisia, and Vietnam) that were serving as term members in that body "blocked an anti-Azerbaijani [presidential] statement [mainly drafted by France and Russia] and blocked the attempt of accusation against Azerbaijan and thus did not allow pro-Armenian global forces to attack Azerbaijan," as Aliyev put it.[40] This lack of consensus was manifested through the breaking of the silent procedure by the aforementioned states, whose representatives insisted that the draft statement include a reference to the four UN Security Council resolutions on the conflict adopted in 1993 (their contents is discussed in other chapters). This insistence was opposed by the draftees and some other members, resulting in irreconcilable differences.

The lack of a presidential statement ensured that the Security Council could not even officially go on record about the war. It also ensured that the UN Secretary-General, who had not been actively involved in the conflict over Karabakh (neither had his predecessors), could continue to choose not to undertake any meaningful initiative. This also ensured the maintenance of the UN's Secretariat's continuing insignificance on this issue.

---

40   Ilham Aliyev, "Address Before the Baku Conference of the Non-Aligned Movement Parliamentary Network," June 30, 2022, at www.president.az.

"One's Own Arms"

A final element to be examined is that of military preparedness. For a number of years, Azerbaijan's armed forces had been trained up to NATO standards, primarily by Türkiye. They had acquired modern sophisticated weapons from countries like Belarus, Israel, Pakistan, Russia, South Korea, and Türkiye, And they had figured out how to incorporate drones into a holistic tactical battle plan (the term of art is 'complex combined arms operations'). Several of the details of this endeavor, as well as commentary on Armenia's lackluster military preparedness, can be found in other chapters of this volume and will not be repeated here.

As noted in our companion contribution to this book, by the onset of the Second Karabakh War, Azerbaijan had acquired what amounted to impeccable geopolitical timing through a sophisticated combination of strategic foresight, limited war objectives, operational artistry, and active diplomacy. This not only brings back to mind the Thucydidean antitheses discussed above, but also one of the great lessons contained in the writings of Niccolò Machiavelli, who in many ways is Thucydides' modern heir:[41] only by having recourse to "one's own arms" might "the state" (*lo stato*) become its own master in both peace and war; this requires the prudential execution of *virtù* (as opposed to the "profession of good") and the opportunities provided by *fortuna*, whose vicissi-

---

41   A useful treatment of Machiavelli's descendance from Thucydides is Thomas L. Pangle and Peter J. Ahrensdorf, *Justice among Nations: On the Moral Basis of Power and Peace*. Lawrence: University Press of Kansas, 1999.

tudes can best be tamed or resisted by its "most excellent" prince (for the formulations in context, see NM, *P.* 6, 13, 15, and 25).[42]

Machiavelli is particularly instructive here because perhaps more than any political philosopher before or since, he understood that the sovereign part of *lo stato* is not the deliberative one, as in classical political philosophy, but rather the executive endowed with "great prudence" acting "decisively" and "alone" (NM, *D.* II:26, II:15, and I:2; see also I:9 and III:6).[43] It is this last characteristic—acting alone or *uno solo*—that stands in contrast to the development of institutional designs intended to domesticate the executive power of the prince. In one of his writings, Harvey Mansfield explains the importance of "effectual acquisition" in coming to terms with Machiavelli's presentation

---

[42] We can note further that *P.* 14 ends with a statement intimating that to tame or resist fortune's adversities appears to be the most that can be achieved by an excellent prince: there is no catch-all remedy (*rimedio*) for accidents, much less a cure. The excellence of a prince is measured in large part by his ability to properly practice Machiavelli's version of moral virtue (NM, *P.* 16-23 provides an account of these). Cf. Riezler, "Philosopher of History," pp. 378-380. Otto von Bismarck would effectually say the same thing centuries later: fortune is a river to be tamed (and, rarely, perhaps even resisted), thanks to the virtues of an excellent prince; but there are limits: the course of a river, like the course of time itself, cannot be simply reversed. This is expressed in two statements he made 40 years apart: "The stream of time flows inexorably along. By plunging my hand into it, I am merely doing my duty. I do not expect thereby to change its course." The second statement: "Man can neither create nor direct the stream of time. He can only travel upon it and steer with more or less skill and experience; he can suffer shipwreck and go aground and also arrive in safe harbors." The two statements can be found in *Bismarck: Die gesammelten Werke*, ed. Herman von Petersdorff et al., Berlin: Otto Stollberg & Co., 1923-1933, XIV:249 and XIII:558, respectively.

[43] Aristotle made the best case for the deliberative as sovereign or authoritative (*kyrios*), which he calls "the work of political joining [or understanding]" as well as "judgments" (*kriseis*); see Arist. *Pol.* IV, in particular 1298a3-4, 1291a28, and 1299a2-3 as well as Arist. *Eth. Nic.* 1112a18-1113a14. Machiavelli's shift away from conceiving the deliberative branch as the sovereign part of the state and replacing it with the executive is an integral part of the case for identifying him as the "father of modern political philosophy." See Leo Strauss, *What is Political Philosophy? and Other Studies*, Glencoe: The Free Press, 1958, 40. Cf. Leo Strauss, *Thoughts on Machiavelli*, Glencoe: The Free Press, 1958, p. 173, where he succinctly portrays the fundamental distinction between classical or ancient philosophy and modern philosophy, again with an emphasis on Machiavelli's parentage: "Classical political philosophy had taught that the salvation of the cities depends on the coincidence of philosophy and political power which is truly a coincidence—something for which one can wish or hope but which one cannot bring about. Machiavelli is the first philosopher who believes that the coincidence of philosophy and political power can be brought about by propaganda which wins over ever larger multitudes to the 'new modes and orders' and thus transforms the thought of one or a few into the opinion of the public and therewith into public power." The term "new modes and orders" is found in NM, *D.* I:pr.

of non-institutional executive power.[44] In another, he interprets this aspect of Machiavelli's teaching to mean that "freedom requires the use of one's own arms, which is virtue as opposed to fortune."[45]

On such and similar grounds, we could thus say that, in the Second Karabakh War, Azerbaijan fulfilled the requirements necessary to consolidate its freedom and, in so doing, produced a vindication of both its deliberate approach to statecraft and carefully fashioned foreign policy posture.[46] Perhaps the fundamental precept that can be derived from the statecraft of Azerbaijan and the statesmanship of Ilham Aliyev is that the conquest of a nation's past represents the liberation of its future liberty.[47]

---

44 Harvey C. Mansfield, "On the Impersonality of the Modern State: A Comment on Machiavelli's Use of *Stato*," *American Political Science Review* 77, no. 4, December 1983, pp. 849-857. The process of the executive power's institutionalization or domestication was first manifested in the works of Thomas Hobbes and then, more directly, in those produced by John Locke, Montesquieu, and the authors of the *Federalist Papers* collectively writing under the pseudonym Publius. The entire lineage of executive power is brought to the surface brilliantly in Harvey Mansfield, *Taming the Prince: The Ambivalence of Modern Executive Power* (New York: The Free Press, 1989). Mansfield also takes up the parentage question noted in the previous footnote: "The whole story of executive power depends on understanding why it is absent in Aristotle" (p. 25) and devotes two (or rather, three) chapters to this topic.

45 Harvey C. Mansfield, *Machiavelli's Virtue*, Chicago: University of Chicago Press, 1996, p. 48. Cf. the last sentence of the passage by Riezler cited in an earlier footnote.

46 The onset of both is traceable back to Heydar Aliyev's return to power in Azerbaijan in mid-1993. Heydar Aliyev's greatest accomplishment was to act as "*uno solo*," and thus to show, in deed, how one could become responsible for one's own "fortune" through the exercise of "virtue" and, in so doing, ensure that a country that was effectually a failing state was able to acquire and then maintain its freedom in both war and peace—motion and rest, as Thucydides would put it (Machiavelli, in contrast, does not acknowledge the possibility of rest in politics, which, as he *does* acknowledge, would constitute "the true political way of life and the true quiet of a city. But since all things of men are in motion and cannot steady steady, they must either rise or fall" (NM, D. I.7.4).). See Svante E. Cornell and S. Frederick Starr, "Heydar Aliyev and the Building of Azerbaijani Statehood," *Baku Dialogues* 6, no 3, Spring 2023, pp. 6-21 and M. Hakan Yavuz, "Heydar Aliyev as Architect and Founder," *Baku Dialogues* 6, no 3, Spring 2023, pp. 24-53.

47 It may very well be that Pashinyan has begun to embrace it, too. In an address to the Armenian parliament in June 2023, he juxtaposed the "duality that exists in each of us [between] historical Armenia and real Armenia. […] This debate is about the following: should the real Armenia serve the historical Armenia, or should the historical Armenia serve the real Armenia? And this is the political and epoch-making question to which we must give an answer." See Nikol Pashinyan, "Final Speech in the Discussion of the Annual Report on the Implementation of the 2022 State Budget in the National Assembly," June 15, 2023, https://www.primeminister.am/en/statements-and-messages/item/2023/06/15/Nikol-Pashinyan-Speech.

In further support of this conclusion, we can reproduce part of the answer Ilham Aliyev provided to a question posed to him in November 2022 during a conference held at ADA University:

> In the case of Azerbaijan, we never heard this straightforward approach or statement from mediators [providing an 'absolutely clear articulation' of support for our territorial integrity]. The narrative was that you have to agree. That was the public narrative. And the messages we sometimes received during private negotiations were that this is a reality and that every country should take into account the reality. And when we were asking what about the UN Security Council resolutions, there was no answer; what about territorial integrity, there was no answer; what about the Helsinki Final Act, there was no answer. And we said, fine if this is the reality, we will change this reality. And we started to prepare ourselves to change reality. And that is how it happened. It was not international law, not the United Nations, and not Armenia's constructive approach that changed the situation. It was our army, our people, and our political will. So, realities must be changed. Do you have the power to do it? If yes, you do it; if not, you accumulate power. If you want a quiet life, you agree with this reality. Our choice was different. I was asked about sleepless nights. Yes, I had many of them during the occupation because of the feeling of anger—not because something will happen, but because of the feeling of anger and understanding

that this injustice is how the world is being regulated. *And my belief in justice only happened after we won the war. I started to believe in justice again.* [...] What we have done is clear. How we approached the situation of restoration of our territorial integrity is also known. So, you have to be strong. Unfortunately, this is the outcome of twenty-first-century international relations. Forget about resolutions, statements, and good words. They are worth nothing: you, your people, your army, and your feeling of justice.[48]

Put differently, war is not like a Hollywood movie where the good guy always wins in the end because, well, that's just how it *should* be. Both Thucydides and Machiavelli teach us that civilization is coeval with conflict, not its Manichean opposite. In world politics, there has never been an apodictic solution to the problem of justice or the sempiternity of upheaval. Freedom is not deserved: it is acquired and then maintained. In many ways, the same can be said of justice. The Armenian understanding of the role of diplomacy in conflict resolution—as either a morality play or an exercise in telling the other side how to avoid perdition—led Yerevan to champion a view of the world that has never been and advocate the use of all means to get there. The Azerbaijani understanding, in contrast, was that what statecraft requires most—everywhere and always—is a clinical examination of what *cannot* be achieved. Only then may the achievable be

---

48 Ilham Aliyev, "Address at ADA University at a Conference Titled 'Along the Middle Corridor: Geopolitics, Security, and Economy'," November 25, 2022, https://president.az/en/articles/view/57968. Emphasis added. This passage should thus serve as evidence that Ilham Aliyev fully understands the necessity to order "one's own arms."

fruitfully contemplated, prudentially planned, and dispassionately executed. Hence the perfect timing of the onset of the Second Karabakh War, which took place at the start of "one of those rare plastic moments of genuine [geopolitical] transformation that come along once or twice a century."[49]

---

[49] William Burns, "The Role of Intelligence at a Transformational Moment," Address at Georgia Institute of Technology, April 14, 2022.

THE FOREIGN AND SECURITY POLICIES OF ARMENIA AND AZERBAIJAN, 1994-2020

Robert M. Cutler

This chapter focuses principally on explicating the evolution of the foreign and security policies of both Armenia and Azerbaijan during the period between the First and Second Karabakh Wars, with occasional references to the events since 2020. It discusses how Armenia's dependence on Iran and Russia grew ever deeper over time, reaching its peak right before the onset of the 2020 war. It also explains how Azerbaijan initially adopted a pro-Western policy but gradually reached out to Russia, strengthened its ties to Türkiye, and developed a global profile as a "middle power." Over the 26 years from 1994 to 2020, Armenia sank deeper into dependence on regimes that sought only to exploit it, while Azerbaijan adopted a multi-vectorial foreign policy leading to a vastly superior international position.

There are two important topics that the chapter does not address directly. One is the Minsk Group of the Organization for Security and Cooperation in Europe (OSCE), which I have addressed elsewhere.⁵⁰ The other important topic is the Armenian diaspora. A few words on the diaspora are therefore appropriate here.

The number of ethnic Armenians living outside Armenia is difficult to ascertain, but a fair estimate is probably between six and seven million. This is over twice the number of ethnic Armenians residing in Armenia itself. Well over half the diaspora resides in France, Russia, and the United States (which are, coincidentally, the three co-chairs of the now-defunct Minsk Group). Russia's president Vladimir Putin estimated its number in his country at "over two million" in 2020.⁵¹ This would be about twice the number in France and the United States together, each of which have an estimated half-million in their respective ethnic Armenian diasporas. It is well known that the diasporas in France and the United States have long been politically very influential. It is less well known that Russia is no different in this respect.

The chapter is organized as follows. These introductory remarks are followed by four sections, respectively devoted to Armenia's and Azerbaijan's relations with the West, Russia, Türkiye, and Iran. Each section has two subsections, one on Armenia and one on Azerbaijan, and each subsection is organized mainly chronologically. Those four main sections are followed by a conclusion in three short sections: one summarizing Armenia's dependence on Iran and Russia, and the inordinate, deleterious influence of the diaspora; one on Azerbaijan's path to the attainment of a "multi-vectorial" foreign policy; and one containing final remarks.

---

50 Robert M. Cutler, "The Minsk Group is Meaningless," *Foreign Policy*, July 23, 2021.
51 Vladimir Putin, interviewed by Pavel Zarubin, "Interview with Rossiya TV Channel," President of Russia, November 13, 2021.

Armenia, Azerbaijan, and the West

Between 1994 and 2020, the foreign and security policies of Armenia and Azerbaijan towards the West were conditioned by their respective geopolitical considerations, security needs, and economic objectives. At the same time, both countries' relationships with the West were influenced by the conflict over Karabakh and the fact that the United States and France were two of the three co-chairs (along with Russia) of the now-defunct OSCE Minsk Group.

Landlocked and reliant on Russia for its security, Armenia sought to cultivate ties with the West by joining NATO's Partnership for Peace (PfP) program in 1994. However, it was difficult for Yerevan to go much further than this, since Russia was Armenia's main security partner, providing it with military support through its main base in Gyumri, large discounts and loans for arms-systems purchase, and border security through its Federal Security Service (FSB) Border Service.

By contrast, Azerbaijan capitalized on its energy resources to forge strategic alliances with the West. The inauguration of the Baku-Tbilisi-Ceyhan (BTC) oil-export pipeline in 2006 was a milestone in Azerbaijan's relationship with the West. This pipeline, bypassing Russia, connected Azerbaijan's vast oil fields to Western and global markets, thereby increasing Azerbaijan's strategic significance overall and to the West in particular. In addition, Azerbaijan demonstrated its commitment to security cooperation with the West through its participation in NATO's International Security Assistance Force (ISAF) in Afghanistan.

Armenia's Relations with the West

During the period between the First and Second Karabakh Wars, Armenia's relations with the West were extremely cordial, in part due to the diaspora's strong political influence. The U.S. extended bilateral relations with Armenia as with every other newly independent state that had been a Soviet union-republic. These relations developed quickly into trade and assistance agreements, even as Armenian military forces were securing their occupation of lands in much of the western part of "mainland" Azerbaijan and ethnically cleansing those territories of their Azerbaijani inhabitants.

Due in part to the diaspora's significance in Democratic Party politics in the U.S., American policy became still more favorable to Armenia after President Barack Obama's inauguration in January 2009. The powerful Armenian lobby in Washington has by and large kept the political elite—if not always the general public—conscious of the conflict with Azerbaijan. Some official representatives of the Armenian diaspora, who need not suffer the consequences of the policies they advocate, did not hesitate to accentuate calls for greater ethnic-Armenian living-space in the South Caucasus. These calls have extended into the post-Second Karabakh War period. Their publicity campaign at the end of 2021 was especially characterized by markedly stronger anti-Azerbaijan sentiments in the mass media, complemented even by territorial claims against Türkiye, Iran, and Georgia.[52]

Armenia's relations with France deserve special mention. The diaspora there (as well as in some American news media

---

[52] For a more general discussion of Western press bias, see Robert M. Cutler, "Western Blind Spot in the South Caucasus: Chronicle of a War Foretold," *Caucasus Strategic Perspectives* 1, no. 2, Winter 2020, pp. 57-70.

outlets) have continually played the "Christian card," depicting the conflict as a "clash of civilizations" with majority-Muslim Azerbaijan. At the very start of the Second Karabakh War, President Emmanuel Macron convolutedly blamed Türkiye for "disinhibiting Azerbaijan regarding what would be a reconquest of North [sic] Karabakh, something that we would never accept," adding, "I say to Armenia and to Armenians that France will play its role."[53] So saying, Macron threw the first shovelful of dirt onto the interred diplomatic casket of what once had been the Minsk Group, of which France was an ostensibly a neutral co-chair.

A few remarks on Armenia's relations with the EU are also in order. These relations have been marked by zigs and zags. In 1996, along with numerous other former-Soviet newly independent states, Armenia signed a Partnership and Cooperation Agreement. This entered into force in 1999. In 2009, Armenia began participation in the EU's Eastern Partnership, which was in 2011 folded into the newly announced European Neighbourhood Policy as its "Eastern direction." In 2010, Armenia began negotiating an Association Agreement (AA) with the EU, which would have included a Deep and Comprehensive Free Trade Area Agreement (DCFTA). These negotiations were successful, but President Serzh Sargsyan broke off the process even as the AA was being prepared for signing in November 2013. This reversal occurred within days of Ukrainian President Viktor Yanukovych's similar rejection of a pending AA with the EU. In contrast to the hostile Western response to Yanukovych's move, which also led to the Maidan demonstrations and Yanukovych's

---

[53] "Karabagh: Emmanuel Macron s'en prend à la Turquie," *Le Progrès*, 30 September 2020. Soon after the conclusion of the Second Karabakh War, both houses of the French legislature encouraged Paris to recognize the so-called "Nagorno-Karabakh Republic," a step that even Yerevan never took.

eventual flight from Kyiv, Western capitals at most expressed mild disappointment over Sargsyan's identical move and engaged in no diplomatic or political campaign against him as they did against Yanukovych.

Yerevan thereupon began negotiations to join the Russia-led Eurasian Economic Union (EAEU) instead. These negotiations were successful: Armenia joined the EAEU, becoming a member of the Eurasian Customs Union (ECU) in 2015. New negotiations with the EU began at the end of that year, but they could not now include the DCFTA, with which the EAEU's provisions conflicted. Yerevan signed instead a Comprehensive and Enhanced Partnership Agreement (CEPA) with Brussels in November 2017. The CEPA's ratification took some time but finally entered into force in March 2021.

Azerbaijan's Relations with the West

Azerbaijan was generally perceived as Western-oriented during the 1990s and 2000s, when mainly Western energy companies first made large investments to develop the country's offshore hydrocarbon resources. The export route for Azerbaijan's oil to Western markets was set with the signature of the Istanbul Protocol at the OSCE's November 1999 summit. This was the framework for a series of subsequent agreements for the construction of the BTC oil-export pipeline.

In order to ensure business investment confidence, Azerbaijan ratified those agreements as international treaties. Shortly thereafter, economists from the International Monetary Fund visited the country for the first time to evaluate developments and discuss policies. These events set the course for Azerbaijani energy development policy in the 1990s and the 2000s.

The 2008 Russian-Georgian war marked a turning-point in Azerbaijan's foreign policy toward both Russia and the West. Up until then, Baku had been "maintain[ing] good relations with Russia while slowly and incrementally moving closer to the West,"[54] using foreign investment to strengthen its own autonomy, all while increasing its international profile. However, the failure by the West—both the U.S. and the EU's major players—to respond to Russia's occupation of Georgian territory with anything other than words and some funding "shook Azerbaijan's political establishment and altered their perception of Russia."[55] The paralysis of American diplomacy was compounded by the election of Obama, under whose presidential administration U.S. military aid and financial assistance to Azerbaijan began to decline as early as 2009. A definite lack of interest demonstrably marked Washington's new attitudes toward the region. The political influence of the Armenian diaspora in Washington and in the Democratic Party in particular (especially the important state politics of California) accounts for much of this shift, along with the failure of the Turkish-Armenian diplomatic rapprochement in which the new U.S. administration had invested significant effort.

Azerbaijan's largely reactive strategic shift away from the West was accentuated following Recep Tayyip Erdoğan's re-election in 2011. In the vacuum of Western engagement, local configurations of Iranian, Russian, and Turkish power acquired greater regional significance for the South Caucasus. Azerbaijan

---
54   Anar Valiyev, "Victim of a 'War of Ideologies': Azerbaijan after the Russia-Georgia War," *Demokratsiya* 17, no. 3, Summer 2009, p. 271.
55   Ibid., 277.

also began to give more attention to multilateral platforms where its distinctive characteristics would give it special advantage. For example, the country joined the Non-Aligned Movement (NAM) in 2011, quickly working to be elected to its chairmanship-in-office from 2019 to 2021. (The term was extended to 2022 due to the effects of the COVID-19 pandemic.) This is an example of the "multi-vectorial" foreign policy that enabled Azerbaijan to broaden its diplomatic portfolio against Iran and especially Russia throughout the 2010s.

The EU extended relations with Azerbaijan, signing a Partnership and Cooperation Agreement (PCA) in 1996 that entered into force in 1999. In 2003, the EU appointed a Special Representative for the South Caucasus. The important 2004 Baku Initiative emerged from the First Ministerial Conference on Energy Cooperation between the EU and the littoral states of the Black Sea, Caspian Sea, and their neighbors, which was held in the Azerbaijani capital. A Transport Ministerial Conference was held simultaneously, producing a framework in support of the EU's Transport Corridor Europe-Caucasus-Asia (TRACECA) program, also with its secretariat in Baku.

Azerbaijan has been part of the European Neighbourhood Policy (ENP), of which the Baku Initiative was a component part, since its launch in 2004. In 2009, the ENP became part of the Eastern Partnership initiative; however, Azerbaijan's relations with the EU stagnated during the first half of the 2010s. In 2016, a Protocol on Azerbaijan's participation in EU programs and agencies was adopted, focusing on economic cooperation, particularly in the energy sector. Azerbaijan and the EU had previously signed a Memorandum of Understanding on a Strategic Partnership in the Field of Energy in 2006 and issued a Joint Declaration on the Southern Gas Corridor in 2011. In February 2017, the EU and Azerbaijan started negotiations to replace the original PCA, but they have not yet finished successfully.

Cooperation on energy issues nevertheless proceeded apace: the two sides adopted a set of "Partnership Priorities" via the EU-Azerbaijan Cooperation Council in 2018; in addition, after the Second Karabakh War, a Memorandum of Understanding on a Strategic Partnership in the Field of Energy was signed in July 2022 and an Agreement on Strategic Partnership on Green Energy in December 2022.

Azerbaijan, Armenia, and Russia

The overall success of Russia's strategy in the South Caucasus has historically depended on its ability to balance actors in the region, and outside it, in such a manner as to keep everyone off-balance. In such a situation, even if Moscow could not fully control others that may try to tip the scales, it could still maintain its own role as a fulcrum. However, this strategy has lately proven increasingly difficult for Russia to implement. Many other players enjoy increasing margins of maneuver and can, at a minimum, play spoiler roles. Together with the outcome of the Second Karabakh War in late 2020, Russia's newly diminished power and prestige following the February 2022 renewal of its war of aggression against Ukraine has altered that dynamic, as have other subsequent events. Russia now needs help from Iran, which has seized the new opportunity provided by this opening: both counted on their (erstwhile) common ally, Armenia, to assist them in that strategy, with Yerevan's attempted turn to the West serving as a complicating factor.

Azerbaijan's Relations with Russia

Moscow's energy and foreign ministries, each having different domestic political constituencies, famously disagreed in public in the early/mid-1990s over whether Caspian Sea national-sector delimitation issues should allow or prevent the development of Azerbaijan's offshore energy deposits. As it was, Russian companies participated, albeit marginally, in the consortia established by Western firms for this purpose. Post-Soviet institutional disarray in the Kremlin, including the parts of the (former) state energy sector transferred to "private" hands, accounted for this confusion.

A rapprochement between Azerbaijan and Russia began in the first years of the twenty-first century. In January 2002, the two countries signed an agreement on the status, principles, and conditions for use of the Gabala Radar Station in Azerbaijan (complemented by a November 2003 protocol). Russia's president Vladimir Putin, supported by Azerbaijan, proposed in June 2007 to use the station as a part of the U.S.-developed missile defense system; however, the proposal was never implemented.[56]

Bilateral relations oscillated in subsequent years. The two defense ministers exchanged visits in 2006-2007, military-personnel exchanges increased, and military-diplomatic relations intensified. Problems arose in the early 2010s, first around the renewal of the Gabala lease to Russia, then around a Russian halt

---

56 Gregory Feifer, "Azerbaijan's Gabala Radar Base Examined," *NPR Morning Edition*, July 2, 2007, https://www.npr.org/templates/story/story.php?storyId=11650207.

of Azerbaijani oil transit through the Baku-Novorossiisk pipeline. As Yerevan began its first attempt at rapprochement with the EU around this time, however, Moscow engaged in a rapprochement with Baku as a warning.[57]

Between 2013 and 2017, Russia supplied two-thirds of Azerbaijan's weapons imports. Russian arms exports to Azerbaijan grew as the West imposed formal or informal restrictions on military procurement. These restrictions hearken back to the "request" in the early 1990s by the OSCE's Committee of Senior Officials that all arms sales to all parties to the conflict should be halted.[58] Russia never honored this request, despite being a co-chair of the Minsk Group, which was charged with resolving the conflict.

During the July 2020 military hostilities in Azerbaijan's Tovuz district, Moscow showed a general lack of even-handedness, tilting decisively toward Armenia, most notably by emergency military re-supply. This demonstrative support for Armenia had a galvanizing effect on Azerbaijani public opinion and arguably shocked the country's political elite. It is not an overstatement to say that these actions created the impression in Baku that it could no longer count on Moscow, and that Ankara was its only true regional friend in facing up to Yerevan.

Russia's relations with Azerbaijan have further changed qualitatively with the withdrawal of Russian "peacekeeping" forces from fully de-occupied Karabakh in the spring of 2024,

---

[57] Sergei Markedonov, "Reviewing Loyalties in Greater Caucasus," *Russia Beyond*, August 16, 2013, https://www.rbth.com/opinion/2013/08/16/reviewing_loyalties_in_greater_caucusus_28973.html.

[58] Organisation on Security and Co-operation in Europe (OSCE), "Decisions based on the Interim Report on Nagorno-Karabakh," https://www.sipri.org/sites/default/files/2016-03/OSCE_Decisions-based-on-the-Interim-Report-on-Nagorno-Karabakh.pdf, reproduced from Committee of Senior Officials, *Journal No. 2*, Annex 1, Seventh Committee on Senior Officials meeting, Prague, February 27-28, 1992.

and the Russian failure to assume proper responsibility in timely fashion for the shoot-down, over Grozny, of the Azerbaijan Airlines plane that crashed in Aktau, Kazakhstan, at the end of 2024.

Armenia's Relations with Russia

One of the reasons why Tsarist Russia implanted ethnic-Armenian populations from the Persian and Ottoman Empires into the South Caucasus in the early nineteenth century was to change the demographic balance in that part of the empire. Just as Ossetians in southern Russia had migrated over the mountains to create South Ossetia inside Georgia, so the ethnic-Armenian drive for territorial expansion resulted from the search for living-space as the population increased, until it became the political dogma that is in evidence today.[59]

Armenia has been a member of the Russian-led Collective Security Treaty Organization (CSTO) since its foundation in 2002 on the basis of the 1992 Collective Security Treaty (CST). Azerbaijan acceded to the CST in 1994 but withdrew in 1999. At the start of the Second Karabakh War, Armenia hosted more than 3,000 Russian soldiers at a military base near Gyumri as well as at an air base near Yerevan. In addition, Russia has since 2016 been integrating Armenian armed forces into the structure of its Southern Military District, including the formation of joint Russian-Armenian ground forces. Also, Armenian forces were not responsible for Armenia's border security; rather, the Border Service of Russia's Federal Security Service (FSB) had this job

---

[59] Tadeusz Swietochowski, *Russia and Azerbaijan: A Borderland in Transition*, New York: Columbia University Press, 1995, pp. 11-12; Taras Kuzio, "Nationalist Myths Drove the Russia-Ukraine and Armenia-Azerbaijan Wars," *The National Interest*, February 16, 2021, https://nationalinterest.org/blog/buzz/nationalist-myths-drove-russia-ukraine-and-armenia-azerbaijan-wars-178278.

up until 2024, when Pashinyan had them (fully or partially) withdrawn from all but the Turkish border.

Russia has been Armenia's main weapons supplier since the 1990s, but Armenia "pays" for Russian arms with targeted ruble-denominated loans from Russia. Azerbaijan, on the other hand, is compelled to pay the significantly higher "normal" international prices charged by Russian arms export bureaucracies, and has done so in hard currency. The Armenian economy is heavily dominated by Russian companies, particularly in the energy sector (up to 80 percent according to some estimates) and also in the financial sector. The state-owned company Armenian Railways was transferred to full ownership by the state-owned company Russian Railways in 2008. There are myriad other examples.

Armenian dependence on Russian arms has had very definite geopolitical results. As mentioned above, Armenia began to negotiate an AA with the European Union in 2010. It was close to being finalized in autumn 2013, but Russia put an end to the process when Armenia announced its decision that year to join the EAEU. This made the DCFTA, which would have been part of the AA, impossible. Armenia's President Serzh Sargsyan announced his country's readiness to proceed with the AA minus the DCFTA, but this never happened. In 2017 he signed instead a CEPA having, despite its name, a much-reduced scope. Armenia's dependence on Russian arms sales was not a small influence that produced this geopolitical result.

Russian deliveries of military equipment and ammunition to Armenia increased just after the military clashes in 2016. Between 17 July and 4 August of that year, there were no fewer than seven flights from Russia that transported arms to Armenia. Georgia refused permission for the overflight of its territory by Russian military transports, so the planes took the roundabout path from Russia over Kazakhstan, Turkmenistan, Iran, and finally into Armenian airspace.

Interestingly, when the current prime minister, Nikol Pashinyan, was in the political opposition in Yerevan in the years before coming to power, he strongly criticized Armenian vassalage to Russia. Since the Second Karabakh War and Pashinyan's subsequent re-election in June 2021, the prevailing view in Moscow has correctly seen Baku as the dominant and most dynamic economic power in the South Caucasus. It evaluates the old Karabakh clan, which held power in Yerevan from 1998 to 2018, as a spent political force, having rotted from the inside due to corruption, and as a blight upon future Armenian social and economic development.[60]

Armenia, Azerbaijan, and Türkiye

In the late 2010s, Russia may have wagered that Türkiye would help Russia in the latter's quest for self-assertion as a great power; however, such a bet has now failed. A few years ago, Türkiye may have seen Russia as a lever for helping to increase its own strategic autonomy, particularly in the broader region including Syria and Libya. Yet that ceased to be the case even before Russia relaunched its war of aggression against Ukraine in February 2022. As demonstrated by its June 2021 Shusha Declaration with

---

60 For background, see Ani Mejlumyan, "Migration Out of Armenia Spikes," *Eurasianet*, November 8, 2021, https://eurasianet.org/migration-out-of-armenia-spikes. Jirair Libaridian drew attention to this danger a decade ago: see his "Emigration Threatens Armenia: Libaridian's Appeal," *IANYAN Magazine*, August 3, 2011, archived at https://archive.md/gefQV.

Azerbaijan, Türkiye seeks to increase its influence in the South Caucasus region, with or without an entente with Russia.

Armenia's Relations with Türkiye

Armenia and Türkiye do not have formal diplomatic relations. Throughout the inter-war period, Türkiye, along with Azerbaijan, maintained an absolute embargo against Armenia, instituted from the time of the First Karabakh War. Armenia's occupation of Azerbaijani lands meant its self-exclusion from negotiations over the BTC pipeline and other transportation and communications links through the South Caucasus in the 1990s. Such links also included the Baku-Tbilisi-Erzurum gas pipeline (which later became the South Caucasus Pipeline, SCP, the first leg in what ultimately became the Southern Gas Corridor thanks to EU support) and the Baku-Tbilisi-Kars railway. Bilateral tensions between Armenia and Türkiye were exacerbated throughout the 1990s by Armenia's insistence on rehabilitating the Metsamor Nuclear Power Plant, which had been shut down after the 1988 Spitak earthquake. Metsamor, only 17 kilometers from the Turkish border, was recommissioned in 1995 after upgrades.

Erdoğan's 2002 election led to some hopes for an improvement in relations. He appointed Ahmet Davutoğlu as a chief advisor (and later foreign minister, and later still, prime minister), and Davutoğlu declared a Turkish foreign-policy doctrine of "zero problems with neighbors." Expert-level consultations led to some early conciliatory moves between Türkiye and Armenia, but they did not get very far. Türkiye gave Armenia limited access to its airspace in 2005, but trade still continued to be routed through Georgia.

Talks about establishing diplomatic relations between the two countries began without publicity in Switzerland in 2007. These bilateral discussions, exploring prospects for reopening the border and exchanging ambassadors, came to public attention with the announcement that Türkiye's president Abdullah Gül would visit Yerevan in September 2008, ostensibly to watch a football World Cup qualification match. Agreement on a roadmap for diplomatic normalization was announced in 2009; in October of that year the two countries' foreign ministers signed the Zurich Protocols, which would have framed that process.

Political opposition to the Zurich Protocols inside Armenia led to their submission to the Constitutional Court for a legal opinion. The Court ruled that their implementation would not imply recognition of the borders drawn by the 1921 Treaty of Kars. Türkiye regarded this official judgment as an unacceptable revision of the agreement, and the Armenian government suspended its ratification. In subsequent years, different Armenian officials made statements seeming to amount to territorial claims against Türkiye.[61]

Bilateral relations between Türkiye and Armenia deteriorated further throughout the 2010s, particularly after the Armenian and Russian defense ministers signed an agreement in December 2015 to create a Joint Air Defense System in the Caucasus. Armenia officially criticized the October 2019 Turkish military offensive in northeast Syria. (Between early 2019 and late 2024, a limited number of Armenian personnel were stationed in

---

61 For example: "Prosecutor General: Armenia Should Have Its Territories Back," *Asbarez*, July 8, 2013.

Syria at the request of the Assad regime, serving alongside Russian troops.) Little else happened and less changed in Armenian-Turkish relations up until the outbreak of the Second Karabakh War in September 2020, although Pashinyan's August 2020 declaration on the centenary of the 1920 Treaty of Sèvres, characterizing the terms of this treaty as "historical fact" and "historical justice," may have played an important role in pushing Türkiye unconditionally to support Azerbaijan's military operations.[62]

Azerbaijan's Relations with Türkiye

The governments of Azerbaijan and Türkiye have cooperated closely on foreign and security matters since Azerbaijan gained independence from the Soviet Union. After the end of the First Karabakh War, this cooperation focused most visibly on the energy sector. Throughout the mid- and late 1990s, agreements about the construction of the BTC oil export pipeline, together with other energy and transportation infrastructure projects described above, were key. They also allowed Ankara to develop a new strategic role as an energy transit country.

In 2000, the armed forces of the two countries implemented cooperation in training and education on the basis of an agreement first signed in 1992. In 2003, Ilham Aliyev visited Ankara to begin setting the foundation for more intensive cooperation between the two countries, which came to pass particularly after Erdoğan's second election victory in 2007—although a very serious dip in bilateral relations took place in 2009-2010 as Baku

---

[62] Robert M. Cutler, "Western Blind Spot in the South Caucasus," p. 66; compare Jirair Libaridian, "A Step, This Time a Big Step, Backwards," *Aravot*, September 1, 2020, who called Pashinyan's remarks "equivalent to a declaration of at least diplomatic war against Turkey."

protested strongly against the Zurich Protocols process. In the late 2000s, Erdoğan began reaching out to other Turkophone countries to establish a cultural, economic, and eventually political community. Azerbaijan had already assumed the role of Türkiye's bridge to the Caspian Sea in energy matters.

Azerbaijan became a bridge from Türkiye not just to the Caspian Sea but potentially across it, into Central Asia. What is now called the Organization of Turkic States was established in 2009 as the Turkic Council. The related but organizationally distinct Parliamentary Assembly of Turkic States (TURKPA) was established in 2008 with its secretariat in Baku. The embedding of Azerbaijani-Turkish relations in such a context drove forward their bilateral cooperation and increased their production of military goods, which spiked in the two months leading up to the Second Karabakh War.

In 2010, a High-level Strategic Cooperation Council mechanism was established at the presidential level to strengthen bilateral relations. That same year, the two countries signed a new gas-supply agreement alongside a landmark document outlining strategic partnership and cooperation in five key security fields: military-political and security issues, military and military-technical cooperation, humanitarian issues, economic cooperation, and other provisions. Additionally, a new Azerbaijani military doctrine adopted in 2010 allowed for the potential establishment of foreign military bases within its territory,[63] and Türkiye, as a guarantor of Nakhchivan's autonomy under the 1921 Treaty of Moscow, has historically provided significant support to Azerbaijan, including its military base in Nakhchivan.

---

63   This was a significant precursor event establishing the military-doctrinal basis for the creation of the joint Russian-Turkish monitoring mechanism near Aghdam just after the 2020 war.

In the 2010s, Azerbaijan became the single greatest source for foreign direct investment in Türkiye. This phenomenon resulted to a significant degree from the massive investment by State Oil Company of the Azerbaijani Republic (SOCAR) in the construction of the Trans-Anatolian Natural Gas Pipeline (TANAP) and associated infrastructure, including enormous petrochemical plants. At the same time, this development, which increased Azerbaijani influence on Turkish diplomacy, may be seen, from a longer-term geo-economic standpoint, as a response by Baku to the 2009 Turkish-Armenian Zurich Protocols. Bilateral Turkish-Azerbaijani relations improved again after 2013-2014, when Ankara's political rhetoric became more nationalistic, after its designs on the Middle East fell apart. Relations deepened further after the 2016 coup attempt in Türkiye increased the nationalist—as opposed to religious—profile of its government's foreign policy. SOCAR constructed TANAP, which runs from east to west across Türkiye, as part of the EU-sponsored Southern Gas Corridor. SOCAR remains TANAP's majority shareholder and operator. SOCAR also owns the enormous and important STAR oil refinery, constructed in Türkiye's Izmir province between 2011 and 2018, which took over $6 billion of Azerbaijani investment. In August 2020, Azerbaijan became Türkiye's largest supplier of natural gas, superseding Russia.

The closeness of the bilateral strategic cooperation is encapsulated in the phrase, "one nation, two states," alluding to the strong cultural ties as well as to the high level of mutual intelligibility between the Anatolian and Azerbaijani Turkish languages. The June 2021 Shusha Declaration on Allied Relations between the two countries only underlines and formalizes this cooperation.

Still, it is instructive to observe that while in Ankara the emphasis is put on "one nation," in Baku it is put on "two states."

Azerbaijan, Armenia, and Iran

Iran and Armenia have for three decades had a strong diplomatic entente that effectively transformed itself, in the immediate aftermath of the Second Karabakh War, into an alliance including enhanced military-industrial, if not overt military, cooperation. In the early 2020s, this alliance appeared to develop in a way that transcends merely bilateral relations in even South Caucasus geopolitics. That is because Russia has shifted, still more directly than before, toward overt military and strategic cooperation with Iran. Such a development was motivated in turn by Russia's redeployment of its armed forces away from Syria and the South Caucasus in order to support its renewed war of aggression against Ukraine. In this period, Iran took steps to exacerbate its military threat against Azerbaijan through unprecedentedly massive military exercises held unprecedentedly close to the border. It also ramped up its subversion against the secular government of Baku through the activities of its agents on Azerbaijani territory.[64] Following the death of Iran's President Ebrahim Raisi with his Foreign Minister, Hossein Amir-Abdollahian in May 2024, however, the complex relationship between Azerbaijan and Iran seems to have entered into a "de-escalation" phase.

---

64 For details, see Heydar Isayev, "Further Strain in Azerbaijan-Iran Relations," *Eurasianet*, March 15, 2023, https://eurasianet.org/further-strain-in-azerbaijan-iran-relations.

Azerbaijan's Relations with Iran

Azerbaijani-Iranian relations between 1994 and 2020 are divisible into two periods, having the year 2012 as their cut-point. During both these periods, Iran's policy toward Azerbaijan has been hostile. During the first period, Tehran sought to undermine if not overthrow, through its special services, the government in Baku. During the second period, Tehran acquired a grudging respect for Baku's efficiency in combating such threats and sought instead to develop economic cooperation, while never moderating what amounted to strategic hostility.

Some Iranian commentators still pretend that a few remarks by then-Azerbaijani president Abulfaz Elchibey in the early 1990s about "southern Azerbaijan" (i.e., northwestern Iran) are a cause for Tehran's hostility; however, no leader since Elchibey has ever repeated those views. This Iranian pretension is a rhetorical smokescreen for the hostility's deeper roots. In 1999, the chairman of the joint chiefs of staff of the Iranian armed forces Hassan Firouzabadi threatened the Baku government by pointing to the presence of "Shi'ite Azer[baijan]is with Iranian blood in their veins" in the region of the Gabala military base. Firouzabadi continued in this manner for over a dozen years. In August 2011, he even personally threatened Azerbaijani President Ilham Aliyev with a "dark future" if the latter did not "pay heed" and cease "to bar Islamic rules."[65]

Iran actively sought to destabilize the Azerbaijani government throughout the 2000s and into the 2010s. Fifteen Iranian and Azerbaijani citizens were convicted in Azerbaijan in 2007

---

65 The various events discussed here are contextualized and sourced in Robert M. Cutler, "Iran Muscles in on Azerbaijan," *Asia Times Online*, March 7, 2012, archived at https://archive.md/wip/6mW7V.

for spying and conspiring to overthrow the government. In 2008, Azerbaijani authorities exposed and thwarted a plot by Lebanese Hezbollah operatives to blow up the Israeli Embassy in Baku with Iranian assistance. In November 2011, the Azerbaijani journalist Rafiq Tagi was murdered in Baku for publishing an article critical of Iran, likely by an Iranian agent or pro-Iranian elements operating in the country.

For its part, Azerbaijan has supported Iran's right to peaceful nuclear program. In January 2011, it signed a five-year agreement to supply least one billion cubic meters of natural gas annually to Iran. Most notably, Azerbaijan pledged that its territory would not be used for military purposes against Iran.

However, Iranian provocations continued. In December 2011, three Azerbaijani men were detained after planning to attack two Israelis employed by a Jewish school in Baku. In late February 2012, members of a terrorist cell established by Iran's Islamic Revolutionary Guards Corps (IRGC) and Lebanese Hezbollah were arrested on suspicion of plotting attacks on the American and Israeli embassies. Later in 2012, Iran recalled its ambassador from Baku, ostensibly over the rejection of its criticisms about Baku's hosting of the Eurovision song contest; Baku later recalled its own ambassador from Iran.

Relations gradually improved after Hassan Rouhani became President of Iran in late 2013. Cooperation was first extended in transportation links. Possibilities for a joint defense commission and cooperation in the petrochemical sector were discussed. In 2018, when Washington reintroduced sanctions against Tehran, Azerbaijan suspended its oil and gas trade cooperation with Iran. When the July 2020 military clashes broke out in Tovuz district, it appeared that Iran was covertly supporting Armenia. During the Second Karabakh War, Iran took a number of steps that reinforced this assessment, including a three-day military incursion into then-recently-liberated territory to delay Azerbaijan's further advance. One factor in Iran's hostility is Azerbaijan's strategic relationship with Israel, but this factor should not be overemphasized, as Iran's complicated relationship with Azerbaijan antedates the latter's relationship with Israel and indeed has cultural roots stretching back centuries.

Armenia's Relations with Iran

Armenia has been an ally of Iran since the early 1990s. It supported Iranian policies in Syria and has always cooperated with Iran against Azerbaijan. Armenian-Iranian relations developed critical mass even as Armenia was waging the First Karabakh War. On 16 March 1992, an Iranian-mediated document was signed by Armenia and Azerbaijan to regulate the conflict, but Armenia immediately violated it by taking the city of Shusha the very next day.

After 1994, the two countries reciprocally appointed ambassadors and began to develop important economic and commercial relations to complement their already strategic political cooperation. A bridge over the Aras River was built, and Iran became an export route for Armenian goods to the Gulf. Hundreds of Armenian-Iranian joint enterprises were established in Armenia, and Iranian banks opened branches there.

Agreements concerning energy cooperation were signed in 1995, and this sector saw significant growth over the next dozen years. A gas pipeline and a high-voltage transmission line between the two countries were constructed, as well as a hydroelectric power station on the Aras River.[66] (Armenia imports gas from Iran through the pipeline and swaps it for electricity exports back to Iran.) Intensive reciprocal high-level visits continued between Yerevan and Tehran from the mid-1990s throughout the first decade of the twenty-first century.

After Robert Kocharyan left the Armenian presidency in 2008, his successor Serzh Sargsyan developed bilateral cooperation with Iran still more intensively. This cooperation went beyond the energy sector to include transport and other industrial sectors, notably investment in the military-industrial sector. In March 2011, on visit to Tehran to celebrate Novruz, Sargsyan strikingly underlined that the Iranian government "has placed no limits on the development of cooperation with Yerevan."[67]

In December 2011, during a visit by Iranian president Mahmud Ahmadinejad to Armenia, a still further expansion of cooperation was launched. Agreements were signed for increased trade and investment from Iran in all the aforementioned sectors of the Armenian national economy. The two sides pursued and intensified these directions throughout the 2010s, during which Iran derived increasing benefit from economic relations not only with Armenia, but also with the Armenian-occupied territories in Azerbaijan. According to Azerbaijan's president Aliyev, speaking to a Heads of State video conference of the Commonwealth of Independent States in October 2021, the IRGC long used the

---

66 Armen Israyelyan, "Iran, Armenia Share Interests in Regional Issues: 20-year-old History of Diplomatic Relations," *Panorama*, February 20, 2011.
67 Gayane Abrahamyan with Gohar Abrahamyan, "Armenia: Iranian Tourists Let Loose in Yerevan for Novruz," *Eurasianet*, April 1, 2011.

occupied territories with Armenia's active assistance, as a kick-off point for smuggling drugs—notably opium manufactured from poppies in Afghanistan—into Europe.[68]

Iran plays the "Armenia card" against Türkiye as well as against Azerbaijan. In the end, this means also playing it against Russia: Iran has never forgotten the Russian Empire's five wars against Persia in the early nineteenth century or the terms of Persia's humiliating capitulation that were the result. As for Russian-Turkish relations today, to put it in the vernacular, it is possible that the Tsar and the Sultan may seem estranged. They traded cards: over Syria, where Russia countered Turkish moves and interests; over Libya, where Russia supported Muammar Gaddafi's son in the presidential election; and over Ukraine, where the Turkish company Baykar has built a plant for producing and modernizing its drones made famous in the Second Karabakh War.[69]

One of the many nuanced recent developments is that Russia—even with its current difficulties and diminished regional influence resulting from its war of aggression against Ukraine—has no incentive structure to work with Türkiye. Türkiye, in turn, can only be unfriendly toward Iran's increased military threats against Azerbaijan and increased military-industrial cooperation with Armenia. In this context, Russia is relying more and more on its own increasing cooperation with Iran over a whole range of fields, as indicated above.

---

68   Jeyhan Aliyev, "Armenia Colluded with Iran on Drug Trafficking to Europe for 30 years: Azerbaijan President," *Anadolu Agency*, October 16, 2021. See also Stephen Blank, "Iran's Latest Misadventure Destabilizes the Caucasus," *War on the Rocks*, June 18, 2020; Mushvig Mehdiyev, "Large Drug Cultivation Site with Cannabis Discovered in Karabakh Region," *Caspian News*, June 30, 2021; and "Drug Trade of Iran's Islamic Revolution Guards Corps with Armenia: Investigation," *APA News*, November 1, 2022. See further the Telegram Cable from the U.S. Embassy in Baku, "Tehran-Baku Tensions Heat Up," October 15, 2009, published by *Wikileaks*, https://wikileaks.org/plusd/cables/09BAKU818_a.html.

69   Clement Charpentreau, "Baykar Drone Factory in Ukraine to be Complete in Two Years: CEO," *Aerotime Hub*, September 13, 2022.

Up until the December 2024 fall of Bashar al-Assad, Russia and Iran largely sided with one another in Syria, whereas Türkiye did not side with them. Since 2022, Russia and Iran have developed what is effectively an alliance. In the Caucasus, they have a joint interest in opposing greater Western and/or Turkish influence. Meanwhile, the Russian-Turkish relationship is increasingly plagued by disagreements, including proxy warfare in Libya and Syria as well as Turkish arms exports to Ukraine; nearly the only factor calming them is the personal relationship between Putin and Erdoğan.

Conclusion

Russia, along with the other two co-chairs of the defunct Minsk Group (France and the United States), has interred the OSCE as a possible mediator, but it remains vitally interested in the South Caucasus. That is because it has wished to broker a deal between the two countries on its own terms and without external interference—or, at the very least, to retain the leverage to block any agreement reached without its explicit consent—while ensuring that the resulting arrangement leaves key issues unresolved. The absence of a comprehensive resolution would then allow Moscow to retain a role in the region. Moscow also has its eye on the North Caucasus, where its role as the controlling security stakeholder (already long overturned in Chechnya) will increasingly come into question, particularly in Karachay-Cherkessia and Kabardino-Balkaria, and possibly also in Ingushetia. Russia has no interest in giving any levers of influence in the North Caucasus to the U.S., Türkiye, Iran, the EU, or any of the EU's member states. Yet a failure by Moscow to regulate the Armenia-Azerbaijan conflict according to its own terms could lead it to lose prestige in the Caucasus as a whole, eventually bringing into question its role as the political hegemon in the North Caucasus.

Armenia's Foreign and Security Policies and Their Fate

The former chief advisor to Armenian president Levon Ter-Petrosyan in the 1990s, Gerard Libaridian, explains Armenia's tragedy of the last quarter-century. The Armenian government, he writes, relied on "dreams rather than hard facts" and "started by the conclusion that corresponded to our dreams, and then asked only those questions that confirmed our conclusions." This meant "adjust[ing] political strategy to our wishes, to what will make us feel good about ourselves rather than tak[ing] into consideration the simple facts that collectively make up the reality around us."[70] It is difficult to find a more poignant or concise expression of the situation.

One might say that a struggle has now started for the soul of Armenia. The victory of Prime Minister Pashinyan in the snap parliamentary elections in June 2021 was extraordinary, insofar as he had headed the government in Yerevan during the catastrophic Second Karabakh War. It signifies the wish by Armenians in Armenia (as opposed to vocal segments of the diaspora) to leave behind the failed policies of the "Karabakh clan" that impoverished the country for two decades. Armenia needs foreign direct investment from the developed capitalist countries of the West to

---

70 Jirair Libaridian, "What Happened and Why: Six Theses," *The Armenian Mirror-Spectator*, November 24, 2020, http://mirrorspectator.com/2020/11/24/what-happened-and-why-six-theses/.

overcome its current dependence for this on Russia and Iran; and for that, it needs a formal peace treaty. It can still be saved from becoming a failed state, but forces are working against it.

Indeed, Iran—in some ways Armenia's closest ally (today strategically even closer than Russia)—has every reason to seek to turn Armenia into a failed state, similar to Lebanon, in order to push its own interests in the South Caucasus. This would be a disastrous development for Armenians in Armenia, the whole of the South Caucasus, indeed also for Türkiye as well as for Russia. A relatively stable Armenia is more in Russia's interest than an unstable Armenia with increased influence from Iran's terrorist and terrorist-sponsoring IRGC.

Yet the "war party" in Yerevan has been recruiting and finding new external allies, even beyond its long reliance on the Armenian diaspora for international publicity and financial support. Members of the Armenian diaspora do not have to suffer the effects of the disastrous policies that they advocate, because they do not live in or even near Armenia. The diaspora's shrillest voices have been working with Iran and calling for a new and catastrophic war. There is also, and always has been, an Armenian lobby in the Kremlin. Iran has moved from covert to overt support of Armenia, although the strength and value of this support is now in question, given Iran's own strategic defeat by Israel in the Iran-Israel proxy war that began on 7 December 2023.

Armenia continues to exchange drafts of a prospective peace treaty with Azerbaijan, although substantive disagreements over important strategic issues persist. Despite bilateral contacts, Armenia engaged in a period of "forum-shopping" for negotiations, favoring mediation either by Russia or by the West (the European Union and the United States), according to the prevailing political winds. Yerevan reached out in this connection to Washington and Brussels (and Paris), all of which became more active in the talks around the start of 2023 and, subsequently, more active in their encouragement of Armenia to move away from both Iran and Russia, including, in a risky and provocative move, arms sales from France. In the background, there is the June 2021 Shusha Declaration between Azerbaijan and Türkiye, which effectively established a mutual defense alliance between those two countries.

Azerbaijan's Foreign and Security Policies and Their Future

The outcome of the Second Karabakh War confirms Azerbaijan as *the* strategic, political, and economic driver among the three South Caucasus states. Its population and gross domestic product are one and a half times the totals of Armenia and Georgia put together. The reconstruction and re-population of the formerly occupied territories will help drive further growth throughout the 2020s. Notably, Azerbaijan has decided to pay for almost all this work directly from its own budget without taking loans from international institutions or private foreign interests.

Despite Iran's grudging respect for Azerbaijan, Tehran still has three motives for hostility to Baku that are sometimes not so well hidden. First, Baku's independence attracts the attention of the sizable ethnic-Azerbaijani minority in northwestern Iran. Second, Baku's cooperation with and closeness to Türkiye and the West—and more recently Israel— in security, energy, and military relations is more than irksome to Tehran. Third, the secularism of the Azerbaijani model of government gives the lie to the millenarian Shi'ite pretensions of the Tehran regime, even if the theocratic elite has been supplanted through a "soft coup" by the IRGC, which has promoted a new and younger stratum of hardline technocrats into administrative power within the state apparatus.[71]

The concept of "strategic hedging" (a post-Cold War theoretical concept designating the combination of cooperative and confrontational elements in a given state's foreign policy) helps to explains the success of Azerbaijan's foreign economic, security, and military policy over the last 10-15 years.[72] Both a motive for and a result of this evolution has been Azerbaijan's self-positioning as a "middle power" or a "keystone state." Its participation in and chairmanship of NAM, as mentioned above, fits neatly into this profile. It is only one of rather many examples about how Baku has enabled itself through becoming a "norm entrepreneur" and thereby facilitating tension-reduction and conflict-limitation among great powers.[73]

Another example of the foregoing is that Baku is the seat of the Secretariat of TURKPA, the inter-parliamentary assembly under the umbrella, but autonomous, of the Organization of Turkic States. This fact takes on significance from the possible construction of a two-way corridor for unimpeded movement

---

71 Saeid Golkar and Kasra Aarabi, *Raisi's Rising Elite: The Imam Sadeghis, Iran's Indoctrinated Technocrats*, London: Institute for Global Change, 2011.

72 Anar Valiyev and Narmina Mamishova, "Azerbaijan's Foreign Policy towards Russia since Independence: Compromise Achieved," *Southeast European and Black Sea Studies* 19, no. 2, 2019, pp. 269-291.

73 Esmira Jafarova, "Is Azerbaijan a 'Middle Power'?" *Modern Diplomacy*, May 16, 2020; see also Christopher Mott, "Inshore Balancers and Reborn Opportunities: Middle Powers and the Silk Road Region," *Baku Dialogues* 5, no. 4, Summer 2022, pp. 6-20.

across southern Armenia, between the Nakhchivan exclave and the main body of Azerbaijan. Such a corridor would open up another direct route (besides the newly renovated BTK railway) for Central Asian transportation and trade to Europe via the South Caucasus and Türkiye.

Azerbaijan's geo-economic significance will also continue to grow as the indispensable hub of the Trans-Caspian International Trade Route ("Middle Corridor") that will run from Southeast Asia and China through Kazakhstan, crossing the Caspian Sea, then through Azerbaijan, Georgia, and further to European countries. Multi-modal ports, already in operation and set for expansion, have been constructed on both the eastern and the western shores of the Caspian Sea. A confluence of events, including Russia's renewal of its war of aggression against Ukraine, propels this development as the use of both the northern and the southern routes correspondingly declines due to sanctions.[74]

Final Remarks

It is no longer the case that Russia, Iran, and Türkiye balance against one another in the South Caucasus. Rather, Russia and Iran have deepened their alignment, particularly as Moscow faces growing isolation due to its war in Ukraine. Nor are Iran and Russia cooperating just on the manufacture of military drones for use against Ukraine (and eventually others). Moscow and Tehran, which together with Beijing seek to revise the status quo established after the international-system transition following

---

74   Robert M. Cutler, "Is Trans-Caspian Corridor Ready for Prime Time?" *Asia Times*, June 2, 2022, https://asiatimes.com/2022/06/is-trans-caspian-corridor-ready-for-prime-time/.

the end of the Cold War, have also increased their north-south cooperation in shipping and commerce. This greater cooperation is in evidence first across the Caspian Sea, and second along its eastern shore. China is also constructing a railway that looks likely to increase both Russian and Iranian influence in Uzbekistan and Turkmenistan.

Throughout the quarter-century covered in this chapter, and especially over the past decade, the South Caucasus has emerged as a microcosm of relations among Iran, Russia, and Türkiye. The result of the Second Karabakh War confirms it as such; developments since then have only deepened such a dynamic.

The relative autonomy of the international system that Azerbaijan's prosperity and diplomacy have provided to the country is like an anchor that will help it to resist the general political turbulence foreseeable in world politics and the Greater Caucasus region during the 2020s and 2030s. Small powers nearby and greater powers further distant would do well to recognize and take into account this "pole of attraction" for economic growth in the region, and its strategic significance.[75]

Azerbaijan is the only South Caucasus country that has enjoyed generally mutual respectful relations with all three long-standing regional powers (Iran, Russia, and Türkiye). However, this balancing act is becoming increasingly complex, as tensions rise over projects like the Zangezur Corridor, which is backed by Türkiye but resisted by Iran and Armenia. I conclude with a short over-simplification of the new post-2020 situation from the standpoint of the regional power balance, but one that sheds light

---

75 The idea of a "growth pole" that would attract economic activity is taken from the influential work on French growth by the economist François Perroux, "Note sur la notion de 'pôle de croissance'," Économie appliquée 8 no. 1-2, January-June 1955, pp. 307-320.

on an important kernel of truth. If we would suppose (1) that Russia has more than half-succeeded in drawing Georgia back into its own sphere of influence under Bidzina Ivanishvili's political hegemony in Tbilisi, and (2) that Azerbaijan's victory in the Second Karabakh War represents an insertion of Turkish influence into the South Caucasus, then we could reasonably conclude (3) that Iran—notwithstanding its recent strategic weakness in the Iran-Israel proxy war—will nevertheless continue to assert itself in the South Caucasus through the instrument of the Armenian military-industrial complex with continuing financial sponsorship from the Armenian diaspora.[76]

Russia's strategic preoccupation with Ukraine since February 2022, which could plausibly be characterized now as a fixation, only strengthens this trend and makes it more evident, although the Armenian economy continues to play an increasingly important role in aiding Russia's circumvention of Western sanctions. Thus, while Russia has not abandoned using Armenia as a South Caucasus lever in its own interests, there is an historical breakthrough by Türkiye, and to a lesser extent by Iran, into the region's geopolitical balance. In this context, one can see that Russia is trying to shore up this loss of influence in the region by reinforcing further its now-hegemonic influence in Georgia. That influence was sealed with Tbilisi's decision in November 2024 to suspend negotiations with the EU on prospective membership, followed by the December 2024 inauguration of Mikheil Kavelashvili from the Georgian Dream party as president of the country.

---

76   For most recent indications, see details of military-industrial cooperation specified in "Iran Is Preparing Armenia for a New War against Azerbaijan," *Aze.Media*, November 3, 2021.

THE EVOLVING ROLE OF THE WEST IN THE ARMENIA-AZERBAIJAN CONFLICT

Svante E. Cornell

The West's Irrelevance in 2020

When the war between Armenia and Azerbaijan broke out in the fall of 2020, the United States and the European Union were blindsided. Although the U.S. and France were, alongside Russia, co-chairs of the OSCE Minsk Group (the international body tasked with finding a negotiated solution to the conflict), their actual influence on the rapid escalation of the conflict in 2019-2020 was negligible.

Nearly a decade before the onset of the Second Karabakh War, the Minsk Group had departed from its previous practice of actively providing proposals for the resolution of the conflict. During negotiations in Kazan in 2011, the Minsk Group put forward what was effectively its last proposal. After this, the Minsk Group was effectively set aside, with the Russian leadership unilaterally providing a platform for negotiations. In 2015, Russian Foreign Minister Sergey Lavrov put forward his own plan, a modification of the Kazan plan, with very limited input from or coordination with the Minsk Group. And following the April 2016 eruption of conflict between Armenia and Azerbaijan, the ceasefire that was reached was negotiated unilaterally by the Russian leadership, without even the pretense of consultation with the Minsk Group.

In the intervening years, the Minsk Group became a body focused almost entirely on process: it mainly facilitated meetings between the foreign ministers of Armenia and Azerbaijan. In early 2019, building on the momentum of the recent change of government in Armenia, the Minsk Group was instrumental in facilitating meetings between President Ilham Aliyev and Prime Minister Nikol Pashinyan. But it rapidly became clear that the Minsk Group was unable to respond to events on the ground. The year 2019 started with great hopes for significant progress in conflict resolution; but as described in this volume, the opposite happened, as the Armenian government veered sharply in a nationalist direction. There was no reaction from the Minsk Group, not even when Yerevan essentially reneged on the Madrid principles in May 2019 (in place since 2007) for the resolution of the conflict. When 2019 saw an escalation of rhetoric, and 2020 a real escalation between the two parties, the EU and U.S. were essentially irrelevant. The only two outside powers that mattered in the end were Russia and Türkiye.

The nail in the coffin of the Minsk Group came during the war, when the Russian president mediated a ceasefire to the conflict unilaterally. But it is, of course, wrong to blame the Minsk Group itself for this failure. The failure belongs in the Western capitals, where policy was (or was not) made regarding the conflict, and the South Caucasus more broadly. The processes in the United States and in the European Union (and within its most relevant member states) were dissimilar but had the same effect: a disengagement from the security affairs of the region. It remains to be seen whether this trend will be reversed following the war in Ukraine.

U.S. Disarray

The United States was the leading force in devising a strategic approach to Central Asia and the South Caucasus in the 1990s. The George H.W. Bush and Bill Clinton administrations understood well the strategic importance of the opening of the Eurasian heartland to the world, and the role of the South Caucasus as the pivotal access point and transit corridor connecting the West and Central Asia. Furthermore, the two U.S. administrations understood the crucial importance to nations in Central Asia and the South Caucasus of the oil and gas resources they possessed, and of the ability to export these resources in an unencumbered manner to international markets. Indeed, this understanding went to the top of the U.S. government, with President Bill Clinton taking a direct role in this endeavor. Clinton ensured the establishment of an inter-agency group on Caspian issues that reported to the "deputies' committee" of the National Security Council.[77] This ensured the coordination of approaches by different U.S. government bodies and top-level political attention, including the

---

77 Jofi Joseph, "Pipeline Diplomacy: The Clinton Administration's Fight for Baku-Ceyhan", Woodrow Wilson School, Case Study 1/99, 1999, pp. 10-11. (https://apps.dtic.mil/sti/pdfs/ADA360382.pdf).

presence of the U.S. president at several signing ceremonies for the Baku-Tbilisi-Ceyhan pipeline project.

This coordinated and strategic approach carried over into the early years of the George W. Bush Administration. For a variety of reasons, however, a decline in the quality and nature of U.S. policy toward the region—and the South Caucasus in particular—developed around 2003-2004. This decline stems from political, conceptual, bureaucratic, as well as ideological issues.

The most obvious cause of U.S. disengagement was the sudden shift of focus in U.S. policy in the aftermath of the 9/11 attacks. Ostensibly, these events led to a rapid intensification of U.S. interaction with the South Caucasus and Central Asia, given the importance of the region in the implementation of U.S. Operation Enduring Freedom in Afghanistan. But at least three factors led, instead, to disarray. First, from 2002 onward, U.S. attention shifted to Iraq amid preparations for an invasion of that country. Because that war did not go according to plan, the U.S. got bogged down in Iraq; salvaging the situation in that country occupied a huge proportion of the U.S. national security bureaucracy's attention. By the time the surge in Iraq was launched in 2007 (and Robert Gates had succeeded Donald Rumsfeld at the helm of the Pentagon) the Department of Defense had little time for anything other than Iraq or Afghanistan, where a similar surge would ensue in 2010. Both in terms of political attention and concrete resources, there was a massive decline in U.S. efforts directed at Central Asia and the South Caucasus, as top political focus had been rerouted to Iraq and its immediate neighborhood.

Second, the shift of U.S. government attention to the War on Terror changed the U.S. government's conceptual approach to the region. Previously, the U.S. had focused on the development of the east-west corridor and on the strengthening of the sovereignty of regional states. This was replaced by an approach that seemed to see the region mainly as a corridor to Afghanistan. In layman's terms, at its most basic the U.S. now came to view Central Asia and the South Caucasus as a highway with a pitstop (the Manas air base in Kyrgyzstan). Baku served as a less formal pitstop on that route as well. This led to a gradual decline of the U.S. strategic understanding of its intrinsic interests in the region itself. This process was aided by the completion of the BTC pipeline linking Azerbaijan's Caspian coast with Türkiye's Mediterranean coast, which allowed U.S. policymakers to view its mission in the region as having been accomplished. Later on, the Obama Administration launched its "Pivot to Asia," an underlying assumption of which was that America's active presence in Europe was no longer necessary—a dramatic miscalculation that required willfully ignoring the visible rise of Russia's neo-imperial agenda and writing off the invasion of Georgia in 2008 as a one-off event of little strategic consequence. The Kremlin, for its part, probably read this as an implicit acknowledgment of a Russian sphere of influence in the former Soviet space.

In parallel, ideological shifts combined to change the nature of America's approach to the region. One such shift was the growing unpopularity of fossil fuels, which resulted from a combination of legitimate concerns over the connection between oil production and authoritarianism, and later on—mainly in the 2020s—growing alarmism concerning climate change. This alarmism made it politically inopportune for U.S. leaders to support oil-producers in the region, but also increasingly established legal obstacles to the financing of new hydrocarbon projects (and even the expansion of existing ones).

More consequential, perhaps, was the launch of the U.S. Freedom Agenda in 2004, through which the Bush Administration made the promotion of democracy and human rights a priority of U.S. foreign policy. This agenda was problematic not because of its inherent goals, but because U.S. officials themselves associated it with revolutionary change of government in countries like Georgia and Kyrgyzstan, where protesters toppled weak authoritarian regimes (regimes that, while imperfect, had considered the U.S. a partner.) This American approach was best captured by Freedom House project director Mike Stone's comment on the toppling of President Askar Akayev in Kyrgyzstan in 2005: "Mission Accomplished."[78] But Akayev had not been a U.S. adversary; quite to the contrary, he had been eager for cooperation with the United States. Under the Freedom Agenda, this mattered little: regimes considered authoritarian now faced the real risk that the U.S. Government, or organizations funded in part by the U.S. government, would work to overthrow them.

This occurred just as Vladimir Putin had consolidated power in Moscow, coming to view such "color revolutions" as an existential threat to Russian interests as well as to his own regime. This inserted a powerful ideological element into the realpolitik of the region. When the U.S. began to prioritize relations with countries it considered more democratic and to downgrade relations with those it considered less so, Moscow actively cast itself as the protector of those demoted by Washington against real or imagined threats of color revolutions. A serious casualty of this

---

78   John Daly, "Kyrgyzstan: Business, Corruption and the Manas Airbase," oilprice.com, April 12, 2009.

dynamic was the near collapse in 2005 of Western relations with Uzbekistan, which was and remains at the geostrategic heart of Central Asia. Meanwhile, the same dynamic also led to a deterioration of ties with Azerbaijan, geostrategically the keystone state of the South Caucasus—whereas the U.S. policy in the region came to focus almost exclusively on supporting Georgia's new government in its reform efforts.

While this was in itself a praiseworthy goal, it led the U.S. to apply a normative rather than a strategic approach to the South Caucasus. Even when U.S. policy sought to counter Russian imperial objectives, this tended to be cloaked in the language of supporting endangered democracies—the refrain being to support "Georgia, Moldova, and Ukraine" and thus disregarding geostrategically more important countries like Azerbaijan, Kazakhstan, or Uzbekistan on account of their lesser commitment to Western democratic values. In other words, the Freedom Agenda led Washington to confuse normative objectives with strategic competition.

In the South Caucasus, this problem was compounded with the Obama Administration's "Reset" with Russia, which was announced only months after Moscow's invasion of Georgia, and its subsequent effort to seek a normalization of relations between Armenia and Türkiye. The "Reset" led the U.S. essentially to push the Georgia issue aside, thus failing to inflict costs on Russia for the invasion—in turn setting up a precedent for Moscow's next move in Ukraine a few years later. Meanwhile, support for the Türkiye-Armenia gambit was based on effectively sidelining the Armenia-Azerbaijan conflict from the list of U.S. priorities. The U.S. government appeared to have accepted the notion promoted by Western NGOs, particularly the International Crisis Group, that a Turkish-Armenian deal would make Armenia more secure, and thereby more inclined to engage in the difficult compromises required to strike a negotiated agreement with Azerbaijan over the conflict with Azerbaijan.[79] In other words, so the argument went, the cause of peace between Armenia and Azerbaijan would be promoted by de-linking the two relationships from one another, under the pretense that Armenia, reassured by a normalization with Türkiye, would be more inclined to make concessions to Azerbaijan. But this premise was logically faulty. It did not provide any reason why a more secure Armenia would be more conciliatory. If it felt more secure, would Yerevan not just double down on its conquest of Azerbaijani territory? In any case, the approach was proven wrong very rapidly. As the Armenian leadership was subjected to nationalist criticism over its nascent normalization process with Türkiye, its belligerent rhetoric toward Azerbaijan actually increased, while Yerevan now also raised its tone on issues regarding the Armenian minority in Georgia.[80]

The ideological fallacies of U.S. policy toward the region were compounded by self-inflicted bureaucratic wounds. U.S. policy has suffered from the geographical divisions that organize U.S. government agencies. Both at the State Department and the NSC, the South Caucasus falls under the "Europe" heading. For the Assistant Secretary of State for European Affairs, or the NSC Senior Director for Europe, the South Caucasus is no doubt among the lesser priorities. Furthermore, when Central

---

79   See detailed discussion in Svante E. Cornell, "Turkey's Role: Balancing the Armenia-Azerbaijan Conflict and Turkish-Armenian Relations" in Cornell, ed., *The International Politics of the Armenia-Azerbaijan Conflict*, London: Palgrave, 2018, pp. 99-100.
80   Ibid, p. 100.

Asia was removed from the Europe Bureau in the mid-2000s and joined with South Asia, the Trans-Caspian connection gradually disappeared from U.S. government thinking—at least until the Russia-Ukraine war forced a rediscovery of this important artery. This rediscovery is nevertheless not necessarily sustainable in the absence of a revision of U.S. government bureaucratic boundaries.[81] Conceptually, the South Caucasus became an easternmost outpost of Europe, where it necessarily compared poorly on many accounts with the rest of the continent. Meanwhile the lumping together of South and Central Asia led the U.S. bureaucracy to think in north-south transportation terms, at the expense of the previously dominant east-west logic. When Secretary of State Hillary Clinton launched the "New Silk Road" strategy in July 2011, she did so with a speech in Chennai, India, and with an initiative that focused exclusively on north-south trade, omitting the South Caucasus entirely.[82] U.S. efforts to develop the Trans-Caspian transportation fell by the wayside, with the U.S. no longer actively promoting a Trans-Caspian pipeline, for example.[83]

A final element in America's strategic myopia is the role of ethnic lobbies in influencing U.S. foreign policy. In the context of U.S. policy towards the South Caucasus, the Armenian lobby has played a most negative role in distorting the priorities of American decisionmakers, particularly on the Democratic side. The prominence of the Armenian cause among Democratic pol-

---

81 See Svante E. Cornell, "Joe Biden's Approach to Eurasia Is Stuck In The Past," 19fortyfive, December 21, 2022.

82 Hillary Clinton, "Remarks on India and the United States: A Vision for the 21st Century," Department of State, July 20, 2011.

83 North-south transport across Afghanistan is a key strategic priority for Central Asian states. This should be promoted as a complement to transportation corridors across the Caspian, not at their expense. Unfortunately, the U.S. foreign policy bureaucracy was unable to maintain the strategic thinking that would have allowed seeing these initiatives as part of a single strategy.

iticians has served to downgrade the perception of Azerbaijan in important sectors of U.S. political life. Granted, Azerbaijan's own shortcomings as seen through Western eyes have contributed to this, but the U.S. criticism directed at Azerbaijan is incomparably larger than that leveled at Central Asian states with similar track records, not to speak of American partners in the Middle East. Indeed, few countries the size of Azerbaijan merited the drafting of no less than eight *Washington Post* editorials in the scope of two years, as Azerbaijan did in 2014-2015—perhaps as a result of the personal bias of editorial page editors.[84] During that period, an apparent alliance of Armenian diaspora groups and human rights campaigners made common cause to disrupt U.S. relations with Azerbaijan, coming very close to convincing the U.S. government to impose sanctions on the country for its human rights deficiencies. Only the intervention of senior defense and national security officials halted such plans, but in the process efforts to rebuild the bilateral relationship were set far back amid mutual recriminations.

This fact of American political life has always been present and is likely to continue to be so. Pro-Armenian politicians have important roles in the Democratic party, including the now-criminally-convicted Senator Robert Menendez, ranking member from 2018 and chairman during 2021-2023 of the Foreign Relations Committee; or Adam Schiff, Chairman of the House Intelligence Committee, who in 2020 called for the U.S.

---

84 These biases were illustrated by former editorial page editor David Ignatius's twitter feed that took statements by the head of the unrecognized Nagorno-Karabakh leadership uncritically at face value. See https://twitter.com/IgnatiusPost/status/1602479381712195588. See the following articles in *The Washington Post*: "Azerbaijan Prosecutes a Prominent Human Rights Defender on Absurd Charges," August 13, 2014; "Jailed without Trial in Azerbaijan," March 1, 2015; "The Country that Diminishes the Olympic Flame," April 15, 2015; "Lady Gaga and Members of Congress Accept the Paychecks of a Tyrant," August 7, 2015; "Azerbaijan's Injustice," August 16, 2015; "Azerbaijani Reporter Sentenced to More than 7 Years After a Farcical Trial," September 2, 2015; "No, This is the Truth about Azerbaijan's Repression," September 25, 2015; "Azerbaijan's Continuing Mistreatment of Rights Activists," November 21, 2015.

recognition of the self-proclaimed Nagorno-Karabakh republic.[85] (in November 2024, he became a U.S. Senator). Then, the September 2022 clashes led to the most senior visit of a U.S. government official to either Armenia or Azerbaijan since they each regained independence in 1991 when then-House Speaker Nancy Pelosi visited Yerevan in a clearly partisan effort to "show support for Armenia."[86] Importantly, however, during periods in which the U.S. executive branch was guided by a broader strategy toward the region, the U.S. government proved able to counterbalance the demands of the Armenian lobby and their supporters in Congress, and ensure that U.S. policy was guided by the U.S. national interest. In the absence of such guidance, however, lobby groups have shown their ability to work for their own narrow goals to be incorporated in the regional policy of successive U.S. administrations.

The EU: Overcoming the Eastern Partnership's Deficiencies

The trajectory of the EU's approach to the South Caucasus contrasts with the U.S. approach, as it has been more linear and has evolved in a more predictable manner. Still, many of the deficiencies found above with regard to U.S. policy reappear in the case of the EU.

The EU's approach to the region has developed in lockstep with the EU's own institutional development. A major breakthrough came with the expansion of the EU to Central and East-

---

[85] "Rep. Adam Schiff Formally Calls for U.S. Recognition of the Republic of Artsakh." Public Radio of Armenia. October 23, 2020.

[86] Carlotta Gall, "Nancy Pelosi Visits Armenia Amid Conflict with Azerbaijan," *New York Times*, September 17, 2022.

ern Europe in 2004, which incorporated new member states with an interest in and an understanding of matters concerning the South Caucasus and Caspian region. That year, the EU updated the newly established European Neighborhood Policy (ENP) to include the South Caucasus whilst also establishing the post of an EU Special Representative for the region. Five years later, the EU's Eastern Partnership was launched, at which point the inclusion of the South Caucasus was considered obvious. However, the EU (just like the United States) made a sharp distinction between the South Caucasus and Central Asia. The EU considers the South Caucasus countries to be European states, while those in Central Asia fall outside this scope.

The EU has faced several key dilemmas with regard to the South Caucasus. One has been the difficulty in adjusting the Eastern Partnership to the differing approaches of the six states covered by that program (i.e., the three from the South Caucasus alongside Moldova, Ukraine, and Belarus). A second has been the EU's insistence on defining its approach depending not on strategic realities but on the specific level of adaptation of a particular region or country to its own *acquis communautaire*. A third has been the difficulty of finessing the Armenia-Azerbaijan conflict.

Unlike the United States, the EU has a formal instrument that covers its relations with the countries of the South Caucasus. The Eastern Partnership was launched in 2009 following a Polish-Swedish initiative, and recognized the European identity of the aforementioned six states. The Instrument was clear in not granting a membership perspective to any of those six, instead aiming at very close approximation of their legal, political, and regulatory systems with the EU. If partner countries followed the steps outlined in the Association Agreements and Deep and Comprehensive Free Trade Agreements (DCFTA) the EU offered to them, they would in practice complete up to 85 percent of the steps needed to qualify for EU membership.[87]

The Eastern Partnership, thus, entirely ignored the geopolitical situation of the South Caucasus, and, specifically, its unresolved territorial conflicts. Of course, these and the accompanying geopolitical constraints undermined both the willingness and ability of those states to utilize the opportunities provided by the Eastern Partnership. This shortcoming would become very clear within a few years, as each of the three South Caucasus states came to approach the Eastern Partnership in fundamentally different ways.

Having been denied a Membership Action Plan at the 2008 NATO summit, Georgia saw the Eastern Partnership as its only road to Euro-Atlantic integration—a process that could indirectly provide it with security from further Russian encroachment. Georgia's leadership did so reluctantly, however, as President Mikheil Saakashvili had on many occasions compared the EU bureaucracy with the Soviet Union, and had previously envisaged an economic model reminiscent of Singapore—something clearly incompatible with the burdensome regulations of the EU.[88] Still, Georgia became recognized as the frontrunner among the six states, earning considerable praise from the EU both during Saakashvili's tenure (2003-2013) and the initial year of the tenure of his successor, Bidzina Ivanishvili. Over time, how-

---

[87] See Bernard Hoekman, "Deep and Comprehensive Free Trade Agreements," European University Institute, Working Paper, 2016.

[88] Zbigniew Dumienski, "Georgia: Singapore of the Caucasus," Rajaratnam School of International Studies, February 16, 2011.

ever, this picture changed, as Georgia began a steady decline in various democracy indices from 2016 onward. In the Economist Intelligence Unit's Democracy Index, Georgia fell from a score of 5.93 in 2016 to 5.12 in 2021; Freedom House's Freedom in the World registered a similar decline, from 64 point in 2016 to 58 points in 2021.[89] In parallel, the EU's approach to Georgia shifted as well, culminating in its decision in summer 2024 to pause Georgia's accession process to the EU on account of the government's repressive turn and anti-Western rhetoric.

Azerbaijan, by contrast, indicated that it was not interested in an EU membership perspective, and thus would not pursue an Association Agreement or a DCFTA. Instead, Azerbaijan sought a Strategic Partnership with the EU. Thus, in 2015, Azerbaijan presented the EU with a draft of a proposed Strategic Partnership Agreement at the Eastern Partnership's Riga summit. As an EU official acknowledged, this surprised the EU: "This is the first time a third country provided the EU with a draft agreement. Not even the U.S. is doing this."[90] In November 2016, the EU decided to launch negotiations on a new comprehensive agreement with Azerbaijan.[91] That agreement has yet to be signed, but in July 2022 Azerbaijan and the EU signed a Memorandum of Understanding on a Strategic Partnership in the Field of Energy (this was followed in December 2022 with an Agreement on Strategic Partnership in the Field of Green Energy Development and

---

[89] See e.g., "Georgia's Score Continues to Fall in Democracy Index," civil.ge, February 11, 2022; https://freedomhouse.org/report/freedom-world

[90] Dirk Schuebel, Head of Division for bilateral relations with the Eastern Partnership countries of the European External Action Service, speaking at a conference organised by the European Policy Centre, on February 8, 2016. See Georgi Gotev, "Azerbaijan's rejection of EU association was an eye-opener for Brussels," *Euractiv*, February 11, 2016.

[91] Georgi Gotev, "EU to launch negotiations for a new agreement with Azerbaijan," *Euractiv*, November 14, 2016.

Transmission between Azerbaijan, Georgia, and two EU member states, Romania and Hungary, the signature of which was witnessed by the President of the European Commission). Thus, Brussels and Baku view each other in a fundamentally different way than do Brussels and Tbilisi (and Brussels and Yerevan). The relationship is much more one of equals, as Azerbaijan does not seek the favors of Brussels or to be included in the Union; and Azerbaijan has economic and strategic assets on offer that are very important to the EU—even more so in the wake of the war in Ukraine.

Armenia's approach to the EU is distinct from both Georgia's and Azerbaijan's. The key difference is that Yerevan must calibrate its outreach to the EU with its political, economic, and security dependence on Russia. Some analysts have gone so far as to claim that Armenia is a Russian satellite.[92] Nevertheless, successive Armenian governments have shown a consistent interest in developing as close relations with the EU as Moscow will tolerate. Up until 2013, Armenia had been pursuing negotiations for an Association Agreement and DCFTA alongside Georgia, Ukraine, and Moldova. But just like President Viktor Yanukovich in Ukraine, Armenian leader Serzh Sargsyan was confronted with a Russian ultimatum in the fall of 2013 that led to Yerevan's decision to jettison the agreement and opt instead to join the Russia-led Eurasian Economic Union (EEU). The circumstances of the decision raised eyebrows. Sargsyan made the announcement in Moscow following a meeting with Putin; reportedly, he had consulted neither his government nor his parliament.[93] Similarly,

---

92   Michael Doran, "Azerbaijan in the Struggle for Eurasia: Restoring America's Geostrategic Approach," *Baku Dialogues* 5, no. 2, Winter 2021-2022, pp. 18-44.
93   Personal communication from Armenian official.

Putin had not deigned to consult with the leaders of Belarus and Kazakhstan (the other members of the EEU) about accepting Armenia into the organization. Nevertheless, Armenia sought to salvage its ties with the EU, opting to sign a Comprehensive and Enhanced Partnership Agreement (CEPA) in 2017. Its ambitious sounding title notwithstanding, this document is more similar to the agreement Kazakhstan had signed with the EU in 2015 than what Georgia and Moldova had signed in 2013. More recent engagement between Armenia and some EU member states as well as the EU itself could be seen as the beginning of a strategic shift in a westerly direction, but this has not yet produced any institutional rapprochement.

In sum, the three states of the South Caucasus have had fundamentally divergent approaches to the EU. But the Eastern Partnership was not set up to accommodate this: it adopted a one-size-fits-all approach. This approach was predicated on the fallacious assumption that all six states would seek the same type of agreements the EU offered and would, in turn, begin to approximate to EU standards in a broad variety of areas without much pushback. This did not happen, as half of the six states took a divergent approach to the one foreseen by the EU—and those that did follow the EU's favored procedure displayed many inconsistencies and setbacks in their cooperation with Brussels. This eventually led the EU to reconsider the one-size-fits-all approach of the Eastern Partnership, forcing Brussels to tailor its policies to each state individually starting around 2015.

Another problem in the EU's approach to the areas to its east has been that Brussels has divided up Eurasia according to its own main key parameter—namely, the extent to which countries are considered candidates for EU accession in the near or distant future. Thus, Brussels divides the world into member states, candidate states, associated states that aspire to membership, and "all others." These categories have tended to guide all EU thinking on these regions—at the expense of considerations regarding trade or security. It has been the EU's understanding of a particular country's prospect of integration into EU structures that formed the strategic guidelines for its policy. Geopolitical, economic, or trade factors have been secondary (at best) in this regard. This may have made sense in the immediate post-Cold War era, when the EU's power of attraction was at its height and geopolitical tensions in Eurasia at their lowest. But it has become clear that the EU's relationship to countries to its east cannot rely solely on the power of its normative values and the prospect of institutional association with the EU. There are signs that recent events have led the EU to focus on European political and economic *interests* to a much greater extent, not solely the bureaucracy-led expansion of European norms and values. The EU is gradually beginning to act not only as a European *project*, but as a European *power*; but it still has a long road to travel in this regard.

The final problem in the EU's approach to the South Caucasus has been its inability to address the Armenia-Azerbaijan conflict. While its more recent approach appeared for a time to be more fruitful, this problem hurt the EU's influence in the region for a long time (and has again more recently). First, the EU was not actively involved in the resolution of that conflict until the Minsk Group was effectively disbanded following the 2020 war. For a brief period following the 2008 war in Georgia, there were discussions and debates in Brussels about a more direct EU role in the conflict, possibly through an expansion or alteration of the Minsk Group format to include the EU. In March 2012, the European Parliament's Committee on Foreign Relations actually voted for an effort to include the EU in the Minsk Group.[94] But such proposals fell on deaf ears, for what appears to be three major reasons: French opposition, Russian opposition, and Armenian opposition. Azerbaijan has also been increasingly uninterested in the Minsk Group as a whole and thus in its composition. Paris has wanted to safeguard it position in the Minsk Group, even as its domestic politics led it to tilt increasingly in a pro-Armenian direction. Russia, of course, has made it a priority to oppose any change of format in the unresolved conflicts of Eurasia, as it would reduce Russia's dominant role in the region. Armenia also made it clear it preferred French mediation to EU mediation, given the strong Armenian diaspora in France—as viewed in November 2022 when Yerevan demanded the presence of French President Emanuel Macron in order to attend an EU-led meeting in Brussels between the two presidents on the conflict.[95] More recently, Baku and Yerevan appear to have concluded that the best form of negotiations is the bilateral format in which no outside powers are involved.

The EU's avoidance of direct engagement with this conflict ran counter to its own pronouncements going back to the beginning of the century. The 2003 European Security Strategy mentioned the South Caucasian conflicts in second place, after the Balkans but before the Arab-Israeli conflict, and promised to "take a stronger and more active interest in the problems of

---

94 "EU to Replace France in OSCE MG?," *Yerkir Media*, March 23, 2012.
95 "Azerbaijan says no to Armenian peace talks if Macron present," France24, November 25, 2022.

the Southern Caucasus."⁹⁶ Similarly, the 2004 Strategy Paper of the EU Commission on the European Neighborhood Policy identified one of its highest priorities "to reinforce the EU's contribution to promoting the settlement of regional conflicts."⁹⁷ EU Commissioner for External Affairs Benita Ferrero-Waldner in 2006 stated that "uppermost in my mind in thinking about the South Caucasus today is the ENP's potential to help support conflict resolution."⁹⁸ This shift led to a "turning point for increased EU involvement in the conflicts in Georgia and Moldova"⁹⁹—but not in the Armenia-Azerbaijan conflict.

Meanwhile, the EU's attempts to pursue Action Plans with both Armenia and Azerbaijan under the ENP actively sowed confusion through efforts to dodge the apparent contradiction between the basic international principles underlying the conflict. When the EU embarked on the process of developing Action Plans under the ENP for Armenia and Azerbaijan in 2005, the language on EU efforts regarding the conflict was identical, but with one crucial exception: the very principles on which the EU committed to base its efforts. The EU's document on Azerbaijan included a clause in the introduction to the Action Plan noting that the common values underlying the relationship includes "the respect of and support for the sovereignty, territorial integrity and inviolability of internationally recognized borders." In the Armenia Action Plan, on the other hand, the language

---

96 Council of the European Union, "A Secure Europe in a Better World: European Security Strategy," September 12, 2013.
97 Commission of the European Communities, *European Neighbourhood Policy—Strategy Paper*, Brussels, May 12, 2004.
98 Benita Ferrero-Waldner, "Political Reform and Sustainable Development in the South Caucasus: the EU's Approach," Speech at the Bled Strategic Forum, August 28, 2006.
99 Nicu Popescu, *EU Foreign Policy and Post-Soviet Conflicts: Stealth Intervention*, London: Routledge, 2011, p. 101.

used in the Azerbaijani text was swapped for "the principle of self-determination of peoples"—a principle included in no other Action Plan, whether for Georgia or Moldova.

This approach to conflict resolution was deeply unserious. It also reflected a shift over time in the EU's approach to the core principles of territorial integrity, particularly (in this context) as regards EU policy on Azerbaijan. In the 1990s and early 2000s, the EU tended to treat the post-Soviet conflicts alike, and it was uncontroversial to include statements of support for Azerbaijan's territorial integrity. But following the launch of the European Neighborhood Policy and the pursuit of Action Plans and subsequently Association Agreements with the countries of the Eastern Partnership, the EU continued to assertively support the territorial integrity of Georgia and Moldova—both textually and politically. By contrast, it slowly moved to a position of neutrality on this key subject regarding the Armenia-Azerbaijan conflict, in particular following the recognition of Kosovo by a majority of its member states in 2008.

Clearly, though, the Russian annexation of Crimea in 2014 reversed this trend. In July 2015, EU President Donald Tusk unequivocally stated that the EU "recognizes Azerbaijan's territorial integrity, sovereignty, and independence. Neither the EU nor its member states recognize Nagorno-Karabakh."[100] Similarly, during Latvia's 2015 presidency of the EU, Latvian diplomats began systematically including Azerbaijan alongside Georgia,

---

100 "EU does not recognize Karabakh and supports territorial integrity of Azerbaijan, Donald Tusk says," Verelq.am, July 25, 2015.

Moldova, and Ukraine in the listing of countries whose territorial integrity the EU supports.¹⁰¹

This happened largely because of the blatant similarities between Crimea and Karabakh, which made it impossible for the EU to show indignation over Russia's behavior in Crimea but remain indifferent to Armenia's behavior in Karabakh. EU officials were at a loss to counter Azerbaijani accusations of double standards in the differentiated treatment of Crimea and Nagorno-Karabakh. High-level EU diplomats privately acknowledged as much, agreeing that their efforts to dodge the issue and cite their support for the Minsk Group as justification was decidedly unsatisfying. Thus, EU officials reverted to a policy of expressing support for Azerbaijan's territorial integrity. As analyst Amanda Paul put it, "the EU cannot pick and choose when it comes to the territorial integrity of its partner states."¹⁰²

New Approaches Post-2020

The aftermath of the 2020 war did not immediately lead to major changes in the approaches of the U.S. and EU toward the South Caucasus. Over time, however, both Brussels and Washington got more directly involved in the resolution process to the Armenia-Azerbaijan conflict, though this has yet to translate into a concrete strategy for the South Caucasus region as a whole. But over time, this Western involvement peaked in part because Western powers appeared to tire when not obtaining immediate results,

---

101 "EU Supports Azerbaijan's Territorial Integrity – Latvian Foreign Ministry," *Trend News Agency*, February 13, 2015; see also Azertac, "Latvia supports resolution of Nagorno-Karabakh conflict within Azerbaijan's territorial integrity," July 4, 2015.

102 Amanda Paul, "Where is EU Support for Azerbaijan?," *Cihan News Agency*, April 16, 2008.

and because the two countries involved found more progress in direct negotiations.

Between the two, it was the EU that had both shown a more systematic approach and been willing to engage at a higher level. EU efforts were led from the very top: by European Council President Charles Michel and Commission President Ursula von der Leyen. Its efforts were also more sustained, with Michel leading several summits between the Armenian and Azerbaijani presidents and Von der Leyen traveling to Baku and subsequently attending several highly publicized top-level events hosted by various EU member states that deepened the strategic energy partnership with Azerbaijan she established. The EU had also taken a more direct approach to the deteriorating situation in Georgia, instituting a clear policy process in March 2021 to incentivize the Georgian government to change course. The decision to provide Georgia with a membership perspective, but to provide a list of twelve concrete steps Georgia had to take to obtain candidate status a year later, is an illustration of this.[103] Still, these efforts failed to reverse Georgia's anti-Western course.

U.S. involvement was slower to emerge and more sporadic, as well as at a lower level. While the White House has had no visible involvement in the Armenia-Azerbaijan conflict, NSC director Jake Sullivan hosted his Azerbaijani and Armenian counterparts in August 2022. Secretary of State Antony Blinken repeatedly convened the foreign ministers of Armenia and Azerbaijan, acting in concert with the EU efforts. On Georgia, the U.S. was less decisive. The State Department official spokesperson in July 2022 responded to the Georgian government attacks

---

[103] European Commission, "Opinion on the EU membership application by Georgia," June 17, 2022.

on Ambassador Kelly Degnan, stating that "disinformation and personal attacks on Ambassador Degnan or her team are not consistent with how partners communicate with one another."[104] Undersecretary for International Security Affairs Bonnie Jenkins publicly sent a similar message on a visit to Georgia in October 2022.[105] But the U.S. has been reduced to watching Georgia move in an increasingly anti-Western direction without much of a policy to reverse the process. By late 2024, the U.S. began to impose sanctions on Georgian officials.

Western engagement in the region remains marred by what can only be called spoilers—high-level politicians that have openly sided with one party to the Armenia-Azerbaijan conflict and in effect undermined EU and U.S. efforts to broker a lasting peace agreement. Yerevan successfully appealed to France to get involved in the EU-led process, sensing perhaps that France resents the demise of the Minsk Group. Pashinyan in November 2022 demanded President Macron's presence at an upcoming Michel-led summit with Aliyev, leading Aliyev to refuse this format, which Baku found prejudiced against Azerbaijan. Macron had commented in October that Azerbaijan had "launched a terrible war" and promised France would not "abandon Armenians," and the French Senate voted in November 2020 to recognize the independence of Nagorno-Karabakh, and in November 2022 to impose sanctions on Azerbaijan.[106] This put Baku in the position of once again dealing with mediators that tilted in Armenia's

---

104 United States Department of State, "Department Press Briefing—July 20, 2022," July 20, 2022.
105 See Statement at https://ge.usembassy.gov/undersecretary-for-arms-control-and-international-security-bonnie-jenkins-remarks-at-the-biosafety-regional-conference/.
106 "Azerbaijan accuses Macron of pro-Armenian 'bias'," Euractiv, October 14, 2022; Ismi Aghayev and Ani Avetisyan, "French Senate calls for sanctions on Azerbaijan and recognition of Nagorno-Karabakh, OC Media, November 16, 2022.

direction, thus undermining the main advantage of the EU's mediation bid—its neutrality between the two sides. In the case of the United States, the fighting between the two states in September 2022—when Armenia accused Azerbaijan of intruding on its sovereign territory—led to an outpouring of support for Armenia, which stood in stark contrast to the broad indifference in the United States toward the three-decade long occupation of Azerbaijani territory by Armenian forces.

Thus, leading Western politicians weakened the influence of Western mediation, and thus undermined the geopolitical interests of the West itself in the region. With regard to Georgia, neither the U.S. nor the EU seem to have a good idea of how to reverse the negative spiral the country is in. The underlying problem is that neither the U.S. nor the EU appears to view the South Caucasus regionally and be taking a strategic approach to the region as such, and how it interlinks with challenges relating to Russia and Ukraine, China, Türkiye, Iran, or Central Asia.

Following the Azerbaijani reassertion of control over all of Nagorno-Karabakh in September 2023, the West's irrelevance to the situation was further cemented. In the short term, the Azerbaijani offensive, and the departure of Armenians from Karabakh, led to widespread condemnation by Western governments as well as Western non-government organizations. The Biden Administration froze much of its relationship with Azerbaijan—a move that achieved very little except marginalizing the role of the United States in the region. Western powers simply lacked leverage to affect the outcome of events in the South Caucasus. Indeed, it is clear that the failure of American and European efforts to bring about a peace settlement between Armenia and

Azerbaijan accelerated the Azerbaijani decision to act unilaterally to bring an end to the conflict.

Going forward, it remains to be seen if the Western powers will prove able to reassess the geopolitical situation in the South Caucasus as it links to Western interests in Central Asia and the Middle East and develop a more realistic and long-term approach to the region.

SITTING ON TWO CHAIRS

Russia's Pragmatic, Transactional Approach
to the Karabakh Question

Nikolas K. Gvosdev

One of the pitfalls in trying to understand the sources and motivations behind Russian actions in the South Caucasus is to ascribe to Kremlin policymaking a single, overarching motive. Russian support for Armenia is said to arise from a centuries-long relationship based on shared cultural and religious identities that serves as the basis for an enduring friendship between the two countries. In contrast, Moscow's shift in support to Azerbaijan is categorized within the context of a preference for authoritarian states, where governments "generally share with the Kremlin a keen interest in their own political longevity, and also a disinclination to allow western notions of free elections, transparent government and human rights to take root."[107]

Both lines of analysis provide useful and important insights into Russian strategic assessments and policy proposals, but they

---

107 Mark Galeotti, "'RepressIntern': Russia's security cooperation with fellow authoritarians," *OpenDemocracy*, November 22, 2016.

are insufficient in conveying the entire picture. Moreover, their starting point assumes that the South Caucasus is itself a *sui generis* region and often overlooks broader themes that categorize Russian national security decision making. In other words, viewing Russian actions in the area, especially in the context of the conflict over Karabakh between the end of the First Karabakh War and the start of the Second Karabakh War, as arising solely or primarily from specific Russian approaches to Armenia and Azerbaijan, risks missing how events in this part of the world are connected to Russia's overall posture in world affairs during this timeframe (1988-2024). Certainly, the situation has become even more complicated in the aftermath of the Russian invasion of Ukraine in February 2022. The greater Silk Road area—of which the South Caucasus serves as a critical keystone interconnector—is now a vital focus of Russian national interest.[108] Thus, when we describe Russia's approach in the region on the basis of a perceived "tilt" towards Armenia or a later effort to rebalance in favor of Azerbaijan, it is critical to have a complete understanding of what drove Kremlin policy, especially in this larger context. Historic sentimentality (in the case of Armenia) or pragmatic transactionalism (in the case of Azerbaijan) is only part of the story.

Situating Karabakh in Overall Russian Foreign Policy

The foundations of the southern/Silk Road vector in Russian foreign policy—prioritizing the importance of the region that in

---

[108] See Nikolas K. Gvosdev, "Moscow's Evolution Towards a G-Zero/Silk Road Paradigm," *Baku Dialogues* 7, no. 4 (Summer 2024), pp. 70-85.

the modern era might be described as the "Caspian-Black Sea macro region" (to use Amur Hajiyev's formulation[109])—began to be laid in the eighteenth century, principally by Prince Gregory Potemkin. This vector was based on the assessment that the projection of Russian power into Central Asia, the Middle East, and Southeast Europe would be critical to the development and maintenance of Russia's position as a great power—and that securing Russian predominance in the Caucasus would be vital in this regard. During the imperial period, a major strategy for maintaining Russian control was to rely both on demographic shifts as a basis for creating pro-Russian constituencies, especially the relocation of ethnic Armenians from the territories of the Ottoman and Persian Empires into Russian-controlled territory, and to forge special relationships with the ethnically Georgian and Azerbaijani nobilities and local elites.[110]

When the Soviet Union replaced the Russian Empire, the ideological coloring of the regime changed but the strategic imperatives remained the same. Even though the nascent Soviet state reconciled itself, at least temporarily, to the loss of Finland, the Baltic States, Poland, what would later be called Moldova, as well as western Belarus and western Ukraine, the Soviet authorities spent a great deal of effort and resources to reabsorb the three Transcaucasian states of Armenia, Azerbaijan, and Georgia that had emerged from the wreckage of the Russian Empire. Once incorporated into the Soviet state, a key part of Soviet nationalities policy—as developed and implemented principally by Josef Stalin in his role as Commissar of Nationalities—was to reduce

---

109   Quoted in "Baku-Ankara-Moscow co-op format based on regional interaction," *Azernews*, October 8, 2019.
110   As discussed in Nikolas K. Gvosdev, *Russia's Southern Strategy*, Philadelphia, PA: Foreign Policy Research Institute, 2019, p. 5; see also Nikolas K. Gvosdev, "Russia's Strategy in the Black Sea Basin," *War on the Rocks*, August 2, 2018.

the viability of any possible independent entity that might re-emerge. Stalin's strategy consisted in part in the redrawing of borders, moving populations, and establishing new political structures to demonstrate—as one of Stalin's key associates, Sergo Ordzhonikidze (who served as the head of the Caucasian Bureau of the Communist Party, or Kavburo, from 1920 to 1926) once stated—"only the Soviet power can solve all the vexed questions related to ethnic strife."[111] Karabakh, which had been an independent khanate at the time of its incorporation into the Russian empire, and subsequently annexed to the Elizavetpol' governorate (which itself became part of the Azerbaijan republic)—but which had acquired a majority-ethnic Armenian population by that time—was created as an autonomous region (oblast) within the Azerbaijani Soviet Socialist Republic in 1923 (this was done despite requests from the Armenian Soviet Socialist Republic to have the territory transferred to its control).[112]

By the mid-1980s, as the Soviet Union began to disintegrate, a new leadership in Moscow, headed by Mikhail Gorbachev, looked for new ways to reinvigorate the USSR. Policies such as perestroika (a restructuring of the economic system), and glasnost (to permit more open discussions and criticisms of Soviet policy) were intended to give the population a sense of having a stake in the system—and Gorbachev's reforms. But these policies also had the unintended consequence of reopening discussions about history and nationalism that eroded the Soviet center's ability to

---

111 Quoted in Farid Shafiyev, *Resettling the Borderlands: State Relocations and Ethnic Conflict in the South Caucasus*, Montreal: McGill-Queen's University Press, 2018, p. 170.

112 See, for instance, Svante E. Cornell, "Undeclared War: The Nagorno-Karabakh Conflict Reconsidered," *Journal of South Asian and Middle Eastern Studies* 20, no. 4, Summer 1997, pp. 2-5; Wendy Betts, "Third party Mediation: An Obstacle to Peace in Nagorno-Karabakh," *SAIS Review* 19, no. 2, Summer-Fall 1999, p. 166.

follow Ordzhonikidze's dictum about the USSR having solved ethnic and national strife. In particular, the question as to how boundaries between republics were drawn, how populations were assigned to territory, and specific governing arrangements all began to be openly discussed—with debates over whether the principle of self-determination or territorial integrity should take precedence. At the same time, Gorbachev increasingly faced resistance to his measures from within the Communist Party and the Soviet "establishment."[113]

Staying in power—and maintaining the Soviet center—became Gorbachev's lodestone. As with so many other issues, Gorbachev did not adopt a standard, consistent approach on the Karabakh question but shifted his policies based on his assessment of whatever measure might strengthen his position at the time. From an initial sympathy for the Armenian claim to have the Nagorno-Karabakh Autonomous Oblast (NKAO) joined to the Armenian SSR (on the basis of a claim of self-determination), to the decision to put the NKAO directly under Moscow's control and supervision, to eventually viewing Armenian separatism in the NKAO as a threat to his plans for the Soviet Union, Gorbachev pursued an inconsistent policy and sent very mixed signals.[114] The end goal, however, as Svante Cornell has argued, was to "enable Moscow to reestablish control over the area."[115]

After 1989, there was an additional complicating factor. As with other issues in the last years of the USSR, a position taken by

---

113   See the discussion in Paul Goble, "Coping with the Nagorno-Karabakh Crisis," *Fletcher Forum of World Affairs* 16, no. 2, Summer 1992, pp. 21-22.
114   Ilya Tsukanov, "How a Senior Gorbachev Advisor's Involvement in Karabakh Conflict Helped Set Region on Fire," *Sputnik International*, October 5, 2020.
115   Svante E. Cornell, *The Nagorno-Karabakh Conflict*, report no. 46, Department of East European Studies, Uppsala University, 1999, p. 18.

Gorbachev and the central Soviet government would increasingly be challenged by an emerging alternate center of power within Moscow: the Russian republican government led by Boris Yeltsin. Some of the pro-democracy intellectuals who rallied to Yeltsin supported Armenian claims to the NKAO, while Soviet efforts to aid the authorities in Azerbaijan in reimposing control over the NKAO in April-May 1991 ("Operation Ring") were seen in light of a possible crackdown against other independence-leaning republican governments, including Russia's. Finally, the "war of laws" between the Soviet center and the Russian republican government—this involved the question of which orders and directives would enjoy supremacy—and the gradual breakdown of control over the Soviet governing and military apparatus, made it unclear as to what "Moscow's" policy was at any given moment, and opened up more avenues for freelance, independent activity. By 1991, Soviet/Russian equipment and even personnel began flowing into the zone of the conflict over Karabakh, but with unclear indications as on whose orders these actions were taken, or whether individuals were simply freelancing. As the Soviet empire collapsed, the Russians (both in the central Soviet ministries that would become "Russian" after 1991 as well as within the Russian republican structures) began supporting their favored groups (either out of ideological and strategic concerns, or from purely mercenary or mercantile motives).[116]

After the August 1991 coup attempt against Gorbachev failed, it became clear that Russian president Boris Yeltsin was increasingly the dominant political figure across the Soviet space. In September 1991, Yeltsin, along with Kazakhstan's president

---

116 Philip Remler, "Russia's Stony Path in the South Caucasus," *Carnegie Endowment for International Peace*, October 20, 2020.

Nursultan Nazarbayev, attempted to mediate a settlement with Azerbaijan's president Ayaz Mutalibov and Armenia's president Levon Ter-Petrosyan. At a series of negotiations at the North Caucasus spa town of Zheleznovodsk, Yeltsin thought he had achieved an agreement on Nagorno-Karabakh that both Armenia and Azerbaijan could accept and that Russia, on behalf of the Soviet center, would enforce. On the one hand, this agreement called for Armenia to renounce any territorial claims to the NKAO and to recognize the territorial integrity of Azerbaijan. On the other hand, it pushed for a maximum degree of autonomy for the NKAO, essentially granting to the Karabakh Armenian community virtual independence from all but the most essential dictates of the government in Baku. The Zheleznovodsk formula reflected Yeltsin's own efforts to reconcile the claims of self-determination for Russia's ethnic republics with maintaining the territorial integrity of the Russian Federation. Finally, the proposed agreement called for the permanent deployment of Russian forces in the NKAO to enforce and police the settlement—with the clear implication that Moscow would need to be part of any post-Soviet regional arrangement.

The Zheleznovodsk talks took place against the backdrop of the ongoing collapse of the USSR, and reflected a view strongly held within Yeltsin's presidential administration that, with the disappearance of the Soviet Union, a post-Soviet Russia would be quickly integrated into the structures of the Euro-Atlantic world, including the NATO alliance, and would be treated as one of the major decision-making components of a post-Cold War security architecture for Europe. Moreover, Yeltsin assumed that Russian efforts to handle conflicts on the territory of the post-Soviet space would be blessed and supported by the West, with Moscow setting the agenda for post-Soviet inclusion into the Western world. In other words, "Russia's interests in the region would be respected and that there would be no serious resistance to Moscow's efforts to maintain hegemony over what it considered to be its vital regional interests."[117]

However, this early confidence of the so-called "Atlanticists" around Yeltsin was dissipated when it became clear that other post-Soviet bloc countries had no intention of letting their own Euro-Atlantic aspirations be subordinated to Russian management, and that the West, especially the United States, was not going to give Moscow any sort of veto over the affairs of the Euro-Atlantic community, especially within NATO. Moreover, the collapse of the Russian economy removed an important source of leverage Russia had over its neighbors.

At the same time, the Yeltsin government attempted to impose a more consistent approach, assessing whether to more directly support Baku or Yerevan, depending on its judgment of what best served Russian interests, especially those concerning the maintenance of Russian influence and leverage.[118] Moscow's previously "balanced" approach (generally reflected in allowing both Armenians and Azerbaijanis access to its weaponry)— whether by design or caused by bureaucratic chaos—gave way to a more pronounced "tilt" on the part of the Russian government towards the Armenians. As the Russian government took control of Soviet forces and redeployed units in the region, Russian forces were in a

---

117 Robert E. Berls, Jr. *Strengthening Russia's Influence in International Affairs, Part II: Russia and Its Neighbors: A Sphere of Influence or a Declining Relationship?* Nuclear Threat Initiative Paper, July 13, 2021.

118 Ibid, p. 165.

position to offer assistance to Armenia and Karabakh Armenian separatist forces in their battles with the Azerbaijani military—both in terms of transferring military equipment and facilitating the transfer of personnel to Armenian control.[119]

In keeping with the Zheleznovodsk principles, and aware of the danger to the integrity of the Russian Federation if any sort of Karabakh principle was acknowledged, Yeltsin stopped short of recognizing the NKAO as an independent state, and in theory remained committed to the principle of Azerbaijan's territorial integrity. At the same time, Moscow did not impose any sort of strict controls over its military and economic assistance to Armenia proper, meaning that Yerevan could "pass along" Russian aid to the separatist regime.[120] Russian security guarantees, weapons sales, and diplomatic support to Armenia shielded Yerevan from major consequences for its continued support for the Karabakh Armenian separatists.

Many Azerbaijanis attributed Russia's tilt towards Armenia to the shared cultural and religious heritage of Armenians and Russians, or pointed to the size of the Armenian diaspora inside of Russia itself (although there was also a substantial Azerbaijani diaspora) as explanations for this "tilt."[121] These were certainly factors, but while shared connections can help sustain a relationship, they are not always the most important or decisive factors. A similar shared culturo-religious connection has not produced a strong bond between Russia and Georgia, while such connections between Russia and Serbia or Russia and Cyprus have not

---

[119] See the discussion, for instance, in Fariz Ismailzade, "The Geopolitics of the Nagorno-Karabakh Conflict," *Global Dialogue* 7, no. 3-4, 2005, pp. 105-108.

[120] Fahimeh Khansari Fard, Mohammad Ali Basiri and Enayatollah Yazdani, "Ethnic Bargaining and Separatism in the South Caucasus," *Region* 8 no. 2, July 2019, p. 186.

[121] Ismailzade, op. cit., p. 105.

prevented the Russian government, in recent years, from forging much stronger linkages with Serbia's historic rivals Croatia and Hungary, or a willingness to preference Russia's relationship with Türkiye, its long-standing opponent, over its ties to fellow Orthodox Greek Cypriots (or Greece itself, for that matter). In that regard, the warning issued by Ekaterina Entina and Alexander Pivovarenko is well-placed: "It would be a gross simplification to consider [Russia's] foreign policy within the logic of civilizational closeness," noting further that a strategic partnership with Russia grounded in "economic cooperation, supplies of arms, and other technical products is not a consequence of civilizational and religious closeness, but rather a result of [...] foreign policy doctrine."[122] And what, then, is that doctrine?

Restoring Russian Primacy in the Caucasus

If the initial assumption of the Yeltsin foreign policy team was that the West would delegate to Russia responsibility for stabilizing the post-Soviet space, when it became clear that neither the West nor many post-Soviet states were desirous of acknowledging a post-Soviet Russian "special responsibility" for the area, the Yeltsin administration, after its initial endorsement of enlarging Euro-Atlantic institutions into the post-Soviet bloc, instead adopted a different approach. This was based on denying other countries in the region access to Western institutions of which Russia was also not a member and denying further expansion of the influence of those institutions to set the agenda for the post-Soviet space. The Yeltsin argument was basically that, left unchecked,

---

122 Ekaterina Entina and Alexander Pivovarenko, "Russia's Foreign Policy Evolution in the New Balkan Landscape," *Croatian Political Science Review* 56, no. 3-4, 2019, p. 195.

an expansion of Western influence into the post-Soviet space, with surrounding countries admitted into the principal Western institutions (while Russia remained outside), could only result in Russia's marginalization and a direct threat to the maintenance of the Russian position in Eurasia, as well as posing a threat to vital geo-economic and geopolitical interests.[123]

As Robert Berls concluded: "It has been one of the Kremlin's highest priorities to preserve as much influence and, where possible, control, over its immediate neighborhood as it can. It has done so through formal institutions and various informal mechanisms—one of which is setting the terms by which it and the outside world define that neighborhood."[124]

From the mid-1990s onward, therefore, Russia embarked on a policy of "pragmatic reimperialization"[125]—finding ways to freeze the process of Euro-Atlantic enlargement and to attempt, as far as possible, to reconnect post-Soviet states with the Russian core. "Pragmatic reimperialization" was designed to prevent the rest of the former Soviet Union from following the westward path of the former Warsaw Pact countries and the Baltic states, and instead to link the rest of the post-Soviet Eurasian space into "economic and security systems dominated by Moscow."[126] Particularly after the failures of the post-9/11 rapprochement and the 2009 "reset" between Russia and the United States to produce a modus vivendi between Moscow and Washington on the Russian role in the former Soviet space, this approach was

---

123 Gvosdev, *Russia's Southern Strategy*, pp. 5-8.
124 Berls, op. cit.
125 Janusz Bugajski, "Russia's Pragmatic Reimperialization," *Caucasian Review of International Affairs* 4, no. 1, Winter 2010.
126 R.J. Krickus, *Russia after Putin*, Carlisle, PA: Strategic Studies Institute and U.S. Army War College Press, 2015, p. 26.

also meant "to present the Americans with a firewall in every part of Eurasia."[127]

In the South Caucasus, the Russian tilt towards Armenia, although buttressed by cultural and historical connections, was driven largely by geopolitical factors. Post-Soviet Armenia initially decreased its connections to Russia in the first several years after the break-up of the Soviet Union (in part driven by hopes that Western powers like the United States and France would step in as alternate providers of security) but Yerevan found itself isolated within the region and extremely dependent upon Russia not only for military protection but for an economic and energy lifeline. At the same time, major energy discoveries in the Caspian basin raised Azerbaijan's profile, enabling the government in Baku to pursue a more multi-dimensional foreign policy, including forging much closer ties with the West. Not only did Azerbaijan demand the accelerated withdrawal of Russian forces from its territory (in 1993), it was open to exploring the possibility of closer security ties with NATO and was a founding member, in 1997, of the Georgia-Ukraine-Azerbaijan-Moldova (GUAM) consultative forum, which evolved into the GUAM Organization for Democracy and Economic Development—an association of post-Soviet states that explicitly excluded Russia.

Azerbaijan's efforts to engage Western partners bore fruit. The United States moved to declare the region—with Baku at the center—strategically vital to U.S. interests in 1994. And Washington played an important role in the deal that produced the "Contract of the Century" in the same year—the first oil pipeline project originating in the former Soviet space that did not pass

---
127 Ibid, p. 26.

through Russian territory. To counterbalance Russian pressure, then-President Heydar Aliyev turned to the United States for support, and his "overall strategy [...] was to resist Russian pressure by combining Azerbaijan's national interests with the U.S. government's regional policy and the large volume of foreign investment by American and other Western oil firms."[128] After the 9/11 attacks, the United States government was able to use the changed conditions provided by the "Global War on Terror" to have provisions limiting U.S. security aid to Azerbaijan waived. These developments gave Azerbaijan the wherewithal to push back against Russian demands. Thus, in the years following the collapse of the USSR, "developments in Azerbaijan and particularly in Georgia [...] made them clear antagonists for Moscow, leaving close cooperation with Armenia as the only viable option, also for securing Russia's rear vis-à-vis Türkiye and Iran."[129]

In contrast, Armenia bowed to geopolitical realities and accommodated not only the stationing of Russian forces on its territory starting in 1992 but also entered the two principal Russian-led organizations of the post-Soviet space: the Collective Security Treaty Organization since the Treaty's founding in 1992 and the Eurasian Economic Union (in 2014).

As Narek Sukiasyan has noted:

> The main determinants of Armenia's foreign policy are security threats—the ongoing Nagorno-Karabakh conflict, the military threats from Turkey and Azerbaijan,

---

128 Pinar Ipek, "Azerbaijan's Foreign Policy and Challenges for Energy Security," *Middle East Journal* 63, no. 2, Spring 2009, pp. 235-236.

129 Árni Þór Sigurðsson & Alyson J.K. Bailes, *"The Bear and the Maiden Fair": Why Does Armenia Side with Russia?* Reykjavík: Félagsvísindastofnun Háskóla Íslands, 2015, p. 4.

and Armenia's closed borders in the east and west. These security threats also explain the rationale behind Armenia's Russia policy, leading it to perceive Russia as the only viable security provider. This has been sealed by extensive bilateral agreements and Armenia's participation in Russia-led regional projects such as the Collective Security Treaty Organization (CSTO) and the Russian-Armenian Treaty of Friendship, Cooperation and Mutual Assistance, and the agreement to establish a Russian military base in Armenia. [...] Russia also exerts powerful economic influence over Armenia. Armenia's overreliance on Russia has come at the cost of ceding the strategic assets of its energy, transport, and other infrastructure, hampering its ability to create new trade partnerships and diversify its economic structure, and consequently deepening asymmetry in its relations with Russia, which has created expectations of loyalty in Moscow.[130]

Prolonging and manipulating the conflict over Karabakh became central to the Russian strategy for retaining influence in the region, both as a lever to pressure Azerbaijan and a cudgel to keep Armenia within the Russian orbit. This is part and parcel of a larger pattern in Russian foreign policy: the instrumentalization of "frozen conflicts" as part of an overall "sharp power" strategy to serve Russian geopolitical aspirations.[131] As then Vice-President Joe Biden noted in 2015, Vladimir Putin looks for any

---

[130] Narek Sukiasyan, "Appeasement and Autonomy: Armenian-Russian Relations from Revolution to War," *European Union Institute for Security Studies Brief*, February 1, 2021.

[131] See, for instance, the discussion in Dov Lynch, "Separatist States and Post-Soviet Conflicts," *International Affairs* 78, no. 4, 2002, pp. 845-846.

"useful tools to be manipulated, to create cracks in the European body politic which he can then exploit."[132] Thus, these tools may be a low-cost means of demonstrating Russia's ability to cause harm. From this perspective, Moscow may use subversion to demonstrate that Russia cannot be ignored. Second, Russia's meddling in both Eastern Europe and in the United States or western Europe may seek to demonstrate the weakness of the West and, consequently, to undermine the hopes U.S. partners and allies place in the United States.[133]

Ever since the collapse of the USSR, "frozen conflicts" across the Eurasian space have played a crucial role in this strategy of "pragmatic reimperialization," serving as instruments to keep post-Soviet states "within the Russian sphere of influence." The exploitation of "frozen conflicts" was seen as essential to preserving the Russian position across Eurasia. If Russia was not to be given a formal veto over the enlargement of the Euro-Atlantic community, "frozen conflicts" would often act as a de facto veto to enlargement. On the other hand, holding out the prospect of Russian support for ending such a conflict can be a powerful tool for Moscow to wield in order to gain important concessions. As Mamuka Tsereteli has observed, "By creating and then manipulating conflicts, Russia is gaining leverage over the decision making on political and economic development, governance issues, and the external alliances of those countries."[134]

Moscow has adopted a very pragmatic, transactional

---

132 Comments of then-Vice President Joe Biden. "Brookings Hosts Viced President Joe Biden for Remarks on the Russia Ukraine Conflict," Washington, DC, May 27, 2015.
133 Andrew Radin, Alyssa Denmus and Krystyna Marcinek, *Understanding Russian Subversion: Patterns, Threats and Responses*, Santa Monica, CA: RAND, February 2020, p. 4.
134 Mamuka Tsereteli, "Can Russia's Quest for the New International Order Succeed?" *Orbis* 62, no. 2, 2018.

approach to the "frozen conflicts" across the former Soviet bloc. Russia does not have a consistent position but varies its policies and approaches "on an ad hoc basis depending on its aims in each instance." Ultimately, as Babak Rezvani has concluded, "Russia wants to be (preferably solely) in charge of intermediation and provision of security."[135]

The endgame for Moscow is a permanent settlement that enshrines its preferred equities.[136] For example, the draft memorandum that was developed by Dmitry Kozak in 2003 to serve as the basis for ending the "frozen conflict" between the Moldovan central government and the breakaway Transnistrian separatists proposed an "asymmetric federal state" that would guarantee that the pro-Russian entity could veto certain foreign decisions of the central government—especially membership in Euro-Atlantic institutions—while cementing permanent links with Russia.[137] Moscow is not wedded to perpetual "frozen conflicts" and will support their resolution and settling regional disputes if "regimes in these countries adopt friendly policies toward Russia, including guaranteeing that the countries consult Russia when making important decisions; are responsive to Russian desires; or, in the case of the inner rings, participate in Russian-led organizations and do not join Western institutions."[138]

So, when we look at Russian actions in the immediate context of the Caspian Basin-Black Sea region, we cannot escape the conclusion reached by Wojciech Bartuzi, Katarzyna Pełczyńska-

---

135 Babak Rezvani, "Russian Interventions in the Post-Soviet and Syrian Conflicts," *Terrorism and Political Violence* 31, no. 6, 2019, p. 1378.
136 Sigurðsson.and Bailes, pp. 4-5.
137 See, for instance, "Moldova: Regional Tensions over Transdniestria," *International Crisis Group*, Report no. 157, June 17, 2004.
138 Radin et al, p.5.

Nałęcz, and Krzysztof Strachota that "the conflicts in the Southern Caucasus have been and remain the main tool with which Moscow makes Azerbaijan, Armenia, and Georgia dependent on Russia and hinders their co-operation with the West."[139]

Of particular importance is how Russia navigates the contradictions between upholding the principles of territorial integrity and non-interference in the domestic affairs of states with a willingness to maintain "official and semi-official contacts with non-sovereign actors [...], especially when they fall into the sphere of Moscow's Realpolitik."[140] In the context of the conflict over Karabakh, this has meant that while Russia officially never recognized the existence of a separate ethnic-Armenian statelet on the sovereign territory of Azerbaijan, the Russian government was prepared to turn a blind eye and even quietly facilitate the efforts of the so-called "Community for Democracy and Rights of Nations," which brought together the unrecognized regimes in Transnistria, Abkhazia, and South Ossetia along with the one established by Armenians in the former NKAO ("Artsakh"), and which sought to strengthen formal ties between these regions and to take advantage of their unofficial economic and political links with Russia—and, coincidentally, grouped together the secessionist entities on the territories of the states that had created the GUAM forum. All of these entities benefitted from sub rosa Russian military and economic support as well as de facto diplomatic support (including blunting efforts by international bodies to take more definitive action to resolve the conflicts). In particular,

---

139   Wojciech Bartuzi, Katarzyna Pełczyńska-Nałęcz, and Krzysztof Strachota, "Abkhazia, South Ossetia, Nagorno-Karabakh: unfrozen conflicts between Russia and the West," *OSW Report*, July 15, 2008.

140   Victor Jeifets and Nikolay Dobronravin, "Russia's Changing Partners: Sovereign Actors and Unrecognized States," *Rising Powers Quarterly* 2, no.1, 2017, p. 225.

Moscow's commitment to upholding the principle of territorial integrity diminished as the brutal crackdown in Chechnya and the tightening of controls over other regions of Russia diminished the threat of separatism within Russia, which had been one of the key motivations behind Yeltsin's Zheleznovodsk approach.

Russian efforts have been aided by the failure of one model of conflict resolution in Europe—the EU approach to Cyprus—and the Western acceptance, at least in the case for Kosovo, of the principle of a unilateral declaration and recognition of independence for a separatist region without the acquiescence of the host government. Both strengthened Moscow's position in dealing with the "frozen conflicts" across the Eurasian space.

During the 1990s, in an effort to break the deadlock over efforts to reunify the island of Cyprus, the European Union undertook a gamble—that permitting the internationally-recognized government of the island to enter the EU (even though it did not control all of its territory) would create incentives for the separatists in northern Cyprus to settle their differences in order to reap the benefits of EU membership, while also providing incentives to Türkiye, the principal patron of the secessionists, to permit reunification of the island. Having relied on the maintenance of "frozen conflicts" as a way to disincentivize the expansion of Euro-Atlantic institutions into the former Soviet space, the Russian government feared that a successful Cyprus settlement would validate the precedent that enlargement did not depend on a Russian willingness to broker settlements and, in fact, would compel Moscow to stop its efforts. Thus, in pushing for the EU and NATO not to allow Russian support for separatist regimes to act as a de facto veto on enlargement, advocates argued that if these problems [the frozen conflicts] could be more easily solved by 'importing' them into NATO, they should be imported. The so-called frozen conflicts [...] can be resolved only if it were pointless for Moscow to fuel them [...] or if Russia had to pay too high a political price for them.[141]

But the perceived failure of the Cyprus gamble has been beneficial to Russia in a number of ways. It demonstrated that offering accession to Euro-Atlantic institutions did not provide a constructive impetus to the solution of "frozen conflicts." It strengthened the perspective that a candidate country would need to solve its internal problems prior to being considered for membership. Finally, the ongoing problems related to the admission of Cyprus to the EU complicated Türkiye's relationship with the European Union, which then spilled over into tensions within the NATO alliance. As Sara Stefanini concluded: "As long as Cyprus remains divided by a UN buffer zone, [...] Turkey hampers NATO efforts to cooperate with the EU, Greek and Turkish relations in NATO remain tense, and Turkey remains reliant on gas deliveries from Russia's Gazprom."[142]

While the Cyprus model failed to produce results, the Kosovo precedent offered Russia a way to discard its Zheleznovodsk formula. After the failure of talks between the Kosovo Albanian secessionist and the central government in Serbia failed to produce a settlement that could accommodate the parameters of UN Security Council resolution 1244 (a maximum degree of self-government for Kosovo while remaining within the juridical confines of the Serbian state), the decision both by the Kosovo

---

141 Indrek Elling and Merle Maigre, *NATO Membership Action Plan: A Chance for Ukraine and Georgia*, Tallinn: Rahvusvaheline Kaitseuuringute Keskus, 2008, p. 3.
142 Sara Stefanini, "Cyprus Fears Russia Could Wreck Reunification," *Politico*, January 12, 2017.

Albanians to unilaterally declare complete independence in February 2008, and by the United States and major European powers to recognize that change in status, helped Russia to itself escape from the self-determination/territorial integrity dilemma. While Russia had opposed Kosovo's attempt at secession, the Russian government embraced a so-called "Kosovo precedent" that would allow for the unilateral recognition of separatist regimes even without any final political settlement between the separatists and the central government. If the Zheleznovodsk communiqué had committed Russia to maintaining the territorial integrity of Azerbaijan (and, by extension, of any other post-Soviet state with one or more "frozen conflicts" on its soil) in terms of any final settlement, the "Kosovo precedent," as defined and embraced by Moscow, now gave the Russian government the right to unilaterally determine when supporting territorial integrity was no longer the overriding consideration.

Over the course of several months in 2008, Russia was able to exploit a collapse in Western credibility directly connected to both the Cyprus failure and the Kosovo precedent. Georgia's request to receive a membership action plan to advance its membership in NATO, expressly requested by then-president Mikheil Saakashvili, was tabled at the Bucharest summit, in part due to concerns as to how the Atlantic alliance could admit a member with two "frozen conflicts" on its territory—a rejection of applying the now-discredited Cyprus approach to conflict resolution.

As Tracey German noted:

It could be postulated that NATO's engagement with Georgia and its statement at the 2008 Bucharest summit that Georgia 'will' become a member of the alliance in the future significantly undermined Georgian security and stability, as well as those of other states in the post-Soviet space who sought to engage with NATO and, ultimately, in the wake of more recent events in Ukraine, the stability of the European subcontinent. Russia's military intervention in Georgia in 2008 revealed the limits of NATO's influence and willingness to engage with states within Russia's 'zone of privileged interest,' as well as its lack of internal unity vis-à-vis relations with Moscow and future engagement with the area.[143]

In the aftermath of the Georgia incursion, Russia demonstrated the effective end of the Cyprus model as a path for pursuing conflict resolution, while it trumpeted the Kosovo precedent to formally recognize the separatist entities of Abkhazia and South Ossetia as independent states. This cleared the way for formal relationships, including agreements on military cooperation and security assistance, and the legitimization of the Russian role and presence in both entities. It also further complicated any future resolution of the conflict, because Moscow now took the position that this was no longer an internal matter to Georgia but an interstate dispute between separate states. After 2014, the Kremlin has also applied lessons taken from both in its approach, first to the Crimea, then to the oblasts of southeastern Ukraine. The first has been to utilize the claim that self-determination overrides territorial integrity, and to use referenda to unilaterally

---

[143] Tracey German, "Heading West? Georgia's Euro-Atlantic Path," *International Affairs* 91, no. 3, May 2015.

alter the status of regions and borders. The second has been the gamble that, over time, the actions not recognized de jure become accepted in a de facto basis.

Bargaining and Balancing

In the immediate aftermath of the 2008 crisis, many predicted that Russia, after having recognized Abkhazia and South Ossetia, might also recognize the independence of the secessionist Karabakh entity, based on statements that had emanated from different Russian officials in the run-up to Kosovo's unilateral declaration of independence. Often, this was paired with assertions about the primacy of historic-cultural ties as the main driver for policy—that if the West had damaged the interests of majority-Orthodox Christian Serbia by recognizing the unilateral secession of largely-Muslim Kosovo Albanians, then Russia ought to balance the score by compensating Christian Armenia for its past losses at the hands of the Turkic-Muslim world by recognizing Christian "Artsakh."

Yet this did not happen. In part, Moscow assessed that it would gain nothing substantially more in geopolitical terms from the Armenians by recognizing the former NKAO's independence, and that it could continue to refuse to change its formal stance on the conflict over Karabakh without risking its relationship with Yerevan. This was made easier for Russia by the fact that Armenia itself never took the formal step of itself recognizing the breakaway entity's independence, or of incorporating it constitutionally into Armenia. At the same time, reducing the perceived "tilt" towards Armenia by adopting a more balanced position offered the possibility of developing a more pragmatic relationship with Azerbaijan, and, in so doing, to balance its close economic and military alliance with Armenia with a more pragmatic partnership with Azerbaijan.

In turn, as it became clear that the United States and the major European powers were not prepared to contest in any major fashion the Russian management of the "frozen conflicts" across the Eurasian space, Azerbaijan began to adjust some of its policies, as they impacted vital Russian interests. This approach, summed up by Anar Valiyev and Narmina Mamishova under the moniker "transactional neutrality," rested on Azerbaijan's willingness "not to transgress Russia's geopolitical red lines in the region, but, in turn, commits Russia to a strategy where it never wants Azerbaijan to feel threatened." Russia compromised on its ideal position—that Azerbaijan become a full member of all Russian-led Eurasian organizations—in favor of Azerbaijan's neutrality, guaranteeing that Western power does not challenge Russian primacy in the immediate region and Russia's ability to be able to connect to the larger Middle East.[144]

As part of its reassurance of Moscow, Azerbaijan formally joined the Non-Aligned Movement (NAM) in May 2011, which foreclosed any option of joining NATO as a full member (while leaving open the possibility of continued cooperation through the Partnership for Peace program, which in turn became the institutional hinge through which the Azerbaijani military was able to receive NATO-standard training, primarily through Türkiye, which in turn can be seen as a precipitating cause of its victory

---

144 Anar Valiyev and Narmina Mamishova, "Azerbaijan's Foreign Policy Towards Russia Since Independence: Compromise Achieved," *Southeast European and Black Sea Studies* 19, no. 2, 2019, pp. 271, 273.

in the Second Karabakh War). Moreover, despite having been a founding member of GUAM, Azerbaijan resisted any efforts, particularly during the tenures of Presidents Viktor Yushchenko of Ukraine and Mikheil Saakashvili of Georgia, to turn the grouping into anything more than a loose consultative association. After the 2014 Crimean annexation, Azerbaijan, while not recognizing this infringement of Ukrainian territorial integrity, nevertheless chose not to join any of the sanctions efforts against Russia. This pattern repeated itself in 2022; although Azerbaijan has condemned the Russian invasion of Ukraine, and refuses to recognize any changes in Ukraine's territorial integrity, Baku has also chosen not to join the full plethora of Western economic sanctions against Moscow whilst sending significant amounts of humanitarian aid to Kyiv.

The parameters of this transactional neutrality are that Azerbaijan will not join NATO or any alliance of which Russia is not also a partner, and while Azerbaijan may have its own linkages, corridors, and export routes that bypass Russia, it will utilize Russia as one of its options and partners, and, more importantly, will never join any effort to contain Moscow or to use its geography to block Russia's access to the south. In return, Moscow accepts that, in other areas, Azerbaijan may choose options that go against Russian preferences and understands that this is the price of keeping Azerbaijan from cementing closer ties with the West.[145]

This transactional neutrality has been especially important for Russia given the changes in the Russia-Türkiye relationship. During the 1990s, Russian support for Karabakh Armenian separatists was designed to counter the prospect of a Türkiye-

---

145   Gvosdev, "Russia's Southern Strategy," p. 11.

Azerbaijan strategic alliance, which, it was feared, would block Russian influence in the greater Black Sea basin and contain Russia.

Yet, as the Russia-Türkiye relationship also changed—with Moscow finding areas of common ground with Ankara and choosing not to let differences define the tenor of their interaction in favor of pursuing mutual benefits —the focus shifted towards emphasizing complementarity, not rivalry, within the framework of a trilateral Russia-Türkiye-Azerbaijan dialogue.[146] Building on Russian-Turkish efforts to prevent possible clashes in Syria from escalating into an open break, this dialogue is not seen as the first steps towards alliance—but a mechanism to pursue deconfliction when interests are in conflict while promoting and safeguarding cooperation wherever possible.

What this means is that, for the moment (that is, in the post-Second Karabakh War period), Azerbaijan has reached a workable and mutually-beneficial modus vivendi with Russia —one that decreases the Russian imperative to continue with its "tilt" towards Armenia. Yet as Azerbaijan over the decade of the 2010s has become more geopolitically accommodating to Russia's security interests, Armenia, believing that it had a lock on its Russian relationship, explored diversifying its partnerships with the West. As George Vlad Niculescu observed:

> [A]ware of the weaknesses entailed in its overdependence on Moscow, Yerevan has continuously struggled to balance its relations with Russia by strengthening ties with the West,

---

[146] As Richard Giragosian, David G. Lewis and Graeme P. Herd have noted, "Russian-Turkish tensions are mitigated by open channels of communication and a history of managing brinkmanship through pragmatic transactionalism." "Russian Crisis Behavior, Nagorno-Karabakh and Turkey?" *George C. Marshall Center Perspectives*, no. 19, January 2021.

including with NATO, the EU, and the US. The signing by Armenia in November 2017 of a Comprehensive Economic Partnership Agreement (CEPA) with the EU has been hailed as the harbinger of a new Armenian multi-vectorial policy.[147]

In seeking to deepen its connection to the Euro-Atlantic world and reduce its dependence on Moscow, Yerevan gambled that its first steps in this direction would not fundamentally rupture its relationship with Russia. Just as Cyprus had discovered, however, it was a mistake for Armenian elites to over-rely on a shared cultural/historical relationship with Russia as the basis for geopolitical associations—particularly once the Ukraine crisis began.

Black Swans: From 2014 in Ukraine to 2020 in Karabakh

Russia's first incursions into Ukraine in 2014 introduced new factors in Russia's approach in the Caucasus, which the full-on invasion that began in February 2022 has only exacerbated. The decision to rely on force to change Ukraine's position was a recognition that, despite its efforts to cultivate support among parts of the Ukrainian elite and to offer a relationship based on the "fraternal bonds" between Ukrainians and Russians as inheritors of the legacy of Rus', an Armenia-style relationship with Kyiv grounded in shared culture and history was not possible. However, despite some glimmers of hope during the presidencies of both Petro Poroshenko and Volodymyr Zelensky, the Ukrainians

---

[147] George Vlad Niculescu, "Armenia's 'Velvet Revolution' and the Karabakh Conflict Resolution," *Worldview*, May 4, 2018.

were uninterested in charting a similar path of "transactional neutrality" along the trail blazed by the Aliyev government, in part because the Ukrainians believed they had a pathway for full integration into the Euro-Atlantic community.[148]

When the Kremlin decided to push, first for the separation of Crimea from Ukraine, and then its formal incorporation into the Russian Federation, it appeared Moscow was emphasizing ethnic self-determination at the expense of upholding territorial integrity. After all, a Crimean precedent could, in theory, be applied to Nagorno-Karabakh as well.[149] At the same time, however, the first efforts by the West to impose economic sanctions heightened the importance of Russia's southern corridor and the necessity of preserving good relations with both Azerbaijan and Türkiye.[150] Finally, the 2018 revolution which brought Nikol Pashinyan to power in Armenia, another apparent "color revolution" that removed a long-standing political ally of the Kremlin (Serzh Sargsyan) from power, opened up the prospect that the new Armenian government might begin to follow some of the same path as the post-Maidan government in Ukraine.[151]

At the same time, Russia's growing involvement in Ukrainian

---

[148] Ukrainian elites increasingly had decided over the past decade not to "embrace the opportunities, as well as the limitations" of a "keystone state" role in the region, emulating the Azerbaijani approach of flexibility in dealing with the major players, in the hopes that "full inclusion in the Euro-Atlantic world would compensate for Ukraine's unfavorable geographic position" vis-à-vis Russia. Ever since the full-scale Russian invasion in 2022, Ukraine is now committed to playing the "frontline" state role in containing Russia—and bearing the brunt of the costs. For a greater discussion of Ukraine's decision not to embrace its keystone potential, see, Nikolas K. Gvosdev, "Keystone States-A New Category of Power," *Horizons* 5, Autumn 2015.

[149] See, for instance, "Crimea Referendum Good Precedent for Karabakh—Expert," *Tert.AM*, March 17, 2014.

[150] See, for instance, "Crimea's Accession to Russia is No Precedent for Karabakh Settlement," *Caucasian Knot*, March 19, 2014.

[151] These sentiments are very present in the letter Congressman Frank Pallone, Jr. sent to then-President Donald Trump on July 31, 2018, urging a bilateral meeting between Pashinyan and the U.S. President. As archived at https://pallone.house.gov/media/press-releases/armenian-pm-pashinyan-during-un-general-assembly.

affairs—and the problems it generated with Russia's relationship with the United States and with Europe—called into question its ability to sustain its approach in the Caucasus and to exclusively keep the conflict frozen on Moscow's terms or preferences. At the same time, advancing Russian interests in Ukraine, Syria, and across the greater Middle East and North Africa required Moscow to adjust some of its positions on the conflict over Karabakh to take into account Turkish preferences in order to facilitate compromises with Ankara in these other areas.[152] The diversion of Russian attention and resources—a trend that has only accelerated since February 2022—also weakened the Kremlin's claim that it was the only power that could guarantee stability in the Caucasus.

By early 2020, therefore, the flirtations of the Pashinyan government with diversifying Armenia's political and security arrangements plus the absolute necessity to keep Azerbaijan within the parameters of "transactional neutrality" meant that the attractiveness, to Moscow, of continuing to support what was effectively no change in the Karabakh status quo declined. Yerevan's assumption that Russia was absolutely committed to maintaining the status quo (and that Russia would actively prevent any effort on the part of the Aliyev government to seek changes) was no longer operative, yet the Pashinyan government, both by deciding not to follow clear hints from the Kremlin that it wanted concessions on the Karabakh issue (to show to Baku the value of its transactional neutrality) and by seeking to rebalance its own relations with Washington and Paris, created a clear incentive for

---

152 Giragosian et al, op. cit.

the Kremlin not to intervene to maintain the pre-2020 status quo at all costs.

When tensions spilled over into open conflict, and, as a result not only of very well-publicized Turkish military assistance (notably the introduction of the Turkish Bayraktar TB-drone which allowed for precision air strikes on Karabakh Armenian armor and artillery as part of an innovative, integrated approach to combat), but also of the sustained sales of military equipment by Russia to Azerbaijan (one of the "transactions" that undergird Azerbaijan's "neutrality"), Azerbaijan changed the situation on the ground by dislodging Armenian forces from many of their positions. Indeed, the expectation that any large-scale conflict between the two would bog down into a protracted military stalemate, with little change on the ground, was disproven by the actual events of the war.[153] Thus, Moscow recalibrated its position. While making clear to the Armenian side that Russia would not intervene to defend Karabakh Armenian positions from Azerbaijani retaliation, Putin could also not allow a complete collapse of Artsakh (nor Azerbaijani military movement into Armenia itself).

An in-depth discussion of the Russian role in bringing the 2020 conflict to an end is beyond the scope of this chapter. What is most critical to note is that Moscow could accommodate a Turkish-assisted Azerbaijani victory against Armenian forces in Karabakh precisely because it served the Kremlin's immediate political needs. The lack of any meaningful help from the United States or Europe, either to aid Armenia or to restrain Türkiye's assistance to Baku, did much to discredit the idea of a "Western

---

153 Giragosian et al, op. cit.

vision" for the Caucasus.¹⁵⁴ It also demonstrated to Azerbaijan that pushing for maximalist goals against Russian opposition would be risky, because there would be no major degree of support from the United States or other NATO countries to counterbalance the Russians—that "Azerbaijan got as close to NATO as possible."¹⁵⁵ Pashinyan needed Russia to help Armenia stave off complete defeat, and Aliyev was prepared to forego the full fruits of battlefield victory in order to secure at the conference table the majority of those gains. Through intensive shuttle diplomacy, and utilizing the Russia-Türkiye channel as well, Putin was able to get an agreement in place to end the war. This agreement represents "more than a narrow ceasefire agreement but less than a general peace treaty: strictly speaking, only its first article deals with the cessation of hostilities in Karabakh; the others lays out various concrete measures aiming towards a future predicated implicitly on the establishment of peaceful relations between two sovereign states: Armenia and Azerbaijan."¹⁵⁶ Azerbaijan thus consolidated its battlefield victory with a diplomatic one that, however, amounts to being seen as a compromise from the Kremlin's perspective.

The critical geopolitical compromise at the heart of the 10 November 2020 deal ending the Second Karabakh War is that Russia became the guarantor of that agreement—especially with the right to deploy peacekeeping forces into parts of Karabakh itself and to serve as guarantor of the various "corridors" that

---

154 Giragosian, op. cit.

155 Ahmad Alili, "Shusha Declaration: Regional Perspectives for Azerbaijani-Turkish Alliance," *Stability Risks and New Conflict Management Platforms in the South Caucasus*, eds. Frederic Labarre and George Niculescu, Vienna: National Defense Academy, 2022, p. 49.

156 Damjan Krnjević Mišković, "Statecraft, European Belonging, and the Second Karabakh War," *Liberated Karabakh: Policy Perspectives by the ADA University Community*, eds. Fariz Ismailzade and Damjan Krnjević Mišković, Baku: ADA University Press, 2021, p. 256.

cross the region—while Moscow accepted a greater Turkish role in the overall question of regional security. Although this might seem to represent a major setback for a Russia that wanted to re-establish its sphere of influence over the region, it was seen in Moscow as a necessary compromise. Türkiye continued to serve as a larger "stand-in" for the West, especially NATO, but President Recep Tayyip Erdoğan has repeatedly stressed that Türkiye will not serve as a proxy or stand-in for the West, but will pursue what it sees as its own best interests in the region, which increasingly appear to be a de facto condominium with Russia through the greater Black and Caspian sea basins.[157] Thus, at the beginning of 2021, despite the battlefield shifts, Karabakh remained essentially a "frozen conflict" in the Russian conception, even as the Russians accepted revisions on terms much more favorable to Azerbaijan. "Pragmatic reimperialization" had been preserved and the terms of the strategic détente with Ankara remained in force. Yet this jury-rigged settlement rested on an important, if largely unstated, assumption: that the Kremlin would continue to be able to devote the level of attention (and necessary resources) to sustain the settlement for the foreseeable future.

After 2022: The Impact of Russia's "Strategic Distraction" In Ukraine On Karabakh

Accepting a diminishment of the Armenian position in 2020 was the strategic price Moscow was willing to pay to keep the Kara-

---

[157] See, for instance, Selim Koru, "The Resiliency of Turkey-Russia Relations," Foreign Policy Research Institute, April 2018; Gülnur Abyet, "The Evolution of NATO's Three Phases and Turkey's Transatlantic Relationship," Perceptions 17, no. 1, Spring 2012, pp. 19-36, and Igor Delanoe, "Russia Extends Black Sea Control," *Le Monde Diplomatique*, February 2019.

bakh issue within the Caucasian family—and not to involve any formal role for the United States, NATO, or the European Union. Between 2020 and 2022, the Kremlin devoted more effort and attention to one part of the "pragmatic reimperialization" portfolio: halting and even reversing the enlargement of Euro-Atlantic influence in the Eurasian space. In December 2021, the Russian Foreign Ministry had mooted two draft treaties that essentially would have mandated a withdrawal of Western influence back to Central-Eastern Europe.[158] Following a successful Russian-led intervention in Kazakhstan in January 2022 against what Putin called a "foreign backed terrorist uprising,"[159] the Russian government, having failed to start a diplomatic process based on the two drafts, undertook a "special military operation" in Ukraine in February 2022. As Putin himself stated, "Further expansion of the NATO infrastructure and the beginning of military development in Ukraine's territories are unacceptable for us." The goal of what was expected to be a military campaign of short duration was the "neutralization" of Ukraine.[160] However, greater-than-expected Ukrainian resistance (and significant Western support), combined with Russian operational shortcomings, punctured the appearance of Russian military supremacy in the greater Eurasian space. In addition, the imposition of severe and punitive Western sanctions accelerated a process of Russian economic

---

158   Steven Pifer, "Russia's draft agreements with NATO and the United States: Intended for rejection? *Brookings*, December 21, 2021, at https://www.brookings.edu/articles/russias-draft-agreements-with-nato-and-the-united-states-intended-for-rejection/.

159   Tamara Vaal, "Putin claims victory in defending Kazakhstan from revolt," Reuters, January 10, 2022, at https://www.reuters.com/world/asia-pacific/kazakhstan-detains-7939-people-over-unrest-2022-01-10/.

160   "'No other option': Excerpts of Putin's speech declaring war," *Al-Jazeera*, February 24, 2022, at https://www.aljazeera.com/news/2022/2/24/putins-speech-declaring-war-on-ukraine-translated-excerpts.

decoupling from Europe—both in terms of the sale of Russian commodities but also impacting Russia's ability to obtain capital and import critical technologies.

After 2022, therefore, Moscow discovered it needed the countries of the greater Silk Road region far more than the reverse, particularly to serve as indispensable economic "roundabouts" to circumvent Western sanctions in both directions.[161] In particular, a key trump card the Kremlin held in 2020—the ability to interrupt the operation of the so-called "Middle Corridor"—had been transformed into Russia needing guaranteed and unimpeded access to these transport and connectivity routes as other connections with the West were severed. Indeed, as Russia's primary geo-economic linkages with Europe were severed as a result of Moscow's invasion of Ukraine, the southern access points are now of even greater importance for Russia's own economic survival. And at a strategic level, this ultimately favors Azerbaijan over Armenia.

Moreover, as the fighting in Ukraine continued, it drew more Russian attention and resources. While the Russians were able (for a time) to keep their peacekeeping and other contingents in the region, the Kremlin lost the capacity to surge personnel and equipment.

Yerevan and Baku both adjusted their strategies. Pashinyan decided that, even as Armenia would serve as a key roundabout, Armenia needed to engage more intensely with NATO and EU member states (and the European Union itself), particularly in

---

161 Gvosdev, "Moscow's Evolution," pp. 77, 79.

security matters.[162] Yet Armenia has discovered that the West's interest in taking up its cause also came with major limitations. The European Union's decision to begin decoupling its economy from Russian energy supplies increased the strategic importance for the EU of Azerbaijan as a major energy producer in its own right as well as its role as a key transit country for other Eurasian sources of supply—including Russia. The NATO focus on sustaining Ukraine's defense capabilities also meant that the United States and the EU would have few resources to divert to Armenia to build up its defensive capabilities.

Russia's need for Azerbaijan to stay the course on its embrace of "transactional neutrality" conveyed the message that Moscow would be prepared to accept more revisions of the South Caucasus map in favor of Azerbaijani preferences. Indeed, the Russian government did not prevent the Azerbaijani military from taking additional border areas in 2022 or, finally, to prevent Azerbaijan from retaking complete control of Karabakh in September 2023, effectively ending the Karabakh "frozen conflict." This shift did not come about because the Russians found new affinities with Baku, or because Azerbaijan's form of government, for instance, was now viewed as more culturally aligned with Russia. Instead, rewarding Baku for its transactional neutrality while rebuking Yerevan for its search for additional or alternative suitors and refusing Russian guidance provided the strategic logic. It also reflected the new Russian view that Armenian setbacks no longer translated into Russian disadvantages. Even in its weakened condition, Moscow still has far more "skin in the game" invested in

---

162 Wojciech Górecki, "Armenia: between the West and the threat of war," OSW, April 10, 2024, at https://www.osw.waw.pl/en/publikacje/analyses/2024-04-10/armenia-between-west-and-threat-war.

the Caucasus than the West. At the same time, while the balance in the relationship has now tilted more in Ankara's favor, a continuation of the Russia-Türkiye partnership in the South Caucasus remains in Türkiye's interests.

This strategic logic explains why Russia acceded to the withdrawal of its peacekeeping forces from Karabakh in April 2024. Not only was the mission now superfluous, the continued presence of Russian forces on Azerbaijani territory was proving counterproductive for Russian strategic goals. Russia was not gaining any advantage in Yerevan since most of Karabakh's Armenian population had departed, while a withdrawal would allow the Azerbaijani government to complete the reunification of the country with no foreign forces present on its territory. Moscow is gambling that the direct presence of Russian troops is not needed as a pressure point to incentivize Baku to continue with the current modus vivendi.[163]

So, while the balance of power has shifted in the region, Russian strategic goals have not. And if the Kremlin's efforts were best suited by a clear tilt towards Armenia in the 1990s, they are now better served by a cold realist calculation whereby preserving good ties with Baku and Ankara overrides any historic ties between Russians and Armenians as a basis for policy. As Anahit Shirinyan puts it, "Russian policymakers have found [...] a comfortable middle-ground of sitting on two chairs."[164] It seems unlikely this will fundamentally change in the time ahead.

---

163 Rusif Huseynov and Murad Muradov, "Why they left: The causes and implications of the Russian peacekeepers' withdrawal from Karabakh," *Middle East Institute*, May 30, 2024, at https://www.mei.edu/publications/why-they-left-causes-and-implications-russian-peacekeepers-withdrawal-karabakh.

164 Anahit Shirinyan, "Assessing Russia's Role in Efforts to Resolve the Nagorno-Karabakh Conflict: From Perception to Reality," *Caucasus Edition: Journal of Conflict Transformation*, February 2013.

GRADUALLY, THEN SUDDENLY

The Evolution of Türkiye's Role in the
Armenia-Azerbaijan Conflict

Michael A. Reynolds

Türkiye played a prominent role in the Second Karabakh War, providing sustained diplomatic and military support that proved essential to Azerbaijan's victory. Observers commonly explain that role by pointing to the linguistic, religious, and cultural links that Türkiye shares with Azerbaijan. The great majority of citizens of Türkiye and Azerbaijan identify as both Muslims and Turks and speak languages that are sufficiently close in grammar and vocabulary to be mutually intelligible without onerous effort (they are also now both written in the Latin script, albeit with a few minor differences—a fact of some symbolic significance in a region where at least five other alphabets are present). In addition, Azerbaijani and Turkish statehoods are intertwined historically in an unusually intimate fashion like that of few other pairs of states.

The Azerbaijan Democratic Republic (1918)[165] and the Turkish Republic (1923) not only emerged out of the wreckage of two empires in virtual simultaneity, but the predecessor of the Turkish Republic, the Ottoman empire, provided critical diplomatic and military assistance that made the creation of the Azerbaijani republic possible. For their part, Azerbaijanis played prominent roles championing republican thought and practice in Turkish politics. The two nations adopted parallel political orientations at birth, embracing a Western republican regime-type resting on secular nationalism, electoral politics, and universal suffrage.[166]

The Republic of Azerbaijan fell to Soviet conquest in 1920. When it regained its independence in 1991, Türkiye was the first state to recognize it, reaffirming the two states' special relationship. Yet on the issue of Karabakh, Ankara provided only qualified—albeit steady—support for over twenty years. It was only when Baku made clear that, after a stalemate of more than two decades in negotiations with Yerevan, it was ready and determined to pursue the option to go to war to recapture Karabakh and its other occupied territories that Ankara delivered the active diplomatic and military assistance that helped Azerbaijan prevail.

Midwifing a Republic

In May 1918, amidst the turbulence of the First World War and the unfolding collapse of the Russian empire, a group of prom-

---

165 "Azerbaijan Democratic Republic" (ADR) is the translation of the Russian language name of the Azerbaijani state founded on 28 May 1918 and is routinely used in English and other languages. The name of the republic in Azerbaijani was somewhat different, "*Azərbaycan Xalq Cümhuriyyəti*," which translates as "Azerbaijan People's Republic. This nomenclature is unfortunate as the phrase "People's Republic" is associated mainly with Marxist-Leninist states, which the ADR was not.

166 The embraces were aspirational. The ADR instituted multi-party parliamentary politics but was overrun before it could hold elections. The Turkish Republic introduced universal suffrage in 1934, 16 years after Azerbaijan, and held its first competitive elections in 1950.

inent Azerbaijanis declared the independence of a new state, known as the Azerbaijan National Republic (*Azərbaycan Xalq Cümhuriyyəti*) or the Azerbaijan Democratic Republic (*Azerbaidzhanskaia Demokraticheskaia Respublika*) or ADR, the latter being the name more commonly used in foreign languages. Azerbaijan thus became the first republic in the Muslim world. The republic's leaders made their declaration in the city of Tiflis (Tbilisi), the former capital of the short-lived Transcaucasian Democratic Federative Republic that had held the South Caucasus together for mere weeks before fracturing into separate Georgian, Armenian, and Azerbaijani states.

The first challenge for the Azerbaijani leadership was to establish control over their republic's envisioned capital city, Baku, then under Bolshevik-Dashnak occupation. As the source of nearly half of world oil production at the turn of the twentieth century, Baku had become the largest city in the Caucasus. The wealth and changes generated by the explosive growth of Baku's oil industry had helped spur a remarkable flowering of modernist cultural and political thought that found audiences throughout the whole of the Muslim world, including the Ottoman empire. Serial publications such as *Hoja Nasraddin* (*Hoca Nəsrəddin*) and *Füyuzat* championed liberalizing cultural and political ideals, including constitutionalism and secularism. Azerbaijani figures such as Ali bey Hüseyinzade (Əli bəy Hüseynzadə) and Ahmed Ağaoğlu (Əhməd bəy Ağaoğlu) played prominent roles in Ottoman intellectual and political life promoting these and related concepts.[167]

---

167   Swietochowski, *Russian Azerbaijan*; A. Holly Shissler, *Between Two Empires: Ahmet Ağaoğlu and the New Turkey*, London: I.B. Tauris, 2003; James H. Meyer, *Turks Across Empires: Marketing Muslim Identity in the Russian-Ottoman Borderlands*, Oxford: Oxford University Press, 2014.

Amidst the chaos of the imploding Russian empire, Baku and its enormous oil reserves in 1918 became the object of a scramble in which Bolshevik Russia, Great Britain, Germany, the Ottoman empire, and the Azerbaijanis were competing. In March of that year, a coalition of Bolshevik and Armenian Revolutionary Federation forces under the leadership of Stepan Shaumian had taken control of the Caspian port following the massacre of several thousand of its Muslim inhabitants. Possession of Baku was essential to the viability of the ADR. As the President of the Azerbaijan National Council, Mamed Rasulzade (Məhəmməd Rəsulzadə), wrote to the Minister of Foreign Affairs, M.G. Gadzhinskii (Məmməd Həsən Hacınski), "If Baku is not taken, everything is over. Goodbye Azerbaijan!"[168]

The Azerbaijanis looked to the Ottoman Turks for assistance. Recognizing the utility of establishing a buffer state against Bolshevik Russia and the necessity of Baku for that state's viability, the Ottoman Minister of War and Deputy Commander in Chief of the Ottoman Army, Enver Pasha, dispatched his brother Major General Nuri Pasha to lead a mixed force composed of Ottoman regulars and Azerbaijani recruits to liberate Baku. Among the difficulties Nuri encountered that summer (1918) was the passivity of the Azerbaijani population in the countryside. Largely illiterate and predominantly Shiite, they were unfamiliar with the concepts that they should constitute a distinct political community with a territorial state of their own or that they should find their historical rivals, the Sunni Ottomans, now to be their allies on the basis of a shared ethnicity. The Azerbaijani General Ali Agha Shikhlinksii (Əli Ağa Şıxlinski) encountered the same

---

[168] "Əgər Bakı alınmazsa, hər şey bitdi. Xuda xafiz Azərbaycan!" Siyasi Sənədlər Arxivi, fond. 227 dosya 7 list' 8. Letter from Rasulzade to the Minister of Foreign Affairs, 03.09.1918.

problem. The Azerbaijani Ambassador to the Ottoman empire Alimardan Topchubashov (Əlimərdan Topçubaşov) accordingly urged the nascent republic's leadership to focus on developing a national army sooner rather than later. The core of a national Azerbaijani army was formed, but it was smaller than what Nuri had hoped.[169]

Nuri nonetheless managed to overcome the military forces of the Bolsheviks, Armenian Dashnaks, and British, as well as the efforts of his ostensible allies the Germans, to delay and sabotage his advance; in September 1918, he liberated Baku. The victory made possible by Ottoman arms allowed Azerbaijan's government to relocate to Baku and begin governing in earnest.

The ADR lasted just short of two years. In April 1920, the Red Army overran it. Facilitating the Red Army's invasion of Azerbaijan was the head of the new Turkish government in Ankara, Mustafa Kemal, who assented to the Bolshevik conquest of Azerbaijan in exchange for financial and military support for his own struggle against the Great Powers and their local allies to establish a sovereign Turkish state encompassing Anatolia. Kemal's military commanders called on the Azerbaijanis not to resist the invading Bolsheviks and then stood aside as the Red Army swept through Azerbaijan, Armenia, and Georgia (in that order). In short, in 1920 the Kemalists sacrificed Azerbaijan's independence to salvage their own vulnerable project, albeit they did use what influence they had to persuade the Bolsheviks in

---

[169] On the Ottoman campaign in the Caucasus in 1918, see Michael A. Reynolds, "Buffers, not Brethren: Young Turk Military Policy in the First World War and the Myth of Panturanism," *Past and Present*, no. 203, May 2009, pp. 137-179. Kurban Said's novel *Ali and Nino* captures this dynamic of evolving identities, shifting loyalties, and confused politics in Azerbaijan in this period. Kurban Said, *Ali und Nino*, Vienna: Verlag E.P. Tal & Co, 1937. On the subject of Azerbaijani identity more generally, see Tadeusz Swietochowski, *Russian Azerbaijan: The Shaping of National Identity in a Muslim Community*, Cambridge: Cambridge University Press, 1985.

the Treaty of Kars to assign the province of Nakhchivan to the Azerbaijan Soviet Socialist Republic and endow it with a special "autonomous" status.[170]

Although Azerbaijan ultimately lost its independence, the Ottoman military intervention had not been in vain. It had made possible the unprecedented—namely, the establishment of an Azerbaijani state and nation. In its brief existence, the ADR had acquired the attributes of modern statehood, such as a constitution, a flag, an anthem, an army, a parliament, and an array of ministries. Notably, the ADR was not only the first democratic and secular republic in the Muslim world, it was a pioneer in other realms, including its embrace of universal suffrage for all adult men and women (two years before the United States, 16 years before Türkiye, and over half a century before Switzerland), guaranteeing of ethnic minority representation in parliament, and its establishment of the first Azerbaijani university, Baku State University (Bakı Dövlət Darülfünunu). Not least important, Azerbaijanis now had a memory—albeit subsequently suppressed under Soviet rule—of independent statehood thanks to the ADR.

Independent Azerbaijan Resurfaces

As the Soviet Union began to splinter decisively following the failed coup against its President and General Secretary of the Communist Party Mikhail Gorbachev in August 1991, the

---

[170] Michael A. Reynolds, *Shattering Empires: The Clash and Collapse of the Ottoman and Russian Empires, 1908-1918*, Cambridge: Cambridge University Press, 2011, pp. 383-385. On the Bolshevik conquest of the Caucasus, see Richard Pipes, *The Formation of the Soviet Union: Communism and Nationalism, 1917-1923*, Cambridge, MA: Harvard University Press, 1954, pp. 193-241. On Türkiye and Bolshevik Russia, see Bülent Gökay, *A Clash of Empires: Turkey Between Russian Bolshevism and British Imperialism*, London: I.B. Tauris, 1997; Samuel J. Hirst, "Transnational Anti-Imperialism and the National Forces: Soviet Diplomacy and Turkey, 1920-1923," *Comparative Studies of South Asia, Africa, and the Middle East* 33 no. 2, 2013, pp. 214-226.

Supreme Soviet of the Azerbaijan Soviet Socialist Republic recalled the precedent of the ADR and declared the "restoration" of Azerbaijan's independence on 30 August 1991.[171] Türkiye, echoing the legacy of 1918, made itself the first state to recognize Azerbaijan's independence, doing so on 9 November 1991. Roughly eight times larger in terms of population and nine times larger in terms of territory, Türkiye stood as a large but benevolent neighbor ready to guide and assist the young, inexperienced, and disoriented Azerbaijan. Türkiye's appeal to Azerbaijan had several dimensions. Its Western orientation meshed with independent Azerbaijan's aspirations to move out from under post-Soviet Russian control whilst avoiding domination by the Islamic Republic of Iran; in contrast, the nationalist and secular principles of Turkish Kemalism offered a model of development that was reassuringly familiar. Not least important, the mutual intelligibility of Turkish and Azerbaijani gave Azerbaijanis a window to the West, a resource for news, education, commerce, business, and popular culture. As a signal of its affinity for Türkiye and the West, Azerbaijan abandoned its Cyrillic script and reverted to a Latin one.

Azerbaijan in the early 1990s had need for a patron. Flanked by an unstable and often meddlesome Russia to the north, a suspicious Iran to the south, the Caspian Sea to the east, and an impoverished Georgia and hostile Armenia to the west, Azerbaijan had no easy access to the wider world, and little reason to attract anyone's concerted interest. It was impoverished and its once formidable oil industry had decayed and obsolesced after decades of Soviet mismanagement. Worse, it was waging a

---

171 "Azerbaidzhan: Vosstanovlena gosudarstvennaia nezavisimost'" *Nezavisimaia Gazeta*, August 31,1991.

losing war with Armenian forces over what had been known in the Soviet period as the Nagorno-Karabakh Autonomous Oblast (NKAO). The struggle for Karabakh had erupted in the turmoil of 1918-1920 as Armenians and Azerbaijanis battled each other for control of that territory. The Bolsheviks imposed a compromise solution of sorts on 5 July 1921 by indicating that "Nagorno-Karabakh shall remain within the Azerbaijan SSR" but as a nominally autonomous region (*oblast*). They pointedly renamed the city of Khankendi (Xankəndi) Stepanakert, in honor of the Armenian Bolshevik Stepan Shaumian, and made it the capital of the NKAO. The compromise did not resolve the conflict over Karabakh, however, but merely papered it over.[172]

The Karabakh Conflict Reignites, Türkiye Stands Aloof

The conflict over Karabakh reignited in the waning years of the Soviet Union. As Gorbachev was easing tight controls on speech as part of his reform program of *Glasnost*, Armenians began to agitate openly for the reassignment of the NKAO from Azerbaijan to Armenia. The conflict soon grew violent and eventually acquired the character of a territorial war fought by armed formations in and around the NKAO. The Armenians' possession of a clear objective—overturning the *status quo* to seize Karabakh and unify it with the Republic of Armenia—coupled with their greater national cohesion gave them the upper hand in that stage of the conflict, and they began seizing Azerbaijani territories

---

[172] Indeed, the Soviet Armenian and Azerbaijani republics continued to maintain a low-key mutual antagonism throughout the Soviet period. See Farid Shafiyev, *Resettling the Borderlands: State Relocations and Ethnic Conflict in the South Caucasus*, Montreal: McGill-Queen's University Press, 2018.

outside as well as inside the NKAO, expelling ethnic Azerbaijanis by the hundreds of thousands.[173]

Notably, Türkiye stood aloof in the early phases of the conflict, even as the Azerbaijanis were suffering battlefield reverses. Indeed, when asked in 1989 about the conflict, Turkish President Turgut Özal replied that because of their Shiite identity most Azerbaijanis were closer to Iran than to Türkiye.[174] Given that the Soviet Union was then still in existence as an enormous nuclear-armed power, Özal's wish to avoid involvement would not be difficult to understand. Yet even after the disintegration of the Soviet Union, Ankara remained reticent to involve itself directly. Several factors explain this. One was the general timidity—or prudence—of Türkiye's leadership, which had long taken guidance from Mustafa Kemal's foreign policy dictum of "peace at home, peace abroad," an admonition to steer clear of foreign entanglements or interventions outside of Türkiye's borders.

To be sure, following the dissolution of the Soviet Union in 1991, Turks initially flirted with the idea that their country should serve as a regional leader and developmental model for the states of Central Asia and the Caucasus. American officials and experts had pushed this idea, seeing NATO member-state Türkiye as geographically and culturally well-suited to serve not only as a Western-oriented counterweight to a potential revived Russia but also as an antidote to Iranian Islamism. As Turkish President Süleyman Demirel put it, the Turkish example demonstrated to

---

173 Two excellent analyses of the first Karabakh War are Thomas de Waal, *Black Garden: Armenia and Azerbaijan through Peace and War*, New York: New York University Press, 2003/2013; and Laurence Broers, *Armenia and Azerbaijan: Anatomy of a Rivalry*, Edinburgh: Edinburgh University Press, 2019.

174 "Flaş Ülke Oluruz," *Cumhuriyet*, January 19, 1990; Mustafa Aydın, "Turkey and Central Asia: Challenges of Change," *Central Asian Survey* 15 no. 2, 1996, p. 160; "Svante E. Cornell, *Azerbaijan Since Independence*, London: Routledge, 2011, p. 364.

the Muslims of the former Soviet Union that "Islam, democracy, human rights, and [the] market economy" could go together hand in hand."[175] Kazakhstan President Nursultan Nazarbayev reflected Türkiye's appeal in the region when in Ankara in September 1991 he described the coming twenty-first century as "the century of Turks," that is, of Türkiye and the Turkic states of the former Soviet Union. Enthusiasm for this role, however, faded quickly inside Türkiye and Central Asia alike.[176]

The internal destabilization and then disappearance of the Soviet Union had opened a vast but also uncharted and unfamiliar arena for Turkish foreign policy. A latent wariness of a diminished yet still potent Russian Federation tempered Turkish ambitions. Expertise on the region was thin and Türkiye's anemic economy could provide only limited resources. Moreover, Türkiye in the early 1990s was facing a myriad of domestic challenges, ranging from a draining insurgency waged by the Kurdistan Workers' Party (Partiya Karkeran Kurdistan, or PKK) to a weak currency. Inhibiting Ankara from assuming a more prominent role in the First Karabakh War in particular was an awareness that a new round of conflict with Armenians could only tarnish Türkiye's international image by revitalizing claims of historical persecution and genocide.[177]

Still, for reasons of geographic, linguistic, and cultural

---

175 Aydin, "Turkey and Central Asia," p. 162.
176 Hakan Fidan, "Turkish Foreign Policy towards Central Asia," *Journal of Balkan and Near Eastern Studies* 12 no. 1, March 2010, p. 113; Philip Robins, "Between Sentiment and Self-Interest: Turkey's Policy toward Azerbaijan and the Central Asian States," *Middle East Journal* 47 no. 4, Autumn 1993, pp. 593-595; Aydin, "Turkey and Central Asia," pp. 157-177. See also Heinz Kramer, *A Changing Turkey: Challenges to Europe and the United States*, Washington: Brookings Institution Press, 2000, pp. 97-116; Graham E. Fuller and Ian O. Lesser, *Turkey's New Geopolitics: From the Balkans to Western China*, Boulder, CO: Westview Press, 1983.
177 Cornell, *Azerbaijan Since Independence*, pp. 370-371; Mustafa Aydin, "Foucault's Pendulum: Turkey in Central Asia and the Caucasus," *Turkish Studies* 5 no. 2, 2004, pp. 2-3.

proximity, as well as of material interest, the mutual attraction between Azerbaijan and Türkiye proved to be more enduring. Soviet Azerbaijan already in January 1990 had expressed its interest in developing economic and cultural ties to Türkiye when the Chairman of the Council of Ministers of Azerbaijan, Ayaz Mutalibov, made the first visit to Ankara by an Azerbaijani at the prime ministerial level in nearly seventy years.[178] The disintegration of the Soviet Union thrust independent sovereignty upon the Azerbaijanis suddenly and with virtually no warning.[179] Azerbaijanis found in secular, nationalist Türkiye—with its cult of personality of Mustafa Kemal and pro-Western orientation—a comprehensible and attractive model as well as a linguistically and culturally accessible one.[180]

For the Turks, fond of repeating to themselves the aphorism that "a Turk's only friend is another Turk," the (re)appearance of a country with pro-Turkish sympathies was both exciting and flattering, and Turks requited that affection. Polls taken between 2019 and 2021, for example, reveal that Azerbaijan is the sole country in the world that a majority of Turkish citizens regard favorably.[181] Ankara was accustomed to being caught between a West that was at best ambivalent and a Middle East that offered

---

[178] Bilâl N. Şimir, *Azerbaycan: Azerbaycan'ın Yeniden Doğuş Sürecinde Türkiye-Azerbaycan İlişkileri*, Ankara: Bilgi Yayınevi, 2011, pp. 71-72.

[179] On the seeming inconceivability of the demise of the Soviet Union, see Aleksei Yurchak, *Everything was Forever, Until It was No More: The Last Soviet Generation*, Princeton: Princeton University Press, 2013.

[180] Elnur Soltanov, "Turkish-Azerbaijani Relations: Brothers in Arms or Brothers in the Dark?'" in Murad Ismayilov and Norman A. Graham, eds. *Turkish-Azerbaijani Relations: One Nation, Two States?* New York: Routledge, 2016, pp. 20-22; Thomas Goltz, *Azerbaijan Diary: A Rogue Reporter's Adventures in an Oil-Rich, War-Torn, Post-Soviet Republic*, Armonk, NY: M.E. Sharpe, 1998, p. 211.

[181] Ragip Soylu, "Turkish public believes Turkey has no friends - but Turks," *Middle East Eye*, January 17, 2020; Mustafa Aydın et. al, *Quantitative Research Report: Turkey Trends 2021*, Istanbul: Kadir Has University Turkey Studies Group, Akademetre and Global Academy, 2021.

little but resentment and headaches, and this new geography offered an attractive alternative.

Geopolitical isolation also spurred Ankara and Baku to embrace one another. Azerbaijan could maintain cordial relations with Russia and respectful relations with Iran, but those relations could never be without elements of fear and tension. As a vastly larger country and the region's former hegemon, Russia was an inherent challenge. The Islamic Republic of Iran, also a past imperial hegemon and larger neighbor with over eight times the population of Azerbaijan, was deeply anxious about independent Azerbaijan's potential to stimulate the national or separatist ambitions of Iran's ethnic Azerbaijani population, which numbers at the very least 20 million and is predominant in the northern part of Iran. Tehran has sought to undermine Baku by consistently assisting Armenia, sometimes subtly and sometimes quite overtly, as well as supporting opposition Islamist groups inside Azerbaijan. Thus, Türkiye was seen as being able to serve as an invaluable counterweight to both Russia and Iran.

Ankara's initial aloofness toward the conflict over Karabakh came under challenge in the wake of the February 1992 Khojaly massacre of over 600 Azerbaijani civilians by Armenian forces. News of the massacre, which was the largest of such crimes committed by either side in the First Karabakh War, aroused public opinion in Türkiye. Here the legacy of the Turks' own conflicts with the Armenians made it difficult for them to remain indifferent to harm inflicted on a fellow Muslim and Turkic nation. Armenian advances in the spring of 1992 discredited the Azerbaijani leadership and spurred the rise to the presidency of Abulfaz Elchibey. Passionately pro-Turkish, Elchibey sought closer ties with Türkiye across all dimensions.[182] Nonetheless, Türkiye refrained from taking any direct military steps against Armenia.

But when in the spring of 1993 ethnic-Armenian forces advanced beyond the borders of the former NKAO to seize the Azerbaijani province of Kelbajar, Ankara decided this was a step too far. As Turkish Prime Minister Süleyman Demirel pointed out to an Armenian presidential envoy in Ankara that April, Kelbajar neither hosted an Armenian population nor was it essential for the security of the Armenians of Karabakh.[183] Ankara thereupon closed its border with Armenia. Turkish President Turgut Özal ominously suggested that Türkiye might go farther and "show its teeth."[184] On a visit to Baku that month (i.e., April 1993), Özal warned that if the Armenians do not cease waging war, Türkiye and Azerbaijan would have to establish a military alliance.[185]

Neither the closing of the border nor Özal's words had any deterrent effect. Armenian forces went on to seize five Azerbaijani provinces outside the former NKAO that summer and fall. Under these blows, the Azerbaijani army's cohesiveness unraveled. Elements of the Azerbaijani army mutinied, causing Elchibey in June 1993 to quit his post and invite Heydar Aliyev back to Baku. Aliyev assumed the post of provisional president. In October 1993, he was formally elected as president in a national vote. Given Aliyev's past as a member of the Soviet Politburo, his return to power was widely interpreted as a win for Russia against

---

182 Goltz, pp. 254-257.
183 Thomas De Waal, *Great Catastrophe: Armenians and Turks in the Shadow of Genocide*, Oxford: Oxford University Press, 2015, p. 206.
184 Hugh Pope, "Turkey 'Must Show its Teeth' to Armenia: Military Help for Azerbaijan Urged," *The Independent*, April 6, 1993.
185 Selma Göktürk Çetinkaya, "Türkiye-Azerbaycan İlişkilerinin Askeri Boyutu ve Jandarma Merkezli Yardımlar (1992-2014)," *Bilecik Şeyh Edebali Üniversitesi Sosyal Bilimler Dergisi* 5, no. 1, 2020, p. 21.

Turkish influence. Aliyev, however, quickly showed that he was independent of Moscow and eager to cultivate ties with Türkiye. Indeed, it was Aliyev who coined the famous apothegm "one nation, two states" to describe the unusually close relationship between Türkiye and Azerbaijan in a speech before the Turkish parliament in 1995.[186]

Aliyev's ascent represented a turning point. While Chairman of the Supreme Soviet of Nakhchivan (a position he held between November 1990 and October 1993), Aliyev had established a good working relationship with Turkish leaders and oversaw the building of a bridge from Nakhchivan to Türkiye that broke Armenia's blockade of the Azerbaijani exclave.[187] Addressing the Turkish parliament on 9 February 1994, Aliyev announced, "The relations between Türkiye and Azerbaijan have a rich history. We are at root one people. Our history is one, our language is one, our religion is one." [188]

That same day (i.e., 9 February 1994), the leaders of the two states signed an "Agreement on Friendship and the Development of Comprehensive Cooperation." Notably, the preamble adopts an unambivalently pro-Western stance. It explicitly defines the agreement as aligned with the goals and principles of the UN Charter, the Helsinki Final Act, and the Organisation for Security and Co-operation in Europe (OSCE), and as being motivated by a joint desire to build democratic legal states based on the principles of human rights, fundamental liberties, a multi-party socio-

---

186 Cornell, *Azerbaijan Since Independence*, 87.
187 Fariz Ismailzade, "Turkey-Azerbaijan: The Honeymoon is Over," *Transatlantic Policy Quarterly*, Winter 2005, pp. 3-4.
188 Musa Qasımlı, *Azərbaycan Respublikasının Xarici Siyasəti, 1991-2003* vol. 1, Baku: Mütərcim, 2015, pp. 444-445.

political system, and free-market economy.[189] The document later commits the parties to cooperate within the frameworks provided by the North Atlantic Cooperation Council,[190] the OSCE, and the UN Charter. With Azerbaijan, Türkiye was indeed fulfilling its role as a shepherd or guide to the West.

The agreement underscored the two parties' commitment to the principles of territorial integrity and opposition to the change of borders by force, and it states in Article Six that if one of the parties suffers an attack from a third state or states, the other party is to aid the first to eliminate the threat by taking necessary measures in compliance with the UN Charter and "other international obligations." It makes no requirement that the other party respond militarily or comprehensively, however. Moreover, Article Seven specifies that the parties will handle issues of national security and defense independently.

Ankara recognized Aliyev's potential and outreach and repaid his enthusiasm by becoming Azerbaijan's most reliable backer in the diplomatic arena, particularly on the question of Karabakh.[191] Turkish diplomats supported Azerbaijan in international organizations like the United Nations and the OSCE, which established in Minsk a working group ultimately co-chaired by Russia, the United States, and France to find a solution to the conflict over Karabakh. In bilateral dealings with Russia and other states, Turkish officials regularly called attention to the need to resolve the conflict over Karabakh.[192]

---

[189] "Azərbaycan Respublikası və Türkiyə Respublikası arasında dostluq və hərtərəfli əməkdaşlığı barədə Mükavilə." Text in *Müqavilələr Toplusu* vol. 1, Baku: Azərbaycan Respublikası Xarici İşlər Nazirliyi, 2008, pp. 24-28.
[190] Later renamed the Euro-Atlantic Partnership Council.
[191] Cornell, *Azerbaijan Since Independence*, p. 360.
[192] Akif Marifli, *Dağlıq Qarabağ Münaqişəsi Azərbaycan-Türkiyə Münasibətlərində*, Baku: Elm, 2020, pp. 124-227.

Institution Building for the Long Term

Although Ankara still refrained from providing direct military support to Azerbaijan in Karabakh, it took an active role in the education and training of the Azerbaijani military. In August 1992 Türkiye and Azerbaijan signed an agreement on cooperation in military education by which Azerbaijani military cadets and junior and midranking officers became eligible for study at the Turkish Military Academy, War Academy, Gülhane Military Medical Academy, and non-commissioned officer schools.[193] The two countries signed another military education agreement in June 1996.[194] In October 1997, the Turkish Gendarmerie and the Azerbaijan Interior Forces Command concluded a protocol on education and training[195] and soon thereafter the Turkish Gendarmerie and Coast Guard Academy began accepting Azerbaijani students.[196] Also in 1997, Türkiye agreed to help reform the education and curriculum of Azerbaijan's Higher Military and Naval schools (Ali Hərbi Məktəbi, Ali Hərbi Dənizçilik Məktəbi) according to NATO standards. Subsequently, Türkiye implemented similar reforms at Azerbaijan's other institutions of military education.[197] Meanwhile, Turkish military schools and academies have graduated hundreds of Azerbaijanis.[198]

Turkish-Azerbaijani military cooperation and NATO-

---

[193] Bilâl Şimşir, *Türkiye ile Türk Cumhuriyetleri Arasındaki Anlaşmalar I*, Ankara: TOBB, 1993, pp. 105-115; Haldun Yalçınkaya, "Turkey's Overlooked Role in the Second Nagorno-Karabakh War," German Marshall Fund of the U.S., January 21, 2021. The text of the agreement can be found here: https://www5.tbmm.gov.tr/tutanaklar/KANUNLAR_KARARLAR/kanuntbmmc076/kanuntbmmc076/kanuntbmmc07603903.pdf

[194] Veliyev, *Azərbaycan-Türkiye Stratejik Ortaklığı*, p. 186

[195] "Ali Hərbi Məktəb," at http://m.dq.mia.gov.az/?/az/menu/92/

[196] "Türkiyə hərbi məktəblərinə kursantların qəbulu üçün müsabiqə elan olunub," apa.az, July 19, 2017.

[197] Cesur Sümərinli, "Azərbaycanda hərbi təhsil problemləri: Silahlı Qüvvələrin NATO standartlarına keçidi peşəkar zabit ehtiyaclarını ortaya çıxarır" *Ayna* no. 22, June 11, 2011, p. 9.

[198] Edward Erickson, "The 44-Day War in Nagorno-Karabakh: Turkish Drone Success or Operational Art?" *Military Review Online*, August 2021, p. 2.

Azerbaijani collaboration have enjoyed a powerful synergy. Azerbaijani units served under Turkish command in the UN Security Council-authorized NATO peacekeeping mission in Kosovo (1999-2008) as well as in Afghanistan (2002-2021).[199] In April 2000, the Turkish and Azerbaijani armed forces agreed to create a Training and Education Center (*Təlim və Tədris Mərkəzi*) to offer an advanced officers course, reserve officers course, and training courses for enlisted ranks and warrant officers. The center, established in March 2001, has as its primary goal to bring the Azerbaijan Armed Forces fully up to NATO standards.[200]

As the ties between Azerbaijan and Türkiye developed, Turkish military officials occasionally hinted that they saw Azerbaijan as more than a partner. Thus, for example, when in 2001 Azerbaijan was experiencing a stand-off of sorts with Iran in the Caspian Sea, the Chief of the Turkish General Staff Hüseyin Kıvrıkoğlu visited Baku where he pointedly warned, "Azerbaijan and Türkiye's skies are one common sky."[201]

Underscoring his personal commitment to developing the military relationship, Azerbaijan President Heydar Aliyev spoke three days later to the graduating class of Azerbaijan's Military Academy. Present were the Chief of the General Staff of the Turkish Armed Forces Major General Kıvrıkoğlu and several other Turkish officers. Noting how the Turkish military had secured the independence of the Turkish Republic under desper-

---

199 Ministry of Defense of Azerbaijan, "Cooperation with NATO," https://mod.gov.az/en/cooperation-with-nato-028/; Aykut Karadağ, "'We're proud of it': Turkish, Azerbaijani soldiers stand shoulder-to-shoulder in Kabul," *Anadolu Ajansı*, August 22, 2021; Mushvig Mehdiyev," Azerbaijan Withdraws Its Peacekeepers from Afghanistan," *Caspian News*, August 26, 2021.

200 "Azərbaycan Ordusunun Təlim və Tədris Mərkəzi," at https://mod.gov.az/az/silahli-quvvelerin-telim-ve-tedris-merkezi-112.

201 Cornell, *Azerbaijan Since Independence*, pp. 360-361; "İran'a gözdağı," *Hürriyet*, August 23, 2001."Kıvrıkoğlu Bakü'de," *Hürriyet*, August 25, 2001.

ate conditions in the 1920s, Aliyev called on the academy graduates "to emulate Turkish soldiers in everything." He reminded the young officers of the Armenian occupation of Azerbaijani territory and the expulsion of one million Azerbaijanis. Although he stressed the need for a peaceful resolution of the conflict over Karabakh, he added, "at the same time, the Azerbaijani army, the Azerbaijani soldier must know that our country's territorial integrity must be secured at all costs."[202]

Nonetheless, Ankara continued to refrain from concluding a formal military alliance or partnership with Baku. While on a visit to Ankara in May 1997, Heydar Aliyev publicly called out Russia's generous military support of Armenia in the hope that, by doing so, he would goad the Turkish government to back Azerbaijan similarly. Then in August 1997, Russia and Armenia signed a Treaty of Friendship and Mutual Assistance that amounted to a miliary alliance. The treaty orients cooperation between Armenia and Russia within the frameworks not only of the UN Charter and OSCE conventions, but also that of the Minsk-based Commonwealth of Independent States. Significantly, in the event of an attack by a third party, the Armenia-Russia treaty obliges each signatory specifically to render military assistance to the other if necessary. It also provides for the joint use of military bases and equipment and commits Armenia and Russia to coordinate their military defense and procurement policies.[203] Heydar Aliyev requested a similar treaty from Ankara. Even so, Ankara remained

---

[202] "Azerbaycan Cumhuriyeti Cumhurbaşkanı Haydar Aliyev'in Azerbaycan Harp Okulu'nda ilk mezuniyet töreninde konuşması," August 26, 2001. Available at: https://lib.aliyevheritage.org/tk/9057131.html.

[203] "Dogovor o druzhbe, sotrunichestve i vzaimnoi pomoshchi mezhdu Rossiiskoi Federatsiei i Respublikoi Armeniia" (Treaty of Friendship, Cooperation, and Mutual Assistance between the Russian Federation and the Republic of Armenia). The text of the Russian-Armenian treaty can be found at https://docs.cntd.ru/document/8306454.

impassive in the face of these entreaties, hesitating to take a step that might provoke Russia.[204]

Family Discord

An especially contentious moment occurred in 1995, when Turkish prime minister Tansu Çiller and several other high-ranking Turkish officials were implicated in a coup attempt against Heydar Aliyev. Years Later, Aliyev would still publicly reprimand the Turks for the offense and their refusal to extradite the plotters.[205] Although it was a disappointment on a far lesser scale, the Turks felt let down by the Azerbaijanis' reluctance to support the claim to statehood of the self-styled Turkish Republic of Northern Cyprus. The Azerbaijanis' worry was that recognition of Northern Cyprus might provide a precedent for the recognition of the self-styled Republic of Artsakh (Armenian-controlled Karabakh) as a state. The fact that the Azerbaijanis' concern was legitimate and that Baku's logic was sound did not prevent Turks from accusing their Azerbaijani "brothers" of betrayal.[206]

Nearly a decade and a half after the ceasefire that ended the First Karabakh War, the conflict over Karabakh came to pose the most severe test to Turkish-Azerbaijani relations. In 2008 Ankara began to flirt with the possibility of opening diplomatic relations with Armenia. Such a step promised both to resolve a chronically nagging issue for Türkiye and win significant goodwill for Ankara in Washington and European capitals. As part of this effort,

---

204 Veliyev, *Azerbaycan-Türkiye Stratejik Ortaklığı*, pp. 187-188.
205 Cornell, *Azerbaijan Since Independence*, p. 372; "Aliyev Criticizes Çiller on Armenia Policy," *Asbarez* May 7, 1997; "The Turkish Underworld," *The New York Times*, January 30, 1998, p. 16.
206 Fariz Ismailzade, "Turkey-Azerbaijan: The Honeymoon is Over," *Turkish Policy*, Winter 2005, p. 8.

Turkish President Abdullah Gül made an unprecedented visit to Yerevan on 6 September 2008 to watch a soccer game between the Turkish and Armenian national teams. While there, he met with his Armenian counterpart Serzh Sarkisian. Although lasting only a matter of hours, the visit of a Turkish head of state to Armenia was symbolically powerful and heralded the possibility of a real bilateral breakthrough.[207]

The prospect of a Turko-Armenian rapprochement, however, alarmed Baku. The fear was that if Türkiye opened its border with Armenia, it would allow Armenia to escape economic isolation and thereby deprive Baku of the only source of leverage short of war that might compel Yerevan to compromise on the Karabakh issue. Thus, when Turkish foreign minister Ali Babacan approved a draft protocol for normalizing relations with Armenia that ignored the Karabakh issue, Azerbaijani President Ilham Aliyev denounced President Gül as a "liar, cheat, and betrayer" in a diplomatic exchange with U.S. envoys, and Azerbaijani officials on multiple levels began pressing their Turkish counterparts to drop the outreach. Prime Minister Recep Tayyip Erdoğan thereafter called on the Armenians to withdraw from occupied Azerbaijani territory at the same time as the Turks would open the border. The Armenians, however, rejected any such linkage and the rapprochement soon died.[208]

---

207   De Waal, *Great Catastrophe*, pp. 216-218.
208   De Waal, *Great Catastrophe*, pp. 223, 301.

Ties Grow Thicker, Diplomatic Support Grows Stronger

The scuffle over the potential normalization of relations with Armenia had shaken Azerbaijani-Turkish relations, but the earlier investments in building connections—particularly in military education and training and in energy—had accumulated such momentum that relations quickly recovered and even deepened. Even as Baku and Ankara were jostling each other in 2008, the Turkish General Staff and Azerbaijan's Ministry of Defense agreed to remodel the Azerbaijani Air Force Academy along the lines of Türkiye's.[209] In August 2010, Türkiye and Azerbaijan signed an "Agreement on Strategic Partnership and Mutual Support."[210] As the phrase "strategic partnership" indicates, the agreement represented an upgrading of ties. It reaffirmed the Treaty of Kars and the 1994 friendship agreement and, in language more precise than that of the 1994 agreement, it underscored the signatories' commitment to the principles of sovereignty, territorial integrity, and the inviolability of internationally recognized borders. In the event that a third state or group of states mounted an armed attack on one of the parties, the partnership agreement committed both signatories to aid each other with their available capabilities, including military force, in the exercise of the right of individual or collective self-defense as provided by Article 51 of the UN Charter. It further expanded the training and education opportunities for Azerbaijani military personnel, including the conduct of joint military exercises and joint production of

---

209 The agreement can be found at https://www.resmigazete.gov.tr/eskiler/2009/02/20090206-1.htm; Cavid Veliyev, "Azerbaijan-Türkiye Military Relations in the Shadow of the Negotiations with Armenia," *Turkeyscope* 7 no. 4, July-August 2023.
210 "Azərbaycan Respublikası və Türkiyə Respublikası arasında strateji tərəfdaşlıq və qarşılıqlı yardım haqqında Müqavilə."

military equipment and ammunition. The partnership agreement thus both reflected a tighter Turkish-Azerbaijani relationship and laid the groundwork for further integration.[211]

Yet even as the Turks were augmenting their rhetorical and institutional backing of Azerbaijan, they advised the Azerbaijanis that any revival of the Karabakh War would produce a "nightmare scenario."[212] Ankara was still wary of getting embroiled in an open conflict that could lead to a clash with Russia and complicate relations with its NATO allies.

It is interesting to note that despite the ongoing and intensifying cooperation between the Azerbaijani and Turkish defense establishments in education and training, Turkish sales of arms and military equipment were minuscule. Over the decade from 2011 to 2020, Türkiye accounted for a mere 2.9 percent of Azerbaijan's military imports, far less than Russia (60.1 percent), Israel (26.6 percent), and Belarus (7.1 percent). Turkish military sales to Azerbaijan—drones, rocket launchers, ammunition, and other equipment and supplies—did surge following the July 2020 clashes (see below), rising in value from just $278,880 in July to $36 million in August 2020 and $77.1 million the next month.[213] Nonetheless, Türkiye had played a remarkably small overall role in arming Azerbaijan.

It was in the diplomatic sphere, however, where Ankara's support grew more pronounced. In early April 2016, amidst rising tensions and provocations along the Karabakh line of

---

211 The text of the agreement can be found at https://e-qanun.az/framework/21158. Shahin Abbasov, "Azerbaijan-Turkey Military Pact Signals Impatience with Minsk Talks – Analysts," *Eurasianet*, January 18, 2011.

212 International Crisis Group, "Armenia and Azerbaijan: Preventing War" *Europe Briefing* no. 60, February 2, 2011, p. 15.

213 Ece Toksabay, "Turkish arms sales to Azerbaijan surged before Nagorno-Karabakh fighting," *Reuters*, October 16, 2020.

contact, the Azerbaijani army mounted a small-scale incursion into Armenian-occupied territory. The combat reached a level of intensity not seen since 1994, involving tanks, multiple launch rocket systems, artillery, and drones. Both sides suffered significant losses. After four days of fighting, the two sides agreed to a ceasefire thanks to Russian mediation. The territory that the Azerbaijanis managed to seize was insignificant, but their demonstration of a will to fight was not. That demonstration was the point, as Baku had grown frustrated with the Armenians' persisting disinterest in negotiations and the Minsk Group's chronic inaction.[214]

Türkiye stood squarely behind Azerbaijan throughout the four-day conflict. President Erdoğan pledged that Türkiye "would continue unto the end to do its best to help" Azerbaijan. He publicly faulted the Minsk Group Co-chairs for their passivity and even accused them of helping to precipitate the fighting.[215] "Karabakh," Erdoğan asserted, "will surely be returned to its rightful owner, Azerbaijan, one day."[216] The Turkish Prime Minister Ahmet Davutoğlu likewise signaled unqualified support of Azerbaijan: "All the world should know: Türkiye will stand with Azerbaijan against Armenia's aggression and occupation until Judgment Day. Every hero (*şehit*) that Azerbaijan loses is a soul of ours, a heart of ours."[217]

Türkiye's diplomatic backing of Azerbaijan was immensely important. Whereas many states recognized the legitimacy of

---

214 Zaur Shiriyev, "Violence in Nagorny Karabakh a Reflection of Azerbaijan's Security Dilemma," *Chatham House*, April 22, 2016.
215 "Azerbaycan'a Elimizden Gelen Yardımları Sonuna Kadar Yapmaya Devam Edeceğiz" *Türkiye Cumhurbaşkanlığı*, April 2, 2016.
216 "Davutoglu says Turkey stands by Azerbaijan in Karabakh conflict," *TRT World*, April 5, 2016.
217 "Davutoğlu Seslendi 'Can Azerbaycan', 'Diyarbakırlı Kardeşlerim'" *Bianet*, April 5, 2016.

Azerbaijan's grievances about the occupation of its lands, none but Türkiye were sympathetic or supportive of Azerbaijan's efforts to change the status quo to fulfill those grievances. As a member of the Minsk Group and of NATO, and as a major regional power, Türkiye had both diplomatic stature and military heft that made it impossible to ignore. Even Russia could not easily intimidate Türkiye. This gave Azerbaijan the room in which to pursue a more proactive strategy of escalating pressure on Armenia when the Minsk Group process stalled.

The message that Baku tried to send to Yerevan through both rhetoric and action was that it was ready and willing to go to war to reassert its claims on Karabakh and the surrounding occupied territories. Baku openly and repeatedly announced its intent to exploit its larger state budget to build up its armed forces to overmatch and overwhelm Armenian forces. It made no secret of its purchases and paraded its arsenal while speaking directly of its intent to deploy that arsenal to retake Karabakh. With the April 2016 clashes, Baku underscored its willingness to shed blood to recover Karabakh.

Yerevan, however, remained oblivious to the shifting balance of power, clinging instead to the comforting conviction that the supposed weakness of Azerbaijani national sentiment, lack of unity, and lower levels of competence were chronic and ensured that Azerbaijan could not impose its will militarily. Thus, Armenian leaders chose to interpret the four-day war of 2016 as a demonstration not of Azerbaijan's resolve to fight but instead of its continuing inability to win a decisive battlefield victory.[218] Meanwhile, Turkish Armed Forces and their Azerbaijani counter-

---

218 Michael A. Reynolds, "Confidence and Catastrophe: Armenia and the Second Karabakh War," *War on the Rocks,* January 11, 2021.

parts grew steadily more integrated, holding seven joint exercises in 2018 and 13 in the following year.[219]

A July Crisis

On 12 July 2020, fighting erupted between the armed forces of Azerbaijan and Armenia in the vicinity of Azerbaijan's Tovuz district and Armenia's Tavush district. Which side initiated the fighting remains in dispute. As the power explicitly threatening force to change the status quo, one could suppose that Azerbaijan was the more likely instigator. Yet it is worth noting that Armenia's rhetoric on Karabakh over the course of the prior year had grown only more belligerent, even swaggering. Armenian Prime Minister Nikol Pashinyan's peremptory declaration in August 2019 that "Artsakh is Armenia, period!" negated the possibility of further negotiations. The Armenian minister of defense's announcement that Yerevan was no longer interested in trading land for peace but would instead wage "new wars for new territories" similarly signaled a new defiant audacity.[220] The fact that fighting broke out not along the line of contact established by the ceasefire that ended the First Karabakh War but on the Armenian-Azerbaijani border near an operational gas pipeline (running parallel to an oil pipeline) that would soon carry Azerbaijani gas to EU markets via the Southern Gas Corridor lends plausibility to the idea that

---

219 Erickson, "The 44-Day War in Nagorno-Karabakh," p. 2. Among these were the tactical exercises "Mustafa Kemal Atatürk" and "Sarsılmaz Kardeşlik" (Unshakeable Brotherhood) in 2019 and "Heydar Aliyev" in 2020 and the series of joint aviation exercises "TurAz Kartalı" (Turkish-Azerbaijani Eagle) in 2017, 2019, and 2020. Azerbaijani forces participated inside Türkiye in the Efes series of tactical training exercises in 2016 and 2018, Kış (Winter), Erciyes, and Anadolu Ankası (Anatolian Phoenix) and in the aviation exercises Tur-Az Şahini (Turkish-Azerbaijani Hawk) in 2016 and 2018. R.N. Pukhov, ed., *Buria na Kavkaze*, Moscow: Tsentr analiza strategii i tekhnologii, 2021, p. 89.

220 Eduard Abrahamyan, "Rationalizing the Tonoyan Doctrine: Armenia's Active Deterrence Strategy," *Eurasia Daily Monitor*, May 2, 2019.

Armenian forces might have initiated the fighting in July 2020 in order to demonstrate their ability to interdict and disrupt Azerbaijan's energy exports.[221]

The deaths of Azerbaijani soldiers and officers sparked demonstrations inside Azerbaijan—including in Baku, where tens of thousands turned out on for street protests on 14 July 2020 to demand the liberation of Karabakh. The demonstrations in Baku culminated with a crowd storming the Azerbaijani parliament at night, a reflection of the building popular frustration with the *status quo*.[222]

The Turkish Foreign Ministry immediately came out in full support of Azerbaijan, stating, "Türkiye will continue to stand by Azerbaijan with all means."[223] Turkish officials made clear that they meant what they said by "all means." On 17 July 2020, the President of Türkiye's Defense Industry Agency (*Cumhurbaşkanlığı Savunma Sanayii Başkanı*) publicly announced while receiving an Azerbaijani delegation, including the Chief of the Azerbaijan Air Force, that Türkiye and Azerbaijan were "one heart" and that all Türkiye's weapons and technology— "from drones, ammunition, and missiles to electronic warfare systems"— were at Azerbaijan's disposal.[224] Also, before the end of the month, the Turkish armed forces were readying to conduct joint military maneuvers with their Azerbaijani counterparts.[225] These were the third joint

---

221 Brenda Shaffer, "The Trigger for War: Energy in the 2020 Armenia-Azerbaijan War," in Turan Gafarlı and Michael Arnold, eds., *The Karabakh Gambit: Responsibility for the Future*, Ankara: TRT Research Centre, November 2021, pp. 100-114.
222 "Pro-war Azerbaijani protesters break into parliament," *Eurasianet*, July 15, 2020.
223 "Azerbaycan-Ermenistan Sınırında Çatışma," *Kanal B*, July 13, 2020.
224 "'Türk SİHA'ları Azerbaycan'ın emrinde'" *Posta*, July 17, 2020.
225 "Türk askerleri Azerbaycan'la ortak tatbikat için Nahçıvan'da" *Habertürk*, July 27 2020; "TurAz Kartalı başlıyor: Türk ve Azeri ordusu bugün ortak tatbikata başlıyor" *Yeni Şafak*, July 29, 2020.

maneuvers in 2020.[226] Aliyev in a phone call to Erdoğan on 31 July 2020 underlined his appreciation for Türkiye's strong support.[227]

Yerevan noted what Ankara was doing. The Armenian Ministry of Foreign Affairs condemned Türkiye's promise to stand by Azerbaijan as destabilizing.[228] Even so, Armenian decisionmakers seemingly ascribed little importance to Ankara's actions. In early August 2020, the Secretary of Armenia's Security Council dismissed Türkiye's expanded collaboration with Azerbaijan as a coping mechanism for Azerbaijani failure and announced that Armenia in response would work with its "strategic ally Russia."[229] One week later, Pashinyan, wittingly or unwittingly, provoked Türkiye when he declared the stillborn Treaty of Sèvres (1920) to be a "living treaty" on its centennial. That agreement had prescribed the partition of Anatolia. Preventing its implementation and overturning it with the Treaty of Lausanne (1923) was a capstone achievement of Mustafa Kemal and the Turkish War of Independence that he had successfully led. Observers of Turkish politics formerly used the phrase "Sèvres Syndrome" as shorthand to refer to lingering Turkish paranoia about chimerical foreign plots and intrigues to subvert and divide Türkiye. By endorsing a largely forgotten and repudiated treaty, Pashinyan roused a monster of the Turkish historical imagination.

It is unknown when exactly Baku took the decision to deliver on its promise to go to war and liberate its occupied territories, but the sudden uptake in arms purchases, especially drones, from

---

226 Pukhov, *Buria*, p. 48.
227 "İlham Əliyev Türkiyə Respublikasının Prezidenti Rəcəb Tayyib Ərdoğana telefonla zəng edib," July 31, 2020.
228 Yerevan condemned the statement as destabilizing. See statement at https://www.mfa.am/en/interviews-articles-and-comments/2020/07/13/MFA_Statement_Turkey/10361
229 Sargis Harutyunyan, "Armenia Seeks to Offset 'Turkish Threat'" *Radio Liberty*, August 3, 2020.

Türkiye in August and September 2020 suggest that it was after the July 2020 clashes, and not before.[230] One Russian analysis, citing unnamed "military-diplomatic sources," asserts that the initiative for the war came from Ankara, not Baku.[231] There is no compelling evidence or good reason to believe this. For over two decades, Baku had been steadily preparing for war and had explicitly and consistently warned that it would resort to war if necessary to recover Karabakh and the surrounding occupied territories.

Along with arms, Turkish military officers arrived in Azerbaijan. Their precise numbers are not known. The above-mentioned Russian analysis suggests that the Turks had 600 military personnel in Azerbaijan assisting the Azerbaijani armed forces, including a battalion tactical group of 200 men, 50 instructors in Nakhchivan, 90 military advisors in Baku, a 120-man unit of aviation technicians in Gabala, 20 drone operators at the airbase in Deller, 50 instructors with Azerbaijan's Fourth Army Corps, and 20 men at both the naval base and the Heydar Aliyev Military Academy in Baku.[232] A less-detailed Russian analysis puts the number of Turkish advisors at 200.[233] No Turkish or Azerbaijani officials have confirmed any reports of direct Turkish participation in the war and the Russian estimates must be treated with circumspection.

Given the novelty of drones, and how quickly the Turkish-

---

230 Although it should be noted that Azerbaijan was planning on purchasing Turkish drones already toward the end of June 2020. Burak Ege Bekdil, "Azerbaijan to buy armed drones from Turkey," *Defense News*, June 25, 2020.
231 "Prinuzhdenie k konfliktu" *Kommersant*, October 16, 2020.
232 Ibid.
233 "Kto iz turetskikh generalov rukovodil atakoi na Karabakh?" *Vzgliad*, November 11, 2020. See also "Raskryt sostav turetskoi voennoi gruppirovki v Azerbaidzhane," *Lenta.ru*, October 17, 2020.

made ones were deployed in combat after delivery in Azerbaijan, it is not implausible to suggest that Turks were likely operating at least some of them.[234] Some Russian analysts further assert that Turkish officers assumed direct command of the ground war around the sixth day of the war, when suddenly the tempo of operations increased.[235] Reports that Turkish reconnaissance aircraft flew along the Turkish-Armenian border, gathering and transmitting intelligence on the positions of Armenian weapons and units are more than plausible, as are those that Russia provided Armenia with intelligence gathered from its base in Gyumri and elsewhere.[236] A small number of Turkish F-16 fighter jets remained on Azerbaijani soil following the joint air exercises, and their presence further underscored Türkiye's commitment to Azerbaijan, sending a clear signal to Russia in particular.[237] Speaking nearly a year after the war, Aliyev expressed deep gratitude for Türkiye's diplomatic support, which in his words not only boosted Azerbaijani morale but also sent a useful warning to other powers in the region and world not to interfere.[238]

Whatever the precise extent of Turkish military involvement, according to some, the Chief of the Azerbaijani General Staff and First Deputy Minister of Defense Necmeddin Sadıkov, found it excessive. A Russian report states he reacted to the deployment of Turkish advisors by asking, "If we are giving the Turks the

---

234 Pukhov, *Buria na Kavkaze*, pp. 44, 81-82; Ruslan Pukhov and Mikhail Barabanov, "Vtoraia karabakhskaia: promezhuyochnye itogi," *Nezavisamaia gazeta Voennoe obozrenie*, no. 38, October 23, 2020.
235 Pukhov, *Buria na Kavkaze*, p. 51.
236 Pukhov, *Buria na Kavkaze*, p. 52; "Turkish Air Force Used E-7A Eagle to Hunt and Destroy S-300 Using TB2 Drones," *Global Defence Corp.*, November 7, 2020.
237 Philip Remler, Richard Giragosian, Marina Lorenzini, and Sergei Rastoltsev, "OSCE Minsk Group: Lessons from the Past and Tasks for the Future" *OSCE Insights*, no. 6, 2020, Baden-Baden: Nomos, 2020, p. 6.
238 "İlham Əliyevin Türkiyənin Anadolu Agentliyinə müsahibəsi," September 28, 2021.

army, maybe we should give them our wives, too?"[239] An ethnic-Lezgin originally from Derbent in the Republic of Dagestan in the Russian Federation, Sadıkov does not speak Azerbaijani, still less Turkish, and his ties to Dagestan and Russia had been the source of some popular controversy several years earlier.[240] Demonstrators during the July 2020 protests had blamed Sadıkov for the deaths of Azerbaijani personnel and called for his sacking, and public resentment may have been a factor in his downfall: Sadıkov apparently was effectively relieved in July 2020.[241] Although the Azerbaijani Ministry of Defense denied this,[242] it removed his name and biography from its official website in October 2020 and in January 2021 confirmed his retirement from active service.[243]

The performance of the Azerbaijani army on the battlefield in 2020 represented an immense improvement over Azerbaijan's performance in the 1990s and 2016, surprising many.[244] The Azerbaijani armed forces in 2020 successfully employed an entirely different, NATO-compatible doctrine. Turkish assistance over a quarter century was essential to this transformation, as it was Turkish education and training that had made it possible. Indeed, Azerbaijani tactical planning and operations bore a powerful resemblance to those conducted by the Turks in Syria

---

239 "Kto iz turetskikh generalov rukovodil atatkoi na Karabakh?"
240 "Lezgin Nadzhmeddin Sadykov – chei on chelovek?" *Lezgi-Yar,* January 06, 2013.
241 "Ministerstvo oborony o napadkakh na Nadzhmeddina Saykova: 'Ego brat ne sluzhit v armianskoi armii'" *Haqqin.az,* July 21, 2020. Some rumors claimed that Sadıkov was accused of treason for betraying to the Armenians of Azerbaijani war plans and the location of General Polat Hashimov. " Nachal'nik Genshtaba Azerbaidzhana obvinen v gosizmene," *Kavkazskii uzel*, October 4, 2020. Sadikov might have been the victim more of public rumors than of internal intrigue or his own behavior.
242 "MN: Nəcməddin Sadıkov hazırda xidmət yerindədir və vəzifələrini icra edir" *APA,* July 21, 2020.
243 "General-leytenant Kərəm Vəliyev Azərbaycan Ordusunun Baş Qərargah rəisi təyin edilib," *BBC News Azərbaycanca,* January 28, 2021. For a good English-language overview of Sadıkov's curious fate, see Ulkar Natiqqizi, "The mystery of Azerbaijan's missing army chief," *Eurasianet,* March 3, 2021.
244 Erickson, "44-Day War," pp. 1, 12-13.

starting in late 2019, especially with regard to the employment of drones.[245]

It would be a mistake, however, to attribute Azerbaijani battlefield success solely or even predominantly to the aid of Türkiye. The commitment to rebuilding and reforming the Azerbaijani army came from Baku, and the determination to reclaim Karabakh came from the Azerbaijani public. At the time of the First Karabakh War, Azerbaijani society was famously disoriented and fractured. Not entirely unlike 1918-1920, Azerbaijanis lacked a strong, binding national identity and this ultimately was reflected on the battlefield. The mutiny that led to Elchibey's overthrow in 1993 was just the most obvious illustration of this. The sting of military defeat and the trauma of expulsion that nearly one-tenth of Azerbaijanis subsequently experienced, however, catalyzed the consolidation of Azerbaijani national resolve. Although Heydar Aliyev and his son and successor Ilham cultivated this resolve, it cannot be reduced to a top-down project. As the July 2020 protests revealed, the determination of ordinary Azerbaijanis to reclaim Karabakh was so widespread that further hesitance to pursue it could be interpreted as putting the legitimacy of the government in doubt. This resolve motivated the Azerbaijani armed forces. By 2020, Azerbaijan had achieved what Rasulzade and the other founders of the ADR had desired more than a century earlier: a genuine national army.

One form of military aid that Türkiye denies providing and Azerbaijan disavows receiving is mercenaries. At the outbreak of the war a number of news outlets, in turn citing alleged French, Russian, Syrian, Iranian, and Armenian intelligence sources as

---

245 Can Kasapoğlu, "Turkey Transfers Drone Warfare Capacity to Its Ally Azerbaijan," Eurasia Daily Monitor, October 15, 2020.

well as "independent" researchers, reported in September and early October 2020 that Türkiye had organized the deployment of, depending on the reports, between several hundred and several thousand Arab fighters from Syria and Libya.[246] This is within the realm of the plausible in so far as Türkiye has worked with militias in those two countries. But there are several strong reasons to be skeptical about these allegations. Many of the initial reports described the fighters as jihadists.[247] When skeptics objected that jihadists who cut their teeth battling Shi'i militias in Syria made unlikely candidates for waging war on behalf of predominantly Shi'i and emphatically secular Azerbaijan, subsequent reports emphasized the indigent state of the fighters to suggest money as the motive. That in turn raises the question of just how useful poorly trained and poorly motivated units would be in a high intensity, combined-arms operation against a determined foe fighting from entrenched positions. Moreover, the Azerbaijani army lacked neither motivation nor numbers. As noted above, public opinion in Azerbaijan was overwhelmingly in favor of retaking Karabakh and the occupied territories by force. Indeed, eyewitnesses described lines in front of military recruitment centers from the first day of the war. Finally, the reports of the fighters or mercenaries all relied heavily or exclusively on hearsay, and some of the stronger forms of alleged evidence they proffered, such as videos and photographs, were revealed to be

---

246 Ron Synovitz, "Are Syrian Mercenaries Helping Azerbaijan Fight For Nagorno-Karabakh?" *Radio Free Europe / Radio Liberty*, October 15, 2020; Ed Butler, "The Syrian mercenaries used as 'cannon fodder' in Nagorno-Karabakh," *BBC News*, December 10, 2020; Kareem Fahim, Isabelle Khurshudyan, and Zakaria Zakaria, "Deaths of Syrian mercenaries show how Turkey, Russia could get sucked into Nagorno-Karabakh conflict," *Washington Post* October 14, 2020.

247 See, for example, John Irish and Michel Rose, "France accuses Turkey of sending Syrian jihadists to Nagorno-Karabakh," *Reuters*, October 1, 2020.

false or highly suspect.[248] Although it is impossible to state definitively that the reports of imported fighters or mercenaries were baseless, it does seem safe to conclude, at a minimum, that such forces had no significance beyond the reports about them.

The Geography of the Peace (Ceasefire)

Azerbaijan has drawn enormous and indisputable benefits from partnership with Türkiye. Through its steadfast provision of military education, training, and assistance, Türkiye acquired substantial and enduring influence inside Azerbaijan and thereby further displaced Russia's fading institutional legacy there. Moreover, the robust diplomatic support and military assistance that Türkiye provided not only facilitated Azerbaijan's victory in 2020 but also challenged Russia's geopolitical dominance of the South Caucasus overall.

But it did not end that dominance, and indeed may have buttressed it temporarily. Moscow's singlehanded brokerage of the truce and deployment of peacekeepers to parts of the former NKAO not only reaffirmed Russia's centrality to the conflict and the region, but it also denied Ankara some of the benefits the patron of a victor of war might normally expect. Moscow nixed Ankara's proposal to deploy its own peacekeeping contingent to parallel the Russian one. Although Moscow did concede to the establishment of a Joint Turkish-Russian Monitoring Center in Ağdam consisting of a few dozen Turkish and Russian soldiers,

---

248 Synovitz notes some of this falsified evidence, but there is more. The video of armed men standing next to an Armenian border marker and thus far from the fighting in Karabakh shows one fighter demonstratively making the hand signal of the Panturkist Grey Wolves, an odd allegiance for an Arab.

this was a consolation prize—not entirely worthless but of less value than the top prize of deploying nearly 2,000 peacekeepers.[249]

Nonetheless, Türkiye has continued to expand and strengthen its ties to Azerbaijan, laying the groundwork for the continued expansion of its influence over the long term. In June 2021, Erdoğan delivered to İlham Aliyev what Heydar Aliyev had requested of Türkiye nearly a quarter of a century earlier. Meeting in the historic town of Shusha in recently liberated Karabakh, the Turkish and Azerbaijani presidents signed a "Declaration on Allied Relations between the Republic of Azerbaijan and the Republic of Türkiye." Citing the Treaty of Kars, the 1994 Friendship Agreement, and the 2010 Strategic Partnership Agreement in its preamble, the Shusha Declaration with its title and content now established a formal alliance between Türkiye and Azerbaijan. It obliged each party in the event of a threat or act of aggression to consult with the other and to coordinate military and other responses as appropriate, albeit always, as the treaty emphasizes, in accord with the principles of the UN Charter and international law. The declaration acknowledges Türkiye's support for Azerbaijan over the course of three decades explicitly while also hailing Azerbaijan's Karabakh victory as a triumph not just for Azerbaijan but also for justice and international law in general. It pledges the signatories to continued cooperation between the security services (including in the realm of cyber security) and, indeed, the defense sectors of the two states as well as to the coordination of their foreign policies. The document provides for a comprehensive alliance. It identifies the spheres of culture, energy, economics, and trade as areas alongside those

---

249 "Türkiyə və Rusiya Qarabağda atəşkəsə nəzarət edəcəklər," *TRT Azərbaycan*, November 12, 2020; Suzan Fraser, "Turkish parliament approves peacekeepers for Azerbaijan," *Associated Press*, November 17, 2020.

of defense and foreign affairs where Azerbaijan and Türkiye will work together. It calls for the integration of transportation links between the two countries via the "Zangezur corridor" and the Kars-Nakhchivan railroad and increased efforts toward the unity and prosperity of the "Turkic World." Although the text of the Shusha Declaration denies that it is directed at any third party, its promise of an alliance between a closely integrated Türkiye and Azerbaijan necessarily puts Armenia, Iran, and Russia on notice.[250]

The Shusha Declaration does, however, also include a clause that reads, "the parties pursue an independent foreign policy aimed at protecting and ensuring national interests." Nothing like the United Arab Republic is emerging. Indeed, the emergence of a formal Azerbaijani-Turkish alliance is unsurprising, given both the economic and cultural complementarity of the two states, their common strategic rivals, and their shared history. Nonetheless, the interests of the two states have differed at various points in the past and undoubtedly will diverge again at various points in the future even if there are no specific reasons at the moment to expect Azerbaijani-Turkish relations will deteriorate.

The Economic Consequences of the Peace (or Ceasefire)

If backing Baku did not yield precisely as many diplomatic dividends as Ankara might have wished, it has delivered concrete economic ones. Economic ties between Türkiye and Azerbaijan

---

[250] The Shusha Declaration was signed in Turkish and Azerbaijani language texts. The Azerbaijani version can be found here: https://report.az/xarici-siyaset/susa-beyannamesinin-tam-metni/. Azerbaijan's Ministry of Foreign Affairs provides an English translation here: https://coe.mfa.gov.az/en/news/3509/shusha-declaration-on-allied-relations-between-the-republic-of-azerbaijan-and-the-republic-of-turkey.

prior to the Second Karabakh War were substantial but far from extensive.[251] Direct investment from Türkiye in Azerbaijan had peaked at $8 billion but in 2019 was only $325 million. Azerbaijani investment in Türkiye that year was substantially more, $6 billion.[252] Even before the war was over, observers were speculating that Türkiye's support for Azerbaijan would pay off economically. After the cessation of hostilities, Baku declared its intention to make major investments in the territories back under its sovereign control, which in the course of three decades had suffered not mere neglect but had indeed been stripped of anything of value by the occupying forces. In January 2021, Azerbaijani officials announced that Turkish firms would receive priority in the awarding of construction tenders in the liberated territories.[253] By July 2022, 30 Turkish companies were operating there and had already invested $1 billion, with more to come.[254] Among the projects in which Turkish firms have played leading roles are the construction of three international airports. In October 2021, Aliyev and Erdoğan inaugurated a new airport in Fuzuli and one year later one in Zangilan. A third is under construction in Lachin and is scheduled to be completed in winter 2024-2025. The airports can accommodate the full range of cargo and passenger jets.[255] In addition to profiting from the construction contracts in

---

251 Elkin Nurmammadov, "Azerbaijan-Turkey Relations Through the Prism of Economic Transactions: A View from Azerbaijan," in Murad Ismayilov and Norman A. Graham, eds *Turkish-Azerbaijani Relations: One Nation Two States?* New York: Routledge, 2016, pp. 88-89.
252 Mustafa Sonmez, "Turkey eyes economic gains in backing Azerbaijan against Armenia" *Al-Monitor,* October 7, 2020.
253 "Azerbaijan to prioritize Turkish firms in reconstruction of liberated Nagorno-Karabakh," *Daily Sabah,* January 18, 2021.
254 "Yakup Sefer: 'Türkiyənin 30 şirkəti Qarabağa 1 mlrd dollarlıq investisiya yatıracaq'" *Report Informasiya Agentliyi,* July 6, 2022.
255 "Azerbaijan opens new international airport in Karabakh" *Airport Technology,* October 27, 2021; Orkhan Baghirov, "The Karabakh Air Gate Opens: Future Prospects for Fuzuli Airport" *Eurasia Daily Monitor,* November 10, 2021.

the short term, Türkiye stands to benefit in the long term from the expansion of trade and tourism in the region that the development of the infrastructure in and around Karabakh will help make possible.

But the long-term development of the broader region will hinge on integrating it logistically. According to the text of the 2020 ceasefire agreement, "the Republic of Armenia shall guarantee the security of transport connections between the western regions of the Republic of Azerbaijan and the Nakhchivan Autonomous Republic in order to arrange unobstructed movement of persons, vehicles, and cargo in both directions."[256] Azerbaijani and Turkish officials interpret this to mean that a transport corridor across Armenia's Syunik Province would be built that would link "mainland" Azerbaijan to its Nakhchivan exclave, thereby providing a unbroken transport connection from Türkiye through Azerbaijan to Central Asia. Aliyev has suggested also that this corridor would become part of a broader regional transport network composed of road and rail connections that would run north to south from Russia to Iran, thereby providing Armenia improved connections to Russia, Iran, and Türkiye.[257] Yerevan, however, has thus far successfully resisted implementing this part of the ceasefire agreement.

Moreover, Ankara paradoxically may have undermined its influence over Baku in the future. Turkish diplomatic support and military assistance were essential to Baku's victory. Now that Baku has recovered effectually all of what it wanted, its need for

---

256 "Statement by President of the Republic of Azerbaijan, Prime Minister of the Republic of Armenia and President of the Russian Federation" *Kremlin.ru*, November 10, 2020.

257 "President Ilham Aliyev attended "New Vision for South Caucasus: Post-Conflict Development and Cooperation" international conference held at ADA University," *Azərtac*, April 13, 2021.

Turkish support is lower. This could potentially afford Baku the latitude and freedom to act more independently of Ankara. Yet given the uncertainties surrounding Russia, Iran, and the future balance of power in the region, Baku will likely continue to value Turkish support.

By helping to break the logjam of the conflict over Karabakh through its support of Azerbaijan, Türkiye may—again paradoxically—find its greatest benefit to be improved relations with Armenia. The end of the Armenian occupation of Karabakh opens up the possibility for Türkiye to normalize relations with Armenia, integral to which would be reopening the border between the two countries. Meanwhile, defeat in Karabakh seems to have shaken Yerevan out of the belief that it could continue to ignore Türkiye indefinitely. Since the end of 2021, Ankara and Yerevan have been actively exploring establishing relations.[258] Ankara's pursuit of normalization, however, may prove a source of tension with Baku if Türkiye decides to realize it before Azerbaijan concludes a peace agreement with Armenia.

---

258 Ani Mejlumyan, "Prospects of Armenia-Turkey normalization appear closer than ever," *Eurasianet*, September 13, 2021; Ani Mejlumyan, "Turkey, Armenia to appoint envoys to normalize relations," *Eurasianet*, December 14, 2021.

IRAN'S ROLE IN THE ARMENIA-AZERBAIJAN CONFLICT

Brenda Shaffer

Iran borders both protagonists in the Armenia-Azerbaijan conflict. For Tehran, this is not some faraway conflict like those in the Gaza Strip or Lebanon. Many of the battles in the countries' two major wars took place close to Iran's borders, and during the first one, there was a major refugee flow into Iran of Azerbaijanis escaping Armenia's troops. Thus, the results of the conflict have high-stake national security implications for Tehran, including those that impact upon Iran's domestic security and potentially the stability of the ruling regime. Iran did not welcome Azerbaijan's independence in 1991: It viewed an Azerbaijani state as a potential magnet for ethnonationalism among its own ethnic-Azerbaijani minority, which comprises approximately one-third of its population.[259] Many Azerbaijanis in Iran share sentiments and ties with the Republic of Azerbaijan. Tehran wanted Azerbaijan engaged in war, so the country could not be seen as an object of attraction for its own ethnic-Azerbaijani minority. Teh-

---

[259] Brenda Shaffer, *Iran is More than Persia: Ethnic Politics in Iran*, Berlin: De Gruyter, 2023, p. 31.

ran's fears were not unfounded: the 2020 Armenia-Azerbaijan War further galvanized the challenge to the ruling regime from Iran's ethnic Azerbaijanis.

While the ruling regime in Iran formally declares that its foreign policy is based on Islamic solidarity, Tehran almost always puts pragmatic concerns above religious fraternity.[260] In the case of the wars between Iran's two northern neighbors, the clash between ideology and pragmatic considerations was unmistakable: In the first war, Christian Armenia had invaded majority-Shiite Azerbaijan, captured close to 20 percent of its territory, and turned almost one million Azerbaijanis into refugees or internally-displaced persons. Yet, Tehran supported Yerevan in its wars with Baku, and Iran has intensified its close cooperation with Armenia following the 2020 war.

This chapter examines Iran's role in the Armenia-Azerbaijan conflict, focusing on Tehran's policies and actions during the 2020 Armenia-Azerbaijan War. It makes several major points. One, the Armenia-Azerbaijan conflict affects Tehran's core national security interests, including Iran's domestic security. In addition, Iran's position toward the conflict is in no way affected by the regime's formally professed Islamic ideology. Next, Iran's positions and policy toward the conflict have been consistent throughout the thirty-year history of the conflict. Iran's behavior during and after the 2020 war echoes its behavior in the early 1990s, often employing the same rhetoric. A component of Iran's position in the conflict is to prevent its resolution. In addition, the main factor in Iran's policy toward the conflict is concern for the

---

[260] For more on this topic, see: Brenda Shaffer, "The Islamic Republic of Iran: Is it really?" in Brenda Shaffer, ed., *Limits of Culture: Islam and Foreign Policy*, Cambridge, MA: MIT Press, 2006.

impact of developments on its control over its domestic ethnic-Azerbaijani community.

Iran has been an active player in the Armenia-Azerbaijan conflict, supporting Armenia in both the First (1992-1994) and the Second Armenia-Azerbaijan War in 2020. During both wars, Iran served as the main channel of supplies to Armenia. In the 2020 war, Iran's involvement in the conflict reached a new height, with Iranian forces both overtly and covertly crossing the border into Azerbaijan's territory several times, where they disrupted the battlefield advances of Azerbaijani forces. Next, Iran sought to maintain Armenia's control of Azerbaijani regions that border Iran and sought to prevent the deployment of foreign forces near its border. Finally, Iran's regional position and security has weakened as a result of the 2020 war. Moreover, the war outcomes also strengthened domestic challenges from Iran's large ethnic-Azerbaijani community, which opposed Tehran's support for Armenia.

Iran's Involvement in the Two Wars

Iran was directly involved in both the First Armenia-Azerbaijan War (1992-1994) and the Second Armenia-Azerbaijan War (2020). This involvement included serving as the main conduit of supplies to Armenia during both wars, sharing military know-how and intelligence with Armenia during the 2020 war, and the direct involvement of Iran's Revolutionary Guard Forces (IRGC).

Iran as Conduit of Supplies to Armenia During the Wars and Subsequently

During both wars, Iran served as the main channel of supplies—military and otherwise—to Armenia. Russia, Armenia's main strategic backer, does not share a border with Armenia. During the first war, in 1992 and 1993, supply routes from all of Armenia's neighbors except for Iran were closed or unreliable; the civil war in neighboring Georgia prevented Russia from providing supplies by land to Yerevan. During the 2020 war, because of Georgia's refusal to allow the transit of military supplies, Moscow depended on transit through Iran to supply Armenia. During the 2020 war, Russian ships arrived at Iran's Caspian port of Anzali and brought Russian arms and other supplies by truck into Armenia and into the battle zone. Russian supply flights to Armenia also transited Iran's airspace. During the wars, ethnic-Azerbaijanis in Iran called on Tehran to halt this transit to Armenia, which, adding insult to injury, passed through Azerbaijani-populated regions in Iran and was directly visible to this community.[261]

During the first Armenia-Azerbaijan War, most of Armenia's fuel and much of its food supplies came from Iran, and these critical supplies allowed Armenia to sustain the war effort. For instance, in April 1992, at one of the most crucial points in the escalation of the conflict between Armenia and Azerbaijan, Iran agreed to supply fuel and to improve transportation links with Armenia.[262] Moreover, according to Armenian statements, Russia often delivered fuel during the war to Armenia by way

---

261 During the 2020 war, the main contractor for trucks to take Russian supplies from Anzali Port was an Iranian ethnic-Azerbaijani, who spoke openly with foreign media about the content of these shipments.
262 Interfax, April 15, 1992.

of Iran, thus further contributing to Yerevan's war effort.[263] Iranian fuel supplies were critical for the war effort and included oil for heavy vehicles and coal for heat and cooking. Hrant Melik-Shahnazaryan, an Armenian specialist on Iran's policies in the South Caucasus, wrote in May 2011 that "Iran [had] provided Armenia's food safety during the war."

Armenian officials publicly thanked Iran several times for the supplies and for serving as a supply route during the war. In fall 2021, Armenian Prime Minister Nikol Pashinyan stated that Armenia would never join efforts against Iran, since Iran had served as "Armenia's lifeline" during the first war.[264] During that war, Armenian Prime Minister and Vice President Gagik Arutyunyan remarked in 1992 at a ceremony commemorating the opening of the bridge over the Araz River that the bridge would contribute to stabilizing the economic situation in the republic by providing alternatives to transport routes blocked by the war.[265] This bridge was opened just after Armenian forces had captured the pivotal city of Shusha. Despite the embarrassing timing of the fall of Shusha that took place literally while Iran was hosting the leaders of Armenia and Azerbaijan for peace talks, Tehran offered no condemnation of Yerevan, and its reaction did not go beyond an expression of "concern over the recent developments in Karabakh."[266]

Following the 2020 war, Iran continued to deliver military equipment and supplies to Armenians in the areas of Karabakh under the control of Russian peacekeepers. In addition to fuel

---

263 SNARK (Yerevan), January 29, 1993.
264 Armenpress, October 3, 2021; "PM Pashinyan: Armenia will never be involved in any anti-Iran conspiracy," *Press TV*, October 4, 2021.
265 Interfax, May 7, 1992.
266 IRNA in English, May 13, 1992.

and consumer goods, Iran delivered surveillance equipment and heavy military equipment to the Armenian forces stationed in parts of Karabakh. This was the main trigger of the fall 2021 tensions between Iran and Azerbaijan. Several of the Iranian trucks that entered the ethnic-Armenian-populated areas of Azerbaijan under Russian peacekeeper control did not depart from the region, because they served as platforms for intelligence and military equipment delivered to the region:

> From 11 August through 10 September [2021], 58 trucks with materials for various purposes, in particular with fuel and lubricants, entered Khankendi, 55 of them later left. [...] It should be noted that illegal transportation from Iran to Karabakh was carried out despite repeated warnings from official Baku about the availability of modern video surveillance systems.[267]

Tehran tried to deceive the Azerbaijani authorities by placing Armenian license plates on the Iranian trucks. Azerbaijani President Ilham Aliyev stated that Tehran was supplying military equipment to the Armenians living in the areas of Karabakh under the control of Russian peacekeepers:

> Of course, we began to monitor the situation and by the beginning of each month we collected information on how many trucks have entered and how many have left, what they brought in and took out. We have all the information, including their license plates, and they have been published

---

267 "Illegal cargo transport to Karabakh - reason to talk about Iran's insincerity, says MP," *Trend*, September 13, 2021.

in the media. But what happened after that? They tried to attach Armenian license plates to Iranian trucks. They committed this falsification in an attempt to deceive us. An extremely incompetent step was taken—a tank truck with a Persian sign but Armenian license plate. I should also note that they attached the same license plates to different cars. So, what does such sloppy work testify to? They wanted to continue this business and just disguise themselves. This took place in mid-August [2021]. We hoped this would be stopped. However, from 11 August to 11 September [2021], about 60 trucks from Iran illegally entered Karabakh again. Today, only 25,000 people live there, in the Karabakh region under the responsibility of the Russian peacekeeping forces. Is this market really so important?[268]

An illustration of lack of respect for Azerbaijan's territorial integrity is the fact that the trucks' travel documents stated that their destination was "Stepanakert, Armenia."[269]

Iran's Direct Intervention in the 2020 War

Iran also intervened directly in the battlefield during the 2020 war in an attempt to prevent or at least slow down Baku's advance. When Azerbaijan's forces reached the Armenian-occupied province of Zangilan, which borders Iran, and were engaged in serious battles with Armenian forces, Iranian forces crossed the border into Azerbaijan on 17 October 2020 and placed large concrete blocks

---

268 "Ilham Aliyev's interview with Turkish Anadolu Agency," president.az, September 28, 2021.
269 "DIN Gorus-Qafan yolunda iki iranlı sürücünün saxlanıldığını" *Modern.Az*, September 15, 2021.

on the road in a section of the Jabrayil region, close to Zangilan, cutting the advancing Azerbaijani forces in Zangilan from supplies and reinforcements.[270] Iranian forces stayed in Azerbaijani territory for three days, claiming they were protecting the Khudafarin hydropower plant, which they had built in cooperation with the Armenian occupation forces. Azerbaijani commanders on the ground attempted to convince the Iranian forces to leave, which was initially refused. The Azerbaijani government brought the Iranian military attaché in from Baku to Jabrayil, where the Iranian troops were located, and sought to discuss their withdrawal. Iranian forces only agreed to leave and permit the removal of the concrete blocks when Baku threatened to publicize the Iranian incursion. Tehran likely feared publicity about its intervention, since this knowledge would further incense ethnic-Azerbaijanis in Iran against the regime. The Iranian roadblock succeeded to cut the two parts of the Azerbaijani forces from each other and thus delayed the arrival of reinforcements and supplies to the forces in battle in Zangilan. Allegedly, six Azerbaijani soldiers were killed by Armenian forces due to the Iranian intervention. The delay in the arrival of those Azerbaijani forces to Zangilan allowed the Armenians to regroup and resupply, and thus indirectly led to additional Azerbaijani casualties. Azerbaijani forces in Jabrayil were forced to use a different, longer route to join their troops in Zangilan. During the 2020 war, Iranian forces also crossed several times into Nakhchivan, Azerbaijan's exclave that borders Iran.[271]

---

270 "How Iran invaded Azerbaijan during 44-Day War in 2020," Contreras Report YouTube, October 10, 2021. Accessed at: https://www.youtube.com/watch?v=iuzJbnl12xw
271 Author's interviews, October 2020.

Provision of Training and Intelligence Information

Iran has provided military knowhow and intelligence to Armenia during the three decades of the conflict. Yerevan maintains strong security cooperation with Tehran and has failed to comply with U.S. and UN sanctions and other policies aimed at isolating Iran. In addition, during the 2020 war, Iran provided Armenia with information on Azerbaijani troop movements in the provinces that border Iran, which it could observe; Iran could also pick up communications from Azerbaijani troops.[272]

Moreover, Iran was likely involved in the development of Armenia's tunnel warfare capacity. In 2018, Armenia adopted a new strategic doctrine of "new wars for new territories," under which it would open new fronts with Azerbaijan in order to deter the latter from attempting to retake its occupied territories. The new doctrine also involved adopting a more dynamic military strategy: using offensive actions as part of its defense, and not remaining in static positions, such as trenches, but moving troops and conducting surprise attacks on Azerbaijani forces. As part of the new Armenian doctrine, Yerevan employed tunnel warfare and built tunnels in the occupied territories, including in Zangilan at the border with Iran, and in Tovuz, in the north of Azerbaijan. There are indications that Armenia gained tunnel expertise from Iran's IRGC: tunnel warfare has been used extensively by Iranian proxies Hizballah and Hamas. The tunnels in the Tovuz region contributed greatly to Armenia's ability to launch a surprise attack on Azerbaijan on 12 July 2020, and thus contributed to the

---

[272] Author's interviews, September 2021; "How Iran invaded Azerbaijan during 44-Day War in 2020," Contreras Report YouTube, October 10, 2021. Accessed at: https://www.youtube.com/watch?v=iuzJbnl12xw; "Иран вторгся в Азербайджан: сенсационные подробности 44-дневной войны," *Caliber*, October 9, 2021.

large number of causalities, including the Azerbaijani General Polad Hashimov.

In the post- 2020 war period, Tehran continued to provide intelligence information and provided surveillance equipment to the Armenians living in the areas of Karabakh under the control of Russian peacekeepers.[273]

Iran's Support for Armenia's Occupation and Economic Exploitation of the Occupied Territories

During the period of Armenia's occupation of Azerbaijan's territories, Iran sought to preserve a large *de facto* border under Armenian control. Notwithstanding formal declarations that it supported Azerbaijan's territorial integrity, Tehran actively opposed Azerbaijan regaining control of its territories under Armenian occupation. Accordingly, Iran had no qualms with engaging in economic cooperation and even making investments in the occupied territories, or with the exploitation of resources and homes of the displaced as well as other Azerbaijani property. An indication that Iranian economic activity was extensive is that following the 2020 war, Iranian state media warned in several articles that Iran could face commercial losses from the change of control over the territories.[274]

During the occupation period, Iran engaged in direct trade

---

273 Author's interviews, June 2021.
274 "Economic Consequences of Azerbaijan-Armenia Agreement for Iran—Loss of Iran-Armenia border belt," *Fars*, November 13, 2020; "Developments in the northern borders and Iran's involvement in traditional approaches to foreign policy," *Tasnim*, November 22, 2020; Brenda Shaffer, "The Armenia-Azerbaijan War: Downgrading Iran's regional role," *Central Asia and Caucasus Analyst*, November 25, 2020.

and cooperation with the Armenian occupation authorities. The most ostentatious Iranian commercial project in the occupied territories was inaugurated in 2010. Iran and Armenia established a hydropower plant complex on the Araz river near the Khudafarin Bridge, which is on the border between Iran and the then-occupied territories.[275] In addition, over 40 Iranian companies operated in Azerbaijan's territories during the three decades of Armenian occupation.[276] An Iranian company conducted restorations of the Yukhari Govhar Agha mosque in Shusha. Moreover, both Iran and Armenia attempted to portray this mosque as "Persian" in order to justify its existence in Shusha and undermine Azerbaijani claims to the city.

During the period of occupation, Iran also sponsored and staffed a radio station in Shusha that broadcasted in the Talysh language, as part of a larger attempt to agitate, in cooperation with Armenia, Azerbaijan's Talysh minority group against Baku.[277]

Several times during the period of occupation, videos were circulated of Iranian trucks bringing supplies to the Armenian occupation authorities. Such videos tended to set off public spats between Baku and Tehran regarding Iran's involvement in the occupied territories. On the eve of the war, in April 2020, an open row emerged between Tehran and Baku.[278] The clear view of the Iranian trucks in the occupied territories also triggered protests by ethnic-Azerbaijanis in Iran.

---

275 After the establishment of the hydropower plant, in 2016 Iran and Azerbaijan signed an agreement formally allowing Iran to use the occupied territories, thus Iran formally recognized of Azerbaijan's sovereignty over the territory.

276 "İşğal zamanı Qarabağda fəaliyyət göstərən İran şirkətləri – Siyahı," *Qavqazinfo.az* October 11, 2021.

277 "The first Talysh radio starts broadcasting from Shushi, Karabakh," Public Radio of Armenia, March 29, 2013.

278 "Состоялся телефонный разговор между МИД Азербайджана и Ирана," *Trend*, April 15, 2020.

For several years, Armenian authorities allowed Iranian citizens to enter the occupied territories and pillage Azerbaijani homes, including the stripping of doors, windows, and metal frames from those homes for a small fee.[279]

In fall 2021, Aliyev noted that Iranian trucks regularly entered the occupied territories both prior to and after the 2020 war:

> This is not the first time that Iranian trucks have entered the Karabakh region. It has happened several times during the occupation. These trucks went there on a regular basis. We saw that trucks keep traveling there even after the war.[280]

Moreover, Iran's main land transportation route to Armenia transited the occupied territories, with no opposition from Tehran. Tehran only protested when Azerbaijan retook control of the road.[281] For example, Fada-Hossein Maleki, a member of the Iranian parliament's National Security and Foreign Policy Committee, threatened Azerbaijan after it retook control of its territories on the road between Iran and Armenia:

> Underlining that blocking Iran's trade with Armenia was not the right thing to do. […] Armenia is an independent country and the Islamic Republic has trade with the region, and Baku should reconsider its recent actions so that no

---

279 The author witnessed in winter 2003 dozens of Iranian cars and trucks in Ağdam, engaging in this pillage. The local occupation authorities explained to the author that they allow the Iranians to enter in order to collect scrap metal and other building materials from the homes of the Azerbaijani refugees.
280 "Ilham Aliyev's interview with Turkish Anadolu Agency," president.az, September 28, 2021.
281 "Iran warns of third-parties malign influence over Tehran-Baku ties," *Tehran Times*, September 24, 2021.

excuses be provided for countries seeking to create problems which will impinge on Baku more.²⁸²

The occupied territories were frequently transited by Iranian drug traffickers. Following the return of the territories to Baku's control in 2020, drug traffickers continued to try to use the territories, and for several weeks in late 2020 and early 2021, there were shootouts between traffickers and Azerbaijani soldiers who enforced the border. Several Azerbaijani soldiers were killed in late 2020 and 2021 in attempts to stop the drug trade from Iran.

Iran's Stance on the Armenia-Azerbaijan Conflict

Unlike other foreign actors involved in the Armenia-Azerbaijan conflict, such as Türkiye and the United States, Iran's position toward the conflict has been consistent since the Soviet breakup in 1991. Even the wording of Tehran's messaging on the conflict and articulation of its interests was almost identical in the early 1990s and in 2020.

Tehran acknowledges that its stance toward the conflict is forged by its national security interests and especially its domestic security concern due to its ethnic-Azerbaijani minority. Mahmoud Va'ezi, who served as Deputy Foreign Minister of Iran and was responsible for the former Soviet region in the early 1990s during the first war, pointed to internal considerations as one of Iran's major factors in its policy toward the Karabakh conflict: ²⁸³

---
282 Ibid.
283 Mahmud Va'ezi in Interfax (in English), March 25, 1992 (FBIS-SOV-92-059). See, also *Tehran Times*, March 10, 1992, p. 2 for reference to the internal Azerbaijan and Armenian factor as affecting its suitability to mediate in the conflict.

Iran was in the neighborhood of the environment of the conflict. Karabakh is situated only 40 km distance from its borders. At that time, this possibility raised that the boundaries of conflict extended [...] beyond [...] Karabakh. Since the[n], Iran's consideration was based on security perceptions. [...] Iran could not be indifferent to the developments occurring along its borders, security changes of the borders, and their impact on Iran's internal developments.[284]

Tehran's concerns regarding the potential impact of the independence of the Republic of Azerbaijan on its domestic ethnic-Azerbaijani minority was one of the most significant factors influencing its policies toward the Armenia-Azerbaijan conflict.[285] Tehran held no special sentiments for Azerbaijanis as co-religionists. Tehran's strategic disposition toward Azerbaijan is primarily rooted in its concern that a strong and prosperous Republic of Azerbaijan could rouse ethno-nationalism among Iran's own sizeable ethnic-Azerbaijani community. Tehran hoped that the devastation and poverty created by the war and occupation in Azerbaijan in the early years of the conflict would serve the regime's goal of discouraging the lure of the neighboring country for its ethnic-Azerbaijani minority. Thus, Tehran adopted a policy in support of Yerevan in the war with Azerbaijan and has continued to engage in close cooperation with Armenia until the present day.

---

[284] Mahmoud Va'ezi, "Mediation in the Karabakh Dispute," *Center for Strategic Research*, January 2008. see also: "Iranian Official on Solution to Conflict," *Interfax*, March 25, 1992.

[285] For more on Iran's ethnic Azerbaijani minority, see Brenda Shaffer, *Iran is more than Persia: Ethnic Politics in Iran*, Berlin: De Gruyter, 2023; Brenda Shaffer, *Borders and Brethren: Iran and the Challenge of Azerbaijani Identity*, MIT Press, 2002; Brenda Shaffer, "The Islamic Republic of Iran: is it really?", in Brenda Shaffer, ed., *Limits of Culture*, MIT Press, 2006.

An oft-repeated misconception is that Iran's adversarial approach to Azerbaijan was formed in response to Baku's close ties with Israel. This is simply incorrect. Tehran was hostile to Azerbaijan from day one of its independence and consequently supported Armenia in its first war with Azerbaijan in 1992-1994, whereas Azerbaijan and Israel began to forge close cooperation only beginning in 1995-1996—that is, more than a year after the First Armenia-Azerbaijan War had come to an end. It is important to understand the timeline here, in order to correctly understand the motivations of Tehran's policies toward Azerbaijan, which are primarily rooted in domestic security concerns and are not about Israel.

Throughout the conflict, Tehran has had several goals. Iran sought to maintain Armenia's control of regions that border Iran. Iran also sought to prevent the deployment of foreign forces near its border. In addition, Tehran aimed to keep Azerbaijan dependent on it for access to the Azerbaijani exclave of Nakhchivan. Thus, Iran has opposed opening roads through Armenian territory, such as the Zangezur Corridor, that would enable Baku's land connection to its exclave without having to traverse Iranian territory. Tehran also sought the continuation of the conflict to leave Baku more vulnerable and thus is actively opposed conclusion of a peace treaty between Baku and Yerevan.

Following both major Armenia-Azerbaijan wars, Iranian officials stated that they did not want any change in the geopolitical status quo near their borders. Iranian Foreign Minister Amir Abdollahian also stated in 2021 that Iran will not tolerate "geopolitical change" in the region near its borders. In addition, Brigadier General Mohammad Pakpour, the commander of the

IRGC's Ground Forces, stated while visiting Iran's northwestern borders in November 2020: "We will not accept change in the geopolitics of borders. This issue is the red line of the Islamic Republic of Iran."[286] This statement echoes Va'ezi's earlier statement on the conflict:

> Iran expressed its opposition to the change of political geography of the region. If this plan could have been somehow implemented it would have had wide political, economic, and security effects on the region. Linking Nakhchivan to Azerbaijan would have reduced the importance of Iran's unique and distinctive position in the Caucasus and interrupted Iran's linkage with Armenia.[287]

Days after the conclusion of the 2020 war, Iranian officials reiterated their longstanding goal of retaining a direct border and uninterrupted transport routes with Armenia.[288] Seyed Abbas Araghchi, then Iran's deputy foreign minister for political affairs, stated in reference to claims circulating that the postwar settlement would lead to a change in its direct transportation links to Armenia that "there will be no change in Iran's transit routes to Armenia or the Republic of Azerbaijan." And, when Azerbaijan retook control of its territory, including a segment of the main land transport road between Armenia and Iran, Tehran protested and did not respect Azerbaijan's sovereignty over part of the road. Ironically, Armenia recognized that the road passed

---

286 "Vague Peace in Nagorno-Karabakh," *Tehran Times*, November 14, 2020.
287 Mahmoud Va'ezi, "Mediation in the Karabakh Dispute," *Center for Strategic Research*, January 2008.
288 "Vague Peace in Nagorno-Karabakh."

through Azerbaijani territory and agreed to withdraw its forces from the road.

Throughout the conflict period, Iranian officials regularly expressed their opposition to the prospect of Yerevan agreeing to a peace settlement that led to Armenia relinquishing control of the occupied regions that border Iran or trading corridors with Azerbaijan, which would entail exchanging territory near Iran. For instance, visiting Yerevan in 1992, Iranian Deputy Foreign Minister Morteza Sarmadi was assured by Armenian leaders that Yerevan would not agree to any border changes.[289]

Iran also conducts policies aimed at preventing the resolution of the Armenia-Azerbaijan conflict, and encourages Yerevan not to sign a peace agreement with Baku. To beef up the confidence of both Armenia and the Karabakh Armenians to resist peace and to increase the likelihood of the re-flaring of conflict, during the period that began with the ceasefire on 10 November 2020 and ended with Azerbaijan's 19-20 September 2023 "antiterrorist measure," Iran sent arms to Armenia and IRGC officers into Armenian-populated parts of Karabakh that were under the control of Russian peacekeepers. Iran also continued to dispatch IRGC specialists to train the Karabakh Armenian forces in various tactics of subversion and sabotage. Moreover, Iran opened a consulate in Armenia in the town of Kafan in late 2022, close to the border with Azerbaijan and an area of clashes between Armenia and Azerbaijan. Tehran likely established this post in order to increase its intelligence gathering inter alia in support of Armenia.

Iran did not want Azerbaijan to regain control of its ter-

---

[289] Paul Goble, "Caucasus Report June 8, 2000," Radio Free Europe/Radio Liberty, June 8, 2000.

ritories that had been under Armenian occupation: during the 2020 war, Brigadier General Kiumars Heidari, Commander of Iran's Ground Forces, made it clear that Iran did not welcome the return of control of the occupied territories to Azerbaijan: "Preserving the geopolitics of the region is our red line, and no power is allowed to change the geography of the region, and we will not tolerate this."[290]

Iranian officials and media regularly echoed Armenia's rhetoric on the conflict. Armenia, in turn, copied Russia's playbook in Abkhazia, South Ossetia, and the Donbas, and claimed that local Armenian authorities control the territories its forces had occupied, in order to deflect responsibility for the occupation.[291] Instead of acknowledging its occupation, Yerevan tried to convince the international community that a second Armenian state—the "Nagorno-Karabakh Republic"—controlled the territories. Tehran adopted Yerevan's rhetoric and would refer to the region as the "Nagorno-Karabakh Republic" or at times by the term used by some Armenians, "Artsakh." Tehran never referred to Armenia's control of Azerbaijan's territories as an "occupation." However, in contrast to the official Iranian rhetorical line, Iranian religious figures of ethnic-Azerbaijani origin and ethnic-Azerbaijani members of the Iranian parliament often articulated more sympathetic positions toward Azerbaijan in the conflict and called for the restoration of Azerbaijan's territorial integrity.

Following the 2020 war, Iran continued to disregard Azerbaijan's legal sovereignty over Karabakh. In December 2022, for instance, close to a dozen Iranian citizens entered the Karabakh

---

290 "No danger threatens Iranian border areas," Mehr News Agency, November 6, 2020.
291 Svante Cornell and Brenda Shaffer, "The United States Needs to Declare War on Proxies," *Foreign Policy*, 27 February 2020.

area through Armenia and the Lachin corridor. Interestingly, most of these Iranians were men of military age and, according to their identity cards, all came from the same town in southwestern Iran, where an IRGC base is located. It did not take long for Azerbaijani security services to understand that the IRGC had dispatched specialists to help train Armenian forces located in the areas of Karabakh under Russian peacekeeping control in various tactics of subversion and sabotage.

Support of Ethnic-Azerbaijanis in Iran in the Armenia-Azerbaijan Conflict

Throughout the conflict period, ethnic-Azerbaijanis in Iran have frequently mobilized to support Baku. The 2020 war was a watershed moment in this community's relationship with the central government in Iran and the results of the war led to heightened ethno-national pride that has had political implications. In addition, Iran's support for Armenia in the 2020 war incensed large swaths of the ethnic Azerbaijani community in Iran, increasing their opposition to the ruling regime in Iran.

During the initial war period (1992-1994), ethnic-Azerbaijani activists in Iran publicly criticized Tehran's policy toward the conflict. The activists distributed petitions, held demonstrations, and ethnic-Azerbaijani members of the Iranian parliament condemned Armenia's occupation of Azerbaijan's lands and Tehran's support for Armenia. In May 1992, 200 students demonstrating at Tabriz University chanted "Death to Armenia" and, alluding to Tehran, described the "silence of the Muslims," in the face of Armenian "criminal activities" as "treason to the

Quran."²⁹² According to the Iranian newspaper *Salam*, the ethnic-Azerbaijani demonstrators in Tabriz urged Tehran to support the Republic of Azerbaijan in this struggle during a march that was marked by "nationalist fervor and slogans." *Salam* reported that the demonstration was held "despite the opposition of the authorities."²⁹³ The next year, Tehran University students held a demonstration in front of the Armenian embassy to show their support for Azerbaijan in the conflict.²⁹⁴ During that demonstration, protestors hurled rocks at the embassy, and subsequently the Iranian ambassador in Yerevan was summoned by the Armenian foreign minister to present an explanation of the incident.²⁹⁵

Iranian Majles deputies from the ethnic-Azerbaijani provinces led campaigns aimed at impelling Tehran to end its support for Armenia in the conflict and they have issued protests against Yerevan. Ethnic-Azerbaijani Majles delegates also participated in demonstrations against Armenia.²⁹⁶ Ethnic-Azerbaijani Majles members distributed petitions and succeeded in gathering the signatures of a majority of the Majles members in a call for a change in Tehran's stance on the conflict. In April 1993, Kamel Abedinzadeh, an ethnic-Azerbaijani deputy from Kho'i, even spoke in the Azerbaijani language in the Majles when he condemned Armenian actions against Azerbaijan. He also issued press releases for publication in *Hamshahri* and other journals on this issue.²⁹⁷ In addition, in an Iranian parliamentary session following Pashinyan's February 2019 visit to Iran, a parliament member from

---

292 *Salam*, quoted by Reuters, May 25, 1992.
293 *Salam*, as quoted by Agence France Presse, May 25, 1992.
294 IRNA, April 13, 1993.
295 Armenia's Radio First Program, April 14, 1993 (FBIS-SOV- 93-071).
296 IRNA in English, April 13, 1993.
297 *Resalat*, April 14, 1993, p. 5.

Urmia, Ruhulla Hezretpur, denounced the visit and Armenia's occupation of Azerbaijani lands. He also condemned the fact that the visit had taken place during the seventeenth anniversary of the 1992 Khojaly massacre of Azerbaijanis by Armenians. He pointed out that according to Supreme Leader Ali Khamenei, "Karabakh is an Islamic land. Now I ask, what is the difference between Palestine and Karabakh?"[298] Hezretpur proceeded to read a nationalist poem in the Azerbaijani language. As stated, ethnic-Azerbaijani members of Iran's parliament often expressed views on the conflict that differed from Iran's official position.

Pashinyan's visit to Iran in February 2019 was a trigger for anti-regime activity by Iranian ethnic-Azerbaijanis. During his visit, in meetings with Pashinyan, Iranian Armenians openly displayed banners stating that "Karabakh is Armenia." The Armenian prime minister posted pictures on his social media accounts with these banners, which appeared widely in the Iranian media, without protest from Pashinyan's Iranian hosts. Ethnic-Azerbaijanis in Iran responded with protests in front of the Armenian embassy in Tehran and stuck posters on the embassy walls stating, "Karabakh is part of Azerbaijan."[299] A few days after Pashinyan's visit to Iran, fans of the main soccer team supported by ethnic-Azerbaijanis in Iran, Traktor FC, burned an Armenian flag during a game. They also waved the flag of the Republic of Azerbaijan and chanted "Karabakh is and will be ours." Iranian security forces arrested 29 ethnic-Azerbaijani citizens for participation in this activity during that soccer match.

---

298 "Urmia representative protests Iran hosting Armenian occupier during anniversary of massacre of Azerbaijanis," *YouTube*, May 17, 2019. (https://www.youtube.com/watch?time_continue=25&v=POi43CQQssY)

299 "Ethnic Azeris protest against Armenian premier's visit to Iran," BBC Monitoring, March 2, 2019.

Ethnic-Azerbaijanis in Iran reacted to an April 2020 release of information indicating that Iran was aiding Armenians in the occupied territories of Azerbaijan. In response, some ethnic-Azerbaijanis suggested blowing up the gas pipeline to Armenia or sabotaging the bridges between Armenia and Iran, all of which run through areas of Iran predominantly inhabited by ethnic-Azerbaijanis.

In response to Armenia's July 2020 attacks in the region of Tovuz in Azerbaijan close to the East-West energy and transit corridor from Azerbaijan to Europe, ethnic-Azerbaijanis in Iran called for protests against Armenia in front of the Armenian embassy in Tehran and in many Iranian cities largely populated by ethnic-Azerbaijanis.[300] Iranian security forces arrested dozens of ethnic-Azerbaijani activists on the eve of the planned demonstrations to preempt them. Consequently, only small numbers of protestors managed to demonstrate against the Armenian attacks of July 2020. In early 2021, the regime put several ethnic-Azerbaijani activists on trial for attempting to organize the July 2020 demonstrations and sentenced them to prison terms.

As noted above, the 2020 war was a watershed moment for ethnic-Azerbaijanis in Iran, setting off a wave of ethnic solidarity with the Republic of Azerbaijan among members of this community. Many personally witnessed Tehran's support for Armenia on the battlefield, observing in real time Iranian trucks transiting Russian arms and supplies to Armenia. Thousands went to the border area with Azerbaijan, observed the battles, and cheered on the Republic of Azerbaijan's soldiers as they regained control of their lands bordering Iran. Azerbaijani soldiers communicated

---

300   Brenda Shaffer, "Armenia-Azerbaijan Conflict poses threat to European energy security," *FDD Policy Brief,* July 17, 2020.

several times with ethnic-Azerbaijanis on the other side of the border.[301] Ethnic-Azerbaijanis in Iran openly expressed encouragement to the Azerbaijani soldiers despite the regime's efforts to prevent them from going to the border area. The Republic of Azerbaijan's subsequent success on the battlefield inspired ethnic pride among many Iranian Azerbaijanis. During the war, several rounds of demonstrations took place in Iranian cities with large ethnic-Azerbaijani populations.[302]

During the 2020 war, ethnic-Azerbaijani activists considered disrupting the supply convoys of Russian weapons to Armenia, which passed mostly through ethnic-Azerbaijani populated provinces. However, they decided to refrain from this activity and continue to carry out non-violent opposition.

These expressions of solidarity worried the regime in Iran. In an attempt to limit this jubilance, Tehran arrested hundreds of protestors and activists who had criticized Iran's support for Armenia.[303] For example, Azerbaijanis were arrested in the town of Tikantapa on 13 November 2020 for celebrating the liberation of the central city of Shusha from Armenia's occupation.[304] Ethnic-Azerbaijani groups in Iran also issued petitions condemning Iran's arms transfers to Armenia. For instance, the ethnic-Azerbaijani university students group based at the University of Tabriz, *Azərbaycan Tanıtım Ocağı*, issued a statement during the war declaring its support for Azerbaijan liberating its territories

---

[301] @Behzad_Jeddi, *Twitter* October 18, 2020; (https://twitter.com/Behzad_Jeddib/status/1317892041456668673).

[302] "Pro-Azerbaijan protestors in Tabriz demand closure of Iran-Armenia border," *Daily Sabah*, October 1, 2020; "Iran Arrests 11 Pro-Azerbaijan Protestors," *Anadolu Agency*, September 30, 2020.

[303] "Hundreds of Protesters Arrested for Opposing Iran's Support of Armenia," *Iran Wire*, October 4, 2020.

[304] Author's interviews, October 2021.

and condemning Tehran's military transfers to Armenia.[305] Many ethnic-Azerbaijanis in Iran received long prison sentences and lashes for their part in the demonstrations against Tehran. [306]

In November 2021, Baku marked the one-year anniversary of the end of the 2020 Second Armenia-Azerbaijan War and the liberation of its territories. Many ethnic-Azerbaijanis in Iran openly celebrated the victory as well. For instance, shopkeepers in bazaars in Azerbaijani-populated areas of Iran distributed sweets and posted pictures of themselves on social media with signs celebrating the victory.

During the military exercises that Iran held at its border with Azerbaijan, which were aimed to intimidate Baku in late 2022 and early 2023, a social media campaign took place and consisted of posts of pictures of ethnic-Azerbaijani soldiers in Iranian army uniforms displaying Azerbaijani nationalist symbols. In its posts, the campaign stated that Iran should not count on the loyalty of its military if it attacks Azerbaijan.

Postwar Security Architecture: Iran is the Major Loser

The results of the 2020 Armenia-Azerbaijan war created significant new challenges for Iran. While Russia and Türkiye gained increased power in the region, the war reduced Iran's influence. With the return of Azerbaijani control of the border regions that

---

305 @Behzad_Jeddi, *Twitter* October 6, 2020 (https://twitter.com/Behzad_Jeddi_B/status/1313541154328244225?s=20)

306 "Urmiyədə Qarabağa dəstək mitinqləri ilə bağlı həbs edilənlər məhkəməyə çağırılıb," VOA Azerbaijani Service, November 24, 2020; "Ərdəbildə Qarabağa dəstək aksiyası ilə əlaqədar 12 vətəndaşa ümumilikdə 15 il həbs və 888 şallaq cəzası kəsilib," VOA Azerbaijani Service, October 11, 2021.

had been under Armenian occupation, Iran lost part of its previously long border with Armenian-controlled territory. Moreover, more Russian forces were deployed close to Iran's border with Armenia, and Ankara and Moscow largely ignored Tehran in setting the postwar security arrangements. Finally, the outcome of the war also strengthened domestic challenges from Iran's ethnic-Azerbaijani community, which mostly opposed Tehran's support for Armenia in the war.

Azerbaijan aims to leverage the war outcomes to end its dependence on Iran for transit and transportation to its exclave of Nakhchivan, depriving Iran of an important policy lever over Azerbaijan. Azerbaijan aims to establish the Zangezur Corridor through Armenian territory. This route would also create new trade and transport options for Armenia, and lower Yerevan's dependence on both Iran and Russia. In parallel, Azerbaijan and Türkiye established in 2023 a new gas pipeline linking Nakhchivan to the Turkish natural gas system, eliminating Azerbaijan's need to transit gas to the exclave via Iran.

Russia and Türkiye's snubbing of Iran reflects an issue of discord in those relationships that may not be apparent at the superficial level. While Russia and Iran are often viewed by the West as allies, Moscow clearly did not create any role for Iran in the postwar security arrangements in the Caucasus. Notwithstanding changes in this bilateral relationship brought on as a consequence of Russian-Iranian cooperation in the context of the Ukraine theater, Russia still resists giving Iran a more prominent role in the Caucasus.

Iran is aware of its geopolitical disadvantages as a result of the 2020 war and Tehran attempts to undo these effects. The geopolitical results of the recent Armenia-Azerbaijan war set off a discussion in Iran on its regional foreign policy in light of a perceived geopolitical setback. The newspaper *Tasmin*, which is close to Iran's Ministry of Intelligence, ran a series of articles analyzing the results of the war for Iran, including the threat from additional Russian troops that will be deployed close to Iran's border with Armenia, and Tehran's perceived "loss of Armenia" due to increased Russian and Turkish power. In one of the articles in the series, the author suggests that Iran adopt a less threatening foreign policy toward its neighbors.[307]

Iran's behavior during the 2020 war brought to the surface and to the public eye in Azerbaijan the fundamental hostile relations between Iran and the Republic of Azerbaijan. Up until the 2020 war, despite their differences, over three decades Tehran and Baku had tried to maintain cordial bilateral rhetoric, develop economic and transportation cooperation, and prevent all-out crises from emerging.[308] However, Iran's military support for Armenia during and after the war triggered a decline in Iran-Azerbaijan relations. In April 2023, Aliyev described the relations between Azerbaijan and Iran as being "at the lowest level ever."[309] Aliyev is one of the few international leaders who openly described Iran's activities as state terror: "in Iran terror is organized on a govern-

---

307 Among the articles, "Developments in the northern borders and Iran's involvement in traditional approaches to foreign policy," *Tasmin*, November 22, 2020.

308 However, there were several peaks in tensions. In 2001, Iran threatened a BP survey boat in a maritime border area of the Caspian Sea. In 2012, Baku thwarted an Iranian plot to kill the U.S. Ambassador to Azerbaijan and attack the Jewish school and other Jewish communal institutions in Baku.

309 "Ilham Aliyev attended international conference on 'Shaping the Geopolitics of the Greater Eurasia: from Past to Present to Future' in Shusha," website of the President of the Republic of Azerbaijan, May 3, 2023; Brenda Shaffer, "President Aliyev: "Relations between Azerbaijan and Iran are at the Lowest Level Ever," *Central Asia-Caucasus Analyst*, May 8, 2023.

mental level."³¹⁰ He further pointed out that Iran held several military drills at the border with Azerbaijan:

> It was difficult to understand it because, during the times of occupation, they never had any military drills in that area […]. So, as always, we responded, and we had two military drills along their border. One, by our special forces […] and second, with our ally, Türkiye, with Turkish F16s and Turkish special forces, it was not a demonstration. But it was a message that we can defend ourselves.³¹¹

Aliyev also described the 27 January 2023 attack on Azerbaijan's embassy in Tehran as an act of state terror:

> Then this terror act on our embassy happened, and that ruined almost everything because there was video footage […]. It was a deliberate, organized act of terror to kill our diplomats and members of their families […]. For 40 minutes, there were no police, no security officers, nothing.³¹²

Following the attack, Aliyev ordered the closing of the Azerbaijani Embassy in Tehran, and there have been reciprocal expulsions of Iranian and Azerbaijani diplomats (from the Azerbaijani consulate in Tabriz, which stayed open). In addition, Aliyev described a subsequent terror attack in Baku in late March

---

310 "Ilham Aliyev attended international conference on 'Shaping the Geopolitics of the Greater Eurasia,'" *Op. cit.*
311 Ibid.
312 Ibid.

2023, which nearly killed a parliamentarian outspokenly critical or Iran, as Tehran "crossing a redline."

Adding to the conflict between Iran and Azerbaijan is the fact that Tehran sponsors forces—the Huseynyun brigades—that operate inside Azerbaijan and broadcast regular television and other media broadcasts from Qom, the aim of which is to overthrow the government of Azerbaijan and end its secular policies. Huseynyun is modeled after Hizballah and other Iran proxy forces it uses in the Middle East.

Azerbaijan has maintained a closed border with Iran (and Russia), which it had initially closed in spring 2020 due to COVID-19 travel restrictions. Baku has subsequently ended visa granting at Azerbaijani airports for Iranian citizens,[313] allowing the only visa option from the Azerbaijani consulate in Tabriz. This is a clear message that Baku is only providing visa services essentially to the ethnic-Azerbaijani population in Iran. Baku has also issued formal travel warnings to its citizens against travel to Iran, after the detention and incarceration of an Azerbaijani citizen in Iran in March 2023.[314]

Iran's status among the wider public in Azerbaijan took a significant downturn due to Iran's support for Armenia in the 2020 war. Up until that war, many citizens in the Republic of Azerbaijan viewed Iran as a favorable place to travel for medical treatment, shopping, family visits, tourism, and small trade. However, after the war, public hostility toward Iran became widespread, even among Shia religious devotees in Azerbaijan.

The war also brought to the surface tensions between Iran

---

313 "Azerbaijan to stop issuing visas to Iranian citizens," news.az, June 16, 2023.
314 "Azerbaijan advises citizens to avoid traveling to Iran," news.az, June 3, 2023.

and Türkiye. In the past, Türkiye and Iran have tended to avoid public airing of disputes over domestic issues. Following the 2020 war, Ankara and Tehran parted from this practice. Türkiye and Iran stood on opposite sides during the war—Ankara supporting Azerbaijan and Tehran supporting Armenia. In addition, Tehran has been increasing its support for the Kurdish PKK, which conducts terror attacks in Türkiye. In remarks made during the victory celebration in Baku in December to mark the 2020 Armenia-Azerbaijan War, Turkish President Recep Tayyip Erdoğan read the lyrics to a traditional Turkic folk poem titled "Oh, Lachin" (also known as the "Araz Song"), which is famous in both Azerbaijan and Türkiye, and speaks of the Araz River, which runs along the Iran-Azerbaijan border, as separating the two parts of the Azerbaijani nation.[315] Tehran viewed Erdoğan's recitation as an attempt to incite Iran's ethnic-Azerbaijani population against Iranian rule. Senior Iranian officials, including then Foreign Minister Mohammad Javid Zarif, severely condemned Erdoğan.

From 2020, the Turkish press increased its coverage of Tehran's human rights abuses against its Azerbaijani minority. Ethnic Azerbaijanis in Iran received Erdoğan's poem-reading gesture enthusiastically.[316] In addition, in October 2021, a period of high tension between Iran and Azerbaijan, Erdoğan referred again to the ethnic-Azerbaijani issue in Iran. Erdoğan remarked that Tehran will not continue its threats to Azerbaijan, "out of concern about its own Azeri speaking population;" Iran's National Security Chief Ali Shamkhani responded that Iran is a "paradise

---

315 "Aras Türküsü'nün Bahtiyar Vahapzade'ye Ait Olduğu İddiası," *Malumat Gurus,* December 11, 2020.
316 Author's observation based on the surge in Azerbaijani-language social media activity in Iran discussing the event.

for its tribes"³¹⁷ and that Türkiye should worry about its own treatment of its minorities. Since 2020, Türkiye has displayed almost unprecedented opposition to Iran's policies in the South Caucasus: Turkish forces participated in Azerbaijani exercises at the border with Iran, conducted in response to Iran's drills there. Türkiye's then Defense Minister Hulusi Akar stood next to Azerbaijan's Defense Minister at one of the exercises at the border with Iran, signaling Ankara's solidarity with Azerbaijan.³¹⁸

The 2020 war results also led to open public tensions between Baku and Tehran. Previously, Azerbaijan, while unhappy about Iranian policies, had sought to keep the public rhetoric between the two countries cordial. At least until the fall of 2022, Baku chose not to make public overtures toward the ethnic-Azerbaijani community in Iran and to treat its lack of cultural and language rights as a domestic Iranian issue.³¹⁹ For instance, in meetings of the world Azerbaijani diaspora held annually in Baku, for many years Baku did not invite representatives from Iran, despite the fact that the Azerbaijanis in Iran are the largest group in the diaspora and even boast numbers larger than the population of the Republic of Azerbaijan itself. However, Tehran's behavior during the 2020 war, culminating in behavior in the latter half of 2022, seems to have changed Baku's policy toward the ethnic-Azerbaijanis in Iran. In parallel, particularly after the wave of protests in Iran in fall 2022, Baku seems to have judged that the regime in Tehran has been weakened domestically, while the anti-regime sentiments

---

317 Iranians often do not refer to the ethnic minorities as ethnic groups or nations, but simply as tribal Iranians.
318 "Turkish, Azeri Armies Hold Drills Near Iran Border Amid Tension," *Bloomberg*, December 6, 2022.
319 In contrast, during the early independence period 1992-1993 under President Abulfez Elchibey, which designated the rights of "south Azerbaijanis" to state policy.

among Iran's ethnic-Azerbaijanis have, in parallel, increased. As a result, Baku no longer refrains from making overtures toward this group. Following the war, the government of Azerbaijan also began to openly call for the protection of the cultural rights of ethnic-Azerbaijanis in Iran, and increased media coverage on the cultural activity of this community and the violation of its rights in Iran. As part of this policy shift, in November 2022, Aliyev openly called for the protection of the cultural rights of the ethnic-Azerbaijani community in Iran[320] and referred to them as Azerbaijan's 40 million compatriots.[321]

Moreover, Aliyev's first trip to the liberated territories in the regions bordering Iran following the war included a visit to the Khudafarin Bridge. The bridge on the Araz River is a symbol for Azerbaijanis of their divided nation between Iran and the Republic of Azerbaijan, akin to the Berlin Wall post-World War II. Aliyev personally hoisted an Azerbaijani flag on the bridge, which generated enthusiasm among ethnic-Azerbaijanis in Iran. Right after having regained this part of its territory, Azerbaijani soldiers had placed a flag on Azerbaijan's side of the bridge, but the Iranians removed this flag. Aliyev thus made a point of himself rehosting an Azerbaijani flag at the bridge. During the president's visit, an Iranian sniper published pictures of Aliyev and his wife taken through his gun's scope, suggesting the ability of Iran to assassinate him.[322]

In addition, in November 2021, Azerbaijan released new

---

[320] "Baku vows to protect civil rights of ethnic Azerbaijanis in Iran," *Azernews*, November 30, 2022.

[321] "Speech by Ilham Aliyev at the 9th Summit of Organization of Turkic States," Azerbaijan President website, November 11, 2022.

[322] "Iranian sniper posts provocative photo taking aim at Azerbaijani President Aliyev," *Daily Sabah*, November 19, 2020.

currency notes to commemorate the victory in the 2020 war, which featured the Khudafarin Bridge on the 500 manat note together with a poets' tomb in Tabriz—a clear message to Tehran and Iran's ethnic-Azerbaijani community. In addition, Azerbaijan placed a large slogan on a mountain facing Iran in the liberated territories, stating, in the Azerbaijani language, that the "Motherland comes first"—a clear attempt to appeal to ethno-linguistic sentiments among ethnic-Azerbaijanis in Iran.

The 2020 war led to increased Israeli influence in the South Caucasus and among the ethnic-Azerbaijani population in Iran. During the war, ethnic-Azerbaijanis in Iran observed that Israel gave the Republic of Azerbaijan extensive support as part of their strategic partnership. In addition, ethnic-Azerbaijanis in Iran noted that Israeli doctors granted extensive medical aid to Azerbaijan's injured soldiers. This increased positive feelings toward Israel among the group, creating another reason for anti-regime sentiment.[323]

Lessons for Research

Over the past three decades, there have been a plethora of articles published on Iran's policy toward the Armenia-Azerbaijan conflict. Many of these have two major methodological flaws: relying on Iran's official statements as an indication of its actual policies toward the conflict; and the assumption that a common religious tradition generally is a major factor in forging strategic

---

[323] @AhmadObali, *Twitter*, March 5, 2021 (https://twitter.com/AhmadObali/status/1367848470556667911?s=20); Itamar Eichner, "Most Iranian people are pro-Israel, expatriate says," *Ynet*, March 23, 2021.

alliances, thus the erroneous conclusion that Iran-Azerbaijan relations are an outlier.

It is common for all states to have a gap between their official statements and actual policy. This is a point that should be obvious to any researcher on foreign policy, but evidently it is not. In the case of Iran's policy toward the Armenia-Azerbaijan conflict, many researchers and Islamic Republic regime sympathizers in the West have pointed to Tehran's official statements on the conflict and taken them at face value. Thus, over the years, there have been many articles asserting that Iran is neutral in the conflict, and that Tehran strives to serve as a good-faith peace negotiator in the conflict. However, as shown in this chapter, it is clear that Iran was not and is not neutral but was and remains an active player supporting Armenia. Yerevan could not have sustained the war effort and captured extensive Azerbaijani territory without supplies from and via Iran during the first war. In the Second Armenia-Azerbaijan War, Tehran escalated its involvement and placed its troops on the battlefield in at least one documented instance (and perhaps others), as well as actively supplying Armenia with intelligence on Azerbaijani troop movements. Publications on Iran's policy toward the conflict have also accepted Tehran's rhetoric that Azerbaijan's relations with Israel are a major factor in its enmity toward Baku. As shown in this chapter, the timeline is simply wrong. Yet, many continue to publish this erroneous assessment, mimicking Iran's official statements.

Lastly, many assessments of Iran's policy toward Azerbaijan claim that despite sharing a common Shia faith, Tehran has not supported Azerbaijan in the conflict. To repeat: the assessment that this policy is exceptional is based on the assumption that common religion is often a basis for alliances. However, there is no evidence of this.[324] The religious factor should not be thought of as a factor in the analysis of the Armenia-Azerbaijan conflict and lack of evidence of this should not be presented as remarkable.

---

[324] For more on the impact (or lack thereof) of religion and culture on foreign policy choices, see Brenda Shaffer, ed., *The Limits of Culture: Islam and Foreign Policy*, Cambridge, MA: MIT Press, 2006.

ARMENIA'S PASHINYAN CONUNDRUM

Implications of the Second Karabakh War

Onnik James Krikorian

The Second Karabakh War between Armenia and Azerbaijan was as inevitable as its conclusion was foregone, culminating in Baku reclaiming almost full control over seven regions surrounding the formerly disputed Nagorno Karabakh Autonomous Oblast (NKAO). This left the ethnic-Armenian entity of a previously self-declared but unrecognized Karabakh in an unsustainable situation,[325] unless, that is, it entered quickly and full-on into a dialogue with Baku. In September 2023, Azerbaijan's victory was cemented by a military operation to disarm ethnic-Armenian forces remaining in the NKAO, separated from the rest of Azerbaijan by a Russian peacekeeping contingent deployed since November 2020.

This significantly impacted over 100,000 ethnic-Armenians that had remained in the remnants of the former NKAO, most of

---
325 Onnik James Krikorian, "Armenia-Azerbaijan: Opening Remarks," April 18, 2021.

whom then fled[326] or were instructed by de facto officials to leave[327] for Armenia. For Armenian Prime Minister Nikol Pashinyan, first in late 2020 and then in late 2023, this new reality was arguably a direct result of two events: the Velvet Revolution that brought him to power in 2018 and his handling of the post-Second Karabakh War environment, especially in relation to Russia.[328]

Remarkably, despite Armenia's defeat in 2020 and the complete loss of Karabakh in 2023, Pashinyan nonetheless remains in power while negotiations with Azerbaijan on a peace agreement continue. His hold on power, however, has largely been due to a disillusioned and apathetic populace in the wake of the defeat. But with little to demonstrate for his tenure to date, Pashinyan's political future might not be certain. Although the political opposition remains weak and unpopular, that could change before the next parliamentary elections set to take place in mid-2026, at the latest.

Compounding these challenges is a new geopolitical rivalry in the region, involving Russia and the West, alongside other international players like Iran, India, China, and Türkiye. All these actors are either currently crucial or will be shortly—not only in shaping Armenia's postwar future, but also that of the entire South Caucasus. Since the latest Russia-Ukraine conflict began in 2022, Pashinyan has had to navigate his new predicament carefully, balancing options without alienating any side. In this uncertain multipolar landscape, the risks are significant, espe-

---

326 Onnik James Krikorian, "Is This How Karabakh Was Meant to End?," *Commonspace*, October 1, 2023.
327 Onnik James Krikorian, "The Challenges and Contradictions of Displacement in Armenia," *Commonspace*, March 18, 2024.
328 Arman Grigoryan, "Armenia's Misguided "Pivot to the West"," *The National Interest*, July 17, 2024.

cially as Pashinyan remains inexperienced and poorly advised, while his leadership style remains erratic.

Nonetheless, the potential remains to resolve the now largely dormant conflict between Armenia and Azerbaijan, as well as foster cooperation in the region; although the opportunity to do so seems to be diminishing with each passing year. Though Armenia accuses Azerbaijan of not being interested in fully resolving the conflict, there is also much criticism of Pashinyan as someone who often changes sides when the opportunity arises—even if it means rejecting previous commitments, agreements, or undertakings. He is now, more than ever, driven most of all by concern with his own survival, no matter the potential cost in other areas, including for landlocked Armenia's survival. In early 2023, I described him as "predictably unpredictable, consistently inconsistent."[329] This characterization still holds true. No analytical post-mortem on the conflict between Armenia and Azerbaijan can be complete without a sustained examination of the individual whose conduct and policies have, more than anyone else in the country, shaped Armenia since May 2018.

The Education of Nikol Pashinyan

Prior to his remarkable and unexpected rise to power following street protests in 2018, Pashinyan was known as a troublemaker in Armenian politics whilst his persona was seen as being bold, confrontational, and unpredictable. His relationship with former leaders Robert Kocharyan and Serzh Sargsyan had been particularly volatile and is now obsessive. Despite this criticism, how-

---

329 Onnik James Krikorian, "The Pashinyan Conundrum: Predictably Unpredictable, Consistently Inconsistent," *Baku Dialogues* 6, no 3, Spring 2023, pp. 130-147.

ever, Pashinyan is also a creation of the regimes led by his two predecessors, themselves also hostage to decades of nationalist, existential narratives.[330]

Born in Armenia's northeastern Tavoush region in 1975, Pashinyan nonetheless represents a marked change in the country's leadership. While Kocharyan and Sargsyan were both widely held to belong to the notorious "Karabakh Clan" and synonymous with authoritarianism, corruption, and falsified elections, Pashinyan is the country's first Armenia-born leader since independence was declared in 1991. Even its first president, Levon Ter-Petrosyan, was born in Syria in 1947, though his parents moved to Armenia two years later (both Kocharyan and Sargsyan were born in Karabakh).

After rising through the ranks of the Communist Party in Karabakh as the Soviet Union was imploding (this culminated in Kocharyan ruling as de facto president in 1994-1997), both Kocharyan and Sargsyan moved to Armenia to serve under Ter-Petrosyan. Then, in 1997, the two joined forces with then Defense Minister Vazgen Sargsyan to oppose a concessionary peace deal with Azerbaijan favored by Ter-Petrosyan.[331] With his legitimacy in tatters because of the contentious 1996 presidential election that saw him secure a second term in office,[332] Ter-Petrosyan had little choice but to resign in 1998, though some of his supporters claim it was to also avoid the risk of civil war. This last demon-

---

330 Arman Grigoryan, "Our Whole Political and Intellectual Field Is Steeped in Myths And Dogmas," *Media.am*, December 7, 2020.
331 Heghine Buniatyan, "What was negotiated and what was demanded by the international community before Ter-Petrosyan's resignation? Declassified government documents," *Radio Azatutyun*, February 3, 2023.
332 Egbert Wessenlink, "Armenia: After the 1996 Presidential Election," *UNHCR*, March 1, 1997.

strated how the Karabakh issue could make or break leaders, something about which Pashinyan remains acutely aware today.

When Kocharyan took over the Armenian presidency in 1998 (though it is questionable whether he was eligible to do so[333]), Sargsyan became his closest confidant and eventually his hand-picked successor when his second and final presidential term ended in 2008. Upon coming to power, Kocharyan also lifted the ban on the Armenian Revolutionary Federation-Dashnaktsutyun (ARF-D). Ter-Petrosyan had banned the nationalist party in December 1994, arresting key figures for allegedly plotting a coup d'état. The ARF-D would remain Kocharyan's main support base and eventually Pashinyan's bitterest of political foes, especially after the Second Karabakh War. Even today, the ARF-D is the main party making up Kocharyan's *Hayastan* (Armenia) faction in the Armenian National Assembly.

During the Kocharyan-Sargsyan era, Pashinyan became best known through his columns in *Haykakan Zhamanak*, the most widely-read newspaper in the country, which he also edited.[334] Constantly criticizing the government, in November 2004 Pashinyan's car blew up in what he claimed was an assassination attempt, or at least a warning, from Kocharyan-ally, oligarch Gagik Tsarukyan.

Even afterward, and despite the publicity generated by the car bombing, Pashinyan still remained a minor political figure, including in 2007 when he led the Alyentrank (Alternative) move-

---

[333] Ruzanna Khachaturian, and Hrach Melkumian, "Armenia: Opposition Divided Over Kocharian's Standing For President," *Radio Free Europe*, February 9, 1998.

[334] Though Pashinyan resigned from these positions when he entered parliament in 2017, the newspaper continues to be associated with him through his wife and is considered an important, if questionable, mouthpiece. See US Embassy in Armenia diplomatic cable, November 2004. (https://wikileaks.org/plusd/cables/04YEREVAN2537_a.html)

ment to contest parliamentary elections as part of the Impeachment bloc. Failing to meet the five percent threshold for entering the Armenian National Assembly, street protests attracted few to the streets. The following year, in 2008, after Ter-Petrosyan's return to politics to dramatically contest that year's presidential election as the main opposition candidate,[335] Pashinyan rose to prominence as a major figure in the campaign that aimed to prevent Kocharyan from passing on power to Sargsyan.

Following the vote held in February 2008, Armenian riot police dispersed a tent camp that had been erected in Yerevan's Liberty Square and Pashinyan took over the organization of barricades erected near the French embassy for the opposition's last stand against the authorities. A state of emergency was declared, with the army called out on 1 March 2008. Ten people died.[336] "We must liberate our city from the Karabakhtsi scum," Pashinyan reportedly said to the demonstrators,[337] presumably referring to Kocharyan and Sargsyan. Pashinyan went into hiding and reappeared only in June 2009, thereupon he was arrested.

Amnestied in May 2011, he was elected to parliament as part of Ter-Petrosyan's Armenian National Congress (ANC) bloc the following year, though he became increasingly critical of its leadership. By 2015, Pashinyan formed the Civil Contract political party and former civil movement that he still heads today. Joining the "Way Out" electoral bloc, Pashinyan again entered parliament in the 2017 elections. If 2008 was defined by attempting to prevent Kocharyan from passing on power to Sargsyan,

---

335 Emil Danielyan, "Armenia's Ter-Petrosian Sets Stage for Tense Presidential Vote," *Eurasianet*, October 29, 2007.
336 Karine Kalantarian, "Police General Defends Break-Up of Opposition Tent Camp," *Radio Azatutyun*, August 5, 2008.
337 Gor Mkrtchian, "Anti-Artsakh Hatred in Armenia," *Oragark*, April 18, 2022.

ten years later it was defined to prevent Sargsyan from becoming prime minister so as to extend his power when his second and final presidential term was due to end. This last had become possible because of the enactment of constitutional changes from a presidential to a parliamentary system of governance in a highly flawed referendum held in 2015 precisely, many believe, to allow that to happen.

A campaign of civil disobedience paralyzed Yerevan to a standstill in Spring 2018, while similar protests occurred nationwide on a scale never seen before. Using his trademark populism and tendency towards confrontation, including a live televised meeting with Sargsyan at the Marriott Armenia hotel on Republic Square on 22 April 2018, Pashinyan demanded that Sargsyan resign. As usual, there was no room for compromise in Pashinyan's playbook and he was detained by masked police after talks broke down in chaotic scenes on Republic Square just hours later.

Tens of thousands gathered in the square later that evening and Pashinyan was released the following day when Sargsyan also resigned. But Sargsyan's Republican Party still controlled the parliament and, again using the politics of the street, Pashinyan called on his supporters to continue blocking traffic, besiege government buildings, and stage a general strike in order to assure that he would be chosen as Sargsyan's replacement. The tactic worked and Pashinyan was eventually elected prime minister on 8 May 2018.

Pashinyan in Power: Populism and Nationalism

While many maintain that Pashinyan's rise to power represented a democratic and peaceful revolution, there were also concerns that most outside observers ignored. Even during the street protests, Pashinyan and his entourage often used nationalist language. Following his election as prime minister, and seeking to shore up support in Karabakh, Pashinyan traveled to the region the following day to mark Victory Day. This tendency towards populism would partially contribute to the inevitability of the Second Karabakh War, as former Armenian diplomat Jirayr Libaridian warned just weeks before it did.[338]

Indeed, during the Velvet Revolution there had already been signs of such a manipulation of nationalist rhetoric, even though it appeared to contradict Pashinyan's earlier position on the conflict. Not only had he donned a military-style camouflage t-shirt for the 2018 Velvet Revolution, but he had also grown a beard in an apparent attempt to resemble a typical Armenian fighter from the First Karabakh War.

And in August 2019, on another visit to Karabakh, Pashinyan declared that "Artsakh is Armenia, and that's it" after having previously declared on numerous occasions during the Velvet Revolution that Karabakh was "an inseparable part of the Republic of Armenia." Though likely intended for domestic political purposes, the interpretation of these words, as well as their ramifications in Azerbaijan, whose leadership had hoped Pashinyan might finally be the one to sign a peace deal, was predictable and obvious.

And in another populist twist, Pashinyan's Minister of

---

338   Gerard Libaridian, "A step, this time a big step, backwards," *Aravot*, September 1, 2020.

Defense, David Tonoyan, revealed a new defense policy doctrine of "new war for new territories" while Pashinyan attended the inauguration of Karabakh's new de facto president following its 2020 unrecognized presidential election and an inauguration ceremony held in then-occupied Shusha. His attendance at the event, coupled with its location (the city is culturally significant to Azerbaijan), was a provocative move that would have devastating consequences later. It had already been planned to move Karabakh's unrecognized but de facto parliament to the mountain citadel by 9 May 2022 in another move that irked Baku.

Adding to the slide towards war, a panel discussion between Azerbaijan President Ilham Aliyev and Pashinyan in February 2020 at the annual Munich Security Conference in Germany descended into a series of mutual recriminations. By the time of the July 2020 clashes on the Armenia-Azerbaijan border, the road to war appeared to be irreversible. In August 2020, for example, Pashinyan's wife, Anna Hakobyan, posed for controversial photographs dressed in military fatigues looking down the sights of an assault rifle as part of an ill-thought-out and highly questionable[339] "Women for Peace" initiative.

Meanwhile, in September 2020, just four days before the Second Karabakh War broke out, Pashinyan ally and speaker of the parliament Alen Simonyan posted a photograph of himself on social media holding a pomegranate with the comment "Akna is my homeland"—a reference to the Armenian nationalist name for Aghdam, a once-bustling Azerbaijani market town located outside the former NKAO that was razed to the ground after Armenian forces captured it in 1993. Even Sargsyan had never

---

339   Zaruhi Hovhannisyan, "Armenia's womanly face of war," *OC Media*, September 21, 2020.

claimed Aghdam as Armenian. In fact, controversially, he had once done the exact opposite. In mid-February 2021, he criticized Simonyan's selfie taken against the backdrop of that very same (at-the-time) ghost town.

Following his participation in the February 2020 debate at the Munich Security Conference, Pashinyan also released a set of six of his own conflict settlement "principles," known as the "Munich Principles." These effectively dismissed the "Basic" or "Madrid" Principles of the OSCE Minsk Group, which had been the basis of negotiations[340] between Armenia and Azerbaijan since 2007. Additionally, in April 2020 Pashinyan had also rejected a modified version of the 2015 "Lavrov Plan," itself a variation of the 2011 "Kazan Plan."

Yet, despite Armenia's crushing defeat in 2020 and the terms of the 10 November 2020 trilateral ceasefire statement that much of Armenian civil society and effectually all opposition parties considered a "capitulation," Pashinyan won snap elections on 20 June 2021. A remarkable feat given the circumstances, Pashinyan had taken another risk that paid off. He was undoubtedly fortunate that his main opponents were those led by his old foes, Kocharyan, Sargsyan, and the Armenian Revolutionary Federation-Dashnaktsutyun (ARF-D).

Nonetheless, some analysts contend that Pashinyan's reelection granted him the legitimacy to engage in peace talks with Azerbaijan even though his own 2021 election manifesto still promoted the idea of "remedial secession" for Karabakh while simultaneously advocating for a "peace agenda." This inconsistency has become a trademark of Pashinyan's leadership, who

---

340   Karen Harutyunyan, "A recap of the 7 plans proposed for the settlement of the Karabakh conflict," *Civilnet*, October 21, 2021.

has the ability to contradict himself sometimes even in the same sentence. In April 2022, Pashinyan also toned down his rhetoric, gradually no longer referring to the entity as "Artsakh" but "Mountainous Karabakh" and stressing the need to "lower the bar" on Karabakh's status. Other leaders might have lost power, but Pashinyan's comments were taken in their stride by most citizens.

The various demonstrations that followed were relatively small and again consisted of opposition supporters allied with Kocharyan and Sargsyan. While some experts predicted that some 50,000-60,000 people would gather outside the National Assembly to unseat him, the protests that lasted for two months typically only drew around 3,000-5,000 people per day, with a maximum of 10,000 on two occasions. A combination of fatigue and a feeling of hopelessness among the general population, as well as deep popular resentment towards Armenia's second and third presidents, again worked to Pashinyan's advantage.

This type of discontent, however, ought to have been understood by Pashinyan to be a warning of sorts, one that increased in potential seriousness on 14-15 September 2022 when clashes across the Armenia-Azerbaijan border resulted in a total of 300 additional deaths on both sides. The popular reaction in Yerevan consisted of thousands more taking to the streets—though only for one night. But it could still turn out to be harbinger of what may come, especially if new leaders emerge ahead of upcoming parliamentary elections in 2026 and popular trust in Pashinyan remains low.

The Peace Talks and Pashinyan's Geopolitical Turn

Under Pashinyan, Armenia has steadily moved away from Russia. While Pashinyan was deferential to Moscow before the Second Karabakh War, it is clear that Moscow never trusted a leader who came to power in what some consider to be a "color revolution," though Pashinyan has always denied that it was. Another factor in Pashinyan's geopolitical change, however, is that Russia has become a useful scapegoat upon which to place the blame for a string of military defeats under his premiership in 2020, 2022, and 2023.

Coinciding with growing tensions between Russia and the West after a new round of fighting began in Ukraine in February 2022, this has emboldened Western actors to step into the vacuum. Though traditionally relying on Russia for its economic and military security, Armenia had been careful to tread a fine line between the West and Moscow following Pashinyan's accession to the premiership in 2018. That changed when he refused to accept a proposed CSTO monitoring team in favor of an unarmed EU civilian mission, confirming that Armenia was indeed distancing itself from Russia.

The 40-person strong European Union Monitoring Capacity (EUMCAP)[341]—announced at the October 2022 meeting in Prague—was deployed on 20 October 2022 and was made up of seconded monitors from the European Union Monitoring Mission (EUMM) in neighboring Georgia. Its original term would last only two months yet was effectively extended for a two-year period in February 2023, when the now-renamed European

---

341 Onnik James Krikorian, "EU Monitoring Capacity deploys on the Armenia-Azerbaijan border," *Osservatorio Balcani e Caucaso, Transeuropa,* November 8, 2022.

Union Mission in Armenia (EUMA)[342] began to operate with an expanded but still unarmed civilian staff of around 100, of which 50 were actual monitors.

Russia reacted with strong diplomatic language but refrained from taking concrete action. Still, many believed that Moscow would now seek to disrupt the delicate normalization process facilitated by Brussels. Although the EU-led Charles Michel-facilitated negotiations between Armenia and Azerbaijan started in December 2021—that is, three months before the 2022 Russia-Ukraine war began—Moscow increasingly felt sidelined, fearing that the Russian-brokered trilateral November 2020 ceasefire and subsequent agreed statements were at risk.

Following the start of the 2022 Russia-Ukraine war, Moscow and Brussels became competitive rather than complementary in the context of the peace process—a situation exacerbated when the United States became directly involved, too. By December 2022, hopes of signing a peace treaty were disappearing fast. With the EUMA's initial two-year term due to expire in February 2025, Azerbaijan continues to voice concern with any further presence of the mission on its border with Armenia. Speaking at the Antalya Diplomacy Forum in March 2024, the then-EU Special Representative for the South Caucasus and Crisis in Georgia Toivo Klaar did indicate that EUMA could be withdrawn after a treaty.[343]

The presence of additional (that is, Western) actors led to the phenomena of "forum shopping"—disrupting progress in

---

342 Onnik James Krikorian, "European Mission in Armenia Completes Its First Year Amid Regional Tensions," *Eurasia Daily Monitor*, March 11, 2024.

343 Ingilab Mammadov, "Baku-Yerevan peace deal to lead to EU mission's withdrawal from Armenia – Toivo Klaar, *Trend*, March 1, 2024.

one track by jumping to another whenever Yerevan and Baku saw it as being more favorable. Deepening disagreements between Yerevan and Baku were also clearly evident in late November 2022, with Aliyev's public statement that Pashinyan insisted on the presence of French President Emmanuel Macron at another EU-facilitated meeting between the two leaders scheduled for 7 December 2022 in Brussels. Indicating this was unacceptable, Azerbaijan pulled out of the meeting as result—especially following what Baku considered to be unacceptable comments made by Macron in an interview on French television aired soon after talks in Prague in early October 2022. Those comments served to confirm Baku's position that the French posture under its current leadership is too one-sided in favor of Armenia to act as an honest broker or mediator in the peace talks.

The Brussels Process was thus brought to a standstill, with even some Armenian analysts remaining confused by what still appears to be Pashinyan again acting on a whim. Pashinyan's pivot towards a more pro-Western stance[344] at the expense of the country's longstanding ties with Moscow provided an opportunity for Russia to destabilize Armenia's domestic political environment. The perceived inaction of the Russian peacekeeping contingent on the Lachin highway throughout 2023 and Moscow's indifference to Azerbaijan reasserting control over Karabakh in September that same year, resulting in the exodus of almost the entire population, added to an already emerging anti-Russian sentiment in Armenia.

The origins of this go back to dissatisfaction with Moscow and the Collective Security Treaty Organization (CSTO) for

---

344 Onnik James Krikorian, "Armenia, one step closer to the EU," *Osservatorio Balcani e Caucaso Transeuropa*, March 21, 2024.

what Yerevan considered an inadequate response to the Second Karabakh War. What came later only deepened this resentment. In September 2024, Pashinyan declared that Armenia's ties with the CSTO were now at the "point of no return," though again he stopped short of saying when he would consider that line actually to have been crossed. For now, Armenia's involvement with the CSTO has been declared by Yerevan as "frozen."

There was also the issue of Iran. Relations with Iran had always been of importance to Armenia and post-Second Karabakh War diplomatic friction between Baku and Tehran definitely emboldened Armenian nationalists and, possibly, the Armenian government, too. This increased in October 2022 when Iranian Foreign Minister Hossein Amir-Abdollahian inaugurated a consulate in the southern Armenian city of Kapan, located very near a part of the border with Azerbaijan over which Baku had regained control during the 2020 war.

The continuing impasse on the "Zangezur Corridor" has also reportedly led to significant disagreement between Iran and Russia.[345] It should be noted, however, that previous peace proposals have always featured such a route—most notably in 2001, when a system of overpasses was discussed at Key West so as not to block or interrupt Armenia's direct access to its southern neighbor. Ironically, Russian FSB border guards continue to patrol that border (as well as the one with Türkiye), although they now no longer man checkpoints on the Iranian border.

As a result of a number of deals made under previous governments, Armenia appears locked into receiving its gas from Gazprom through Georgia via fully Russian-owned pipelines

---

345 Vasif Huseynov, "Putin's Visit to Baku Stirs up Iran-Russia Tensions on Zangezur Corridor," *Eurasia Daily Monitor*, September 12, 2024.

until 2043.[346] Only 12.5 percent of its gas supply comes from Iran in a barter deal with Armenia for electricity in exchange. Under the terms of these contracts, Armenia cannot purchase gas from any country other than Russia.

Some have suggested purchasing gas from Azerbaijan in the context of a post-peace deal situation, but unless new pipelines are built, this gas would still have to pass through the Russia-owned pipeline network—unless, of course, an arrangement between Baku and Moscow was to materialize. Azerbaijan would also have to match prices offered by Moscow, heavily subsided in a form of soft power, though Aliyev has said this could be possible in case of normalization.

Confounding the situation is the Soviet-era Metsamor nuclear reactor plant,[347] which has had its termination date extended several times over the years. Armenia also receives its nuclear fuel from Russia. Armenia has been in negotiations with Russia, the U.S., and what it describes as a "third country" regarding the replacement of its aging nuclear reactor. This also includes modular reactors from the U.S., a geopolitical tool that Washington views as a way to wean various countries away from Moscow, especially in the former Soviet space.

But this still doesn't address the issue of nuclear fuel, which would have to be transferred by land or air via Russia, though one Armenian political scientist suggests Kazakhstan could be an alternative.[348] For that to happen, however, Kazakh fuel would

---

346   Onnik James Krikorian, "Armenia-Azerbaijan Gas Co-operation: Pipe Dream or Reality," *Commonspace*, May 7, 2024.
347   Onnik James Krikorian, "Armenia Looks West to Reduce Nuclear Energy Dependency on Russia," *Eurasia Daily Monitor*, July 22, 2024.
348   Areg Kochinyan, "Armenia Should Use This Window of Opportunity to Leave Russia's Orbit," *Carnegie Politika*, May 21, 2024.

still have to be transported via Russia and Georgia, Iran, or Azerbaijan. The first would still be controlled by Moscow, the second is unlikely to be acceptable to the United States, and the third is hardly feasible until normalization—and even then, it might not be welcomed by Baku.

Even though the UN's main nuclear energy specialist in Armenia believes that the country should continue its tried and tested cooperation with Russia on a replacement nuclear reactor, Pashinyan says he finds the prospect of working with the U.S. to be "politically appealing." In July 2024, Armenia's Security Council Secretary Armen Grigoryan stated that talks in Washington on this issue were in a "substantive phase," calling for the legislative basis in the U.S. for cementing a deal to be expedited. Visiting Yerevan that same month, USAID Administrator Samantha Power underlined this would be central for diversification away from Moscow.

However, it is unclear to what extent Armenia might be swayed by its trade and other relations with Iran, given that this also potentially runs counter to improving relations with the West. Neither the EU nor the U.S. so far seems willing or able to provide Yerevan with hard security or economic guarantees.

COP29 and a Constitutional Conundrum

In mid-2024, Aliyev floated the idea of *initialing* a set of agreed basic principles by or even at COP29 in Baku in November 2024. This would leave the signing of a comprehensive treaty until after the Armenian constitution is changed.[349]

[349] Onnik James Krikorian, "Constitutional Delay in Armenia Threatens to Derail Peace Talks with Azerbaijan," *Eurasia Daily Monitor*, June 15, 2024.

Baku's objection centers on the constitution's controversial preamble, which refers to its authority as stemming from "the fundamental principles of the Armenian statehood and nation-wide objectives enshrined in the Declaration on the Independence of Armenia." This last document, which dates back to 23 August 1990, itself contains a preambular clause indicating that it is in part "based on the 1 December 1989 Joint Resolution of the Supreme Council of the Armenian Soviet Socialist Republic and the Artsakh National Council of 1 December 1989 [titled] 'On the Reunification of the Armenian Soviet Socialist Republic and the Mountainous Region of Karabakh.'"

If a compromise could have allowed Armenia a year to put constitutional amendments to a nationwide referendum, the announcement of a new deadline to draft amendments or a new constitution by the end of 2026 at first seemed more like a tactic to delay the process in the hope that Baku would drop its demands. This deadline falls six months after the latest possible date for holding parliamentary elections in Armenia, where Pashinyan's political future is uncertain.

Moreover, even if a referendum were held, its outcome would be far from guaranteed. For the amendments to pass, a simple majority of 50+1 percent of the electorate must vote in favor, and their total should also exceed one quarter of all registered voters. Analysts opposed to a peace deal quickly point out that in the 2023 city council elections, voter apathy was so significant that only 28 percent participated, meaning even fewer voted for Pashinyan's mayoral candidate, Tigran Avinyan. For Pashinyan, it is also crucial to implement structural changes in the constitution to ensure the political system benefits him, just as it did for his predecessor. This could be another reason for delaying any referendum.

While Pashinyan views the West as a potential savior, powers closer to home are likely more important. In short, numerous obstacles and lingering Russian influence could firmly keep Armenia at least partially within Moscow's orbit. Additionally, the outcome of the Ukraine war will significantly impact the region. If Russia emerges victorious, Moscow may return to the South Caucasus with renewed assertiveness, starting with Armenia. Although it is unlikely to leave the Eurasian Economic Union, Pashinyan's increasing criticism of Russia and his diminishing involvement in the CSTO are actions Russian President Vladimir Putin is unlikely to forget.

Crossroads of Peace

The sensitivity[350] of what Azerbaijan refers to as the "Zangezur Corridor" and Armenia (marginally) includes in its "Crossroads of Peace" proposal is not new. Even Pashinyan himself is on record as having written about the restoration of an overland route from Azerbaijan to its exclave of Nakhchivan via southern Armenia as early as May 2001 in a *Haykakan Zhamanak* newspaper column.[351] When then-President Robert Kocharyan was believed to be negotiating a territorial swap to facilitate such a route in talks held in Key West in March 2001, it was considered tantamount to treason. Pashinyan made it clear that control should remain with Yerevan and Armenia should benefit from transit fees. In October

---

350   Onnik James Krikorian, "Baku, Yerevan, and Moscow Clash Over Regional Transit," *Eurasia Daily Monitor*, June 25, 2024.
351   Nikol Pashinyan, "We and Our Interests," *Haykakan Zhamanak*, May 23, 2001.

2024, he repeated the same claims,[352] albeit without any relevant study that would have put a monetary figure to it.

"If Turkey or Azerbaijan wants to communicate through Meghri, let them communicate. Let them use our territory, let them use our railway and pay for it, as is customary in the world," he wrote in his 2001 article. "Turkey has no railway connection with Nakhchivan and […] the Turks will have to use our railway on the Gyumri-Yerevan-Yerask line and pay for it. Let the economists calculate how many millions of dollars that would be for our budget," he concluded.

Two decades ago, Pashinyan argued that if the route was to fall out of Yerevan's control, then Armenia would turn into a "dead end," no longer able to become the "heart of the region" or the "crossing point of West and the East." This appears to be the position he maintains today, and it is one of which Biden Administration officials like Assistant Secretary of State James C. O'Brien seemed to tacitly approve, terming the "Crossroads of Peace" a step toward "encouraging and strengthening regional trade and connectivity through a just and durable peace."

The "Crossroads of Peace" proposal is an extension of Pashinyan's earlier "Armenian Crossroads" initiative that he put forward at the end of 2021, which was in turn an expansion of the North-South Road Corridor project under construction in Armenia since the Sargsyan presidency. While an East-West component does include the mainland Azerbaijan-Nakhchivan route, its main focus is on a north-south road connection from Iran to

---

352 "Prime Minister Pashinyan explains why Azerbaijan is concerned over Crossroads of Peace project," *ArmenPress*, October 12, 2024.

Georgia through Armenia and rail transportation between Armenia and Türkiye.

However, in his two-page "Crossroads of Peace" proposal, Pashinyan does not prioritize the route to and from Nakhchivan, even though it was a central component of many peace documents in the past, including the 10 November 2020 trilateral ceasefire statement. It also fails to include a specific road, instead preferring to use existing roads further north, something that Azerbaijan opposes. Instead, Armenia's focus remains as it has for decades on the opening of the border with Türkiye and the restoration of the Gyumri-Kars railway line,[353] a route that could potentially be extended to Azerbaijan's northwestern Gazakh region.

In short, "Crossroads of Peace" appears to be primarily a geopolitical project, not a geo-economic one. The absence of any sort of feasibility study suggests strongly that it hypes the political importance for Western audiences of supporting the proposal without any consideration of whether it is economically viable. This, of course, does not mean that the sort of support articulated by the likes of O'Brien will not eventually materialize in concrete form, but it does decrease the likelihood that the billions of dollars surely needed to bring the "Crossroads of Peace" proposal to life is unlikely to produce an economic return in the short to midterm. Azerbaijan and Türkiye continue to oppose the plan,[354] as do those who understand the geo-economics of both the Middle Corridor and the Belt and Road Initiative.

---

353 Arshaluis Mgdesyan, "October 2024, The Kars-Gyumri Railway Could Become Armenia's New Gateway to Europe – Deputy Minister," *Business Media,* October 2, 2024.

354 Onnik James Krikorian, "Armenia and Turkey meet on closed border," *Osservatorio Balcani e Caucaso Transeuropa,* August 1, 2024.

Church and Opposition

In 2024, Pashinyan faced a new headache: Archbishop Bagrat Galstanyan, Primate of the Tavush Diocese and former head of the Canadian branch of the Armenian Apostolic Church. That the government and the Church would go head to head had been clear since Armenian Public Television refused to air the annual New Year's Eve message by the Catholicos of All Armenians, Karekin II, on 31 December 2023. The snub was taken harshly by the Church and interpreted by observers as the most serious escalation between the Catholicos and the Prime Minister since Armenia's defeat in the Second Karabakh War, when Karekin II began calling for Pashinyan's resignation. "For the Church, the approach of the authorities to resolving the conflict, which boils down to recognizing Artsakh [Karabakh] as part of Azerbaijan, is unacceptable," Galstanyan said in June 2024.

Initially starting with small protests and acts of civil disobedience near the location of the border delimitation and demarcation process with Azerbaijan that had recently been agreed and begun, Galstanyan embarked on a roughly 170-kilometer march to Yerevan. Upon arriving in the Armenian capital on 9 May 2024, he organized a protest demonstration in the central Republic Square that attracted about 31,000 people. This was the largest rally since Pashinyan's own in 2018 and was enough to surprise the government—or at least until the next two rallies held in the following days, which were attended by only 11,000 and 9,000 persons, respectively. Part of the reason for the huge drop in numbers could have been that, rather than talk about the situation on the border, Galstanyan instead called for Pashinyan's resignation.

Claiming that he was acting individually and not as a proxy for the Church itself, some Armenians saw Galstanyan as an outsider untainted by the disillusionment associated with traditional political parties and the current government. Even Western media picked up on the cleric's personage, incorrectly presenting him as a lone crusader for justice who had reluctantly entered politics to speak up for the residents of Tavush. That too could not have been further from the truth. Galstanyan had been visible in the Dashnaktsutyun-led protests in 2022 and later that year described himself as a revanchist eager to take revenge against Azerbaijan to regain land lost in the Second Karabakh War.

That same year, former Armenian Foreign Minister Raffi Hovannisian had also proposed the establishment of an interim government in case Pashinyan was ousted. Galstanyan was again included as an integral part of that structure. All of this was long before the issue of border delimitation and demarcation came up.

Besides, at Galstanyan's first small gathering held in the Tavush village of Voskepar on 13 April 2024, Dashnaktsutyun members were present—including from its radical youth wing, the Armenian Youth Federation (AYF). By his side at all times was Dashnaktsutyun MP Garnik Danielyan, raising doubts about his claims of having no direct political linkages with the main party in Kocharyan's parliamentary faction. Galstanyan, by his own admission, also said that he was engaged in politics with the blessing of Karekin II, just as he was in 2022. [355]

Indeed, the Armenian Government was quick to make such claims from the outset. "A cleric cannot say a political text without the permission or instructions of the Catholicos of All Arme-

---

[355] "Artsakh has the right to have rights': Bishop addresses rally in Yerevan," *Panorama*, May 11, 2022.

nians, Karekin II," stated Pashinyan in a live televised address before Galstanyan's first rally. "It is obvious that the leader of the [demonstrations] is the Catholicos of All Armenians, and the beneficiary is Robert Kocharyan." [356]

Among his supporters were also individuals such as Hampig Sassounian, sentenced to life imprisonment for assassinating the Turkish Consul General in Los Angeles in 1982 until his controversial release on parole in 2021. Others included ultranationalist groups such as the National Democratic Pole and militias such as Combat Brotherhood. A fourth rally on 26 May 2024 did see numbers increase from the two previous protests but still only attracted 23,000 people, which is average for Armenia even during the Kocharyan period. As expected, and ignoring his constitutional ineligibility, Galstanyan declared himself to be the opposition's nomination for the post of Armenian prime minister.[357]

The Church became ever more outspoken in its criticism of Pashinyan, resorting to stereotypical and nationalist slurs against him. "I have said several times that these authorities are not Armenian. [...] Everything can be expected from the antinational authorities," Archbishop Mikael Adjapahyan, Primate of the Diocese of Shirak said of him.[358] "It is quite logical that [...] the interests of 'old men,' such as ex-presidents Sargsyan and Kocharyan, and the Armenian Church found each other [and]

---

[356] "Pashinyan: Leader of "Tavush for the Homeland" is Catholicos of All Armenians and Beneficiary is Robert Kocharyan," *The Armenian Report*, May 9, 2024.

[357] "Protest-Leading Armenian Archbishop Says He Will Challenge Pashinyan for Premiership," *Radio Free Europe*, May 26, 2024.

[358] Zarouhi Dilanyan, "Tomorrow, the memorial complex of Sardarapat will be assembled – Archbishop Mikael Adjapahyan," *168 Hours*, May 28, 2024.

decided to use the image in the cassock as a new tool for active confrontation with Pashinyan," concluded one Russian analyst.[359]

On 12 June 2024, around 3,600 gathered outside the National Assembly amid significantly bolstered security measures. State officials had already warned the demonstrators publicly that significant precautions had been readied both inside and out in case they planned to storm the building while Pashinyan spoke inside. Clashes broke out and police fired stun grenades[360] at those among the crowd who had attempted to break through. Around 100 people required medical treatment, with on-the-ground footage showing Galstanyan and Dashnaktsutyun leader Ishkhan Saghatelyan attacking the police line and using force.

Tensions were also high in parliament, with government and opposition lawmakers confronting and jeering each other. Pashinyan had launched a ferocious tirade against Dashnaktsutyun MPs, accusing them of being responsible for the exodus of 100,000 ethnic-Armenians from Karabakh following Baku's military operation to disarm Armenian security forces in September 2023. He also accused the nationalist party of paying 5,000 Armenian Drams (around $13) to individual Karabakh Armenian refugees to attend the protests in Yerevan.

In the days that followed, several Dashnaktsutyun activists were detained by police. Some Western commenters—especially those who had anyway been critical of Pashinyan and his apparent willingness to deal with Azerbaijan—were quick to condemn the former revolutionary leader for the use of police to suppress

---

[359] Vadim Mansurov, "The Armenian Church is pushing Yerevan towards self-destruction with its revanchist ideas," *Caliber*, June 2, 2024.

[360] Onnik James Krikorian, "Azerbaijan-Armenia Border Demarcation to continue despite violent protests in Yerevan," *The Caspian Post*, June 19, 2024.

the crowd. This was their mistake, too. The 2018 Pashinyan-led Velvet Revolution was more about replacing the deeply unpopular Serzh Sargsyan than bringing about a truly democratic society and all that it entailed. Pashinyan's methods have always been populist and manipulative. Ironically, Galstanyan was just copying them.

But by 2024, widespread disappointment and disillusionment with the results of the Velvet Revolution and the Pashinyan government had set in—even if the opposition has yet to fully capitalize on it. Given the sensitivity of changes afoot in the country, and especially in terms of normalizing relations with Azerbaijan, the Armenian prime minister's situation remains incredibly fragile in case of the emergence of a new figure—one who is able to instill confidence and hope among the population. Galstanyan's movement demonstrated this last, even if it failed.

Election Headaches

This raises concerns about parliamentary elections scheduled for no later than 2026, but which may end up taking place earlier. Even if Pashinyan were still to garner a higher number of votes than his rivals, it is also quite possible that he would not be able to achieve a sufficient majority in these parliamentary elections—whenever they end up taking place. That could create unfortunate obstacles in the post-2026 segment of the normalization process with Azerbaijan. There is also a lot riding on Pashinyan being able to go to the polls having signed a peace deal with Azerbaijan and perhaps even with Türkiye (which is expected to follow from the first one) in order to justify what are perceived as unpopular unilateral concessions.

When Pashinyan's Civil Contract party came to power in 2018, it garnered 70 percent of the vote. Following the war, snap elections held in June 2021 saw that fall to 53.95 percent. In September 2023, in municipal elections held in the capital, it was just 32.6 percent. By December 2023, in a survey conducted by the International Republican Institute (IRI), only 20 percent of respondents said they would vote for Civil Contract if elections were held that weekend. And in May 2024, in a poll by MPG, that had dropped further to just 12.8 percent.

All subsequent surveys have indicated that Pashinyan's ratings fluctuate between 12 and 20 percent. None of his opponents or rivals came close even to those dismal numbers. But it gets worse. In various polls, around two-thirds of respondents say they trusted no leader, clearly signaling the existence of a vacuum that might one day be filled. And only about one quarter of respondents believe the country is moving in the right direction.

Moreover, since Aliyev strongly reiterated his position in June 2024 that no peace agreement could be signed until Armenia removed a controversial preamble to the country's constitution that effectively lays claim to Karabakh, somewhere between two-thirds and three-quarters (or more) of respondents indicated that they were against changing this document at all. That figure was 34.2 percent in a poll conducted in January 2024.

Such numbers are arguably existential in nature, but they also indicate the reality that the opposition hardly fares any better, only drawing equal when the ratings of individual parties are combined into a single block. Most of the electorate still remains either against all political forces or is simply non-engaged and apathetic. Even the April 2024 agreement between Armenia and Azerbaijan to demarcate 12.7 kilometers of their mutual border, with Yerevan also handing over four non-enclave villages in the Gazakh region of Azerbaijan it had controlled since the early 1990s, failed to ignite popular anger (or support).[361]

What the Armenian opposition really needed was a populist to take on another populist—a professional orator to take on another. Towards the end of May 2024, Galstanyan was present at an international conference held by Dashnaktsutyun in Yerevan devoted to *Hai Tahd* (Armenian Cause). With him was a special representative sent from Etchmiadzin and Kocharyan's former foreign minister, Vartan Oskanyan. The event was unreported in the local media, but was covered by the pro-Dashnak press in the diaspora. And in June 2024, Galstanyan was present at another meeting convened by the Ararat Alliance, a body established by the head of the Union of Russian Armenians, businessman Ara Abrahamyan, who is widely described not only as pro-Putin but also as a Kremlin insider.

With them was Seyran Ohanyan, the head of Kocharyan's mainly Dashnaktsutyun Hayastan parliamentary faction. Several pro-Galstanyan Telegram channels voiced their displeasure at this apparent endorsement of a Russian platform given earlier assurances that there were no such links. This part of the opposition's apparent connection to Abrahamyan could also prove a major problem for Pashinyan going forward. Few believe that Armenia's economic diversification can become a reality in the foreseeable future. Armenia's main market remains Russia,

---

361 Onnik James Krikorian, "Armenian Government Faces Domestic Pressure Over Handling of Border Dispute," *Eurasia Daily Monitor*, April 8, 2024.

and it seems unlikely that it can expand into other markets so easily unless new trade routes materialize. This would, of course, require normalization and open borders with both Azerbaijan and Türkiye.

Conclusion

The 2020 war between Armenia and Azerbaijan was inevitable after years of unsuccessful negotiations, but Pashinyan's leadership—both his speeches and deeds—arguably expedited its onset. Since then, his trademark populism has also at times disrupted the resulting peace process. His tendency to look for foreign support and intervention hasn't helped, either. Indeed, the Armenian prime minister's unpredictable political adaptability continues to pose risks. For instance, in early June 2024, though Pashinyan had acknowledged the problem in 2023, Baku's demand that a peace agreement cannot be signed without amendments to Armenia's constitution, which it claims includes territorial demands on Azerbaijan, continue to be rejected.

But even then—by now calling for a total rewriting of the entire constitution—it is highly likely that the controversial preamble will be removed, but only in 2027 at the earliest. This would mean that it would follow the 2026 parliamentary elections. It remains unclear whether Pashinyan, who won snap elections in 2021 by promoting a *peace agenda*, could again face the nation without having delivered on his core promise. It remains to be seen if Pashinyan's populism can regain traction amidst the growing skepticism, disillusionment, and apathy of the voting public.

Ironically, however, it could be Pashinyan's populist messaging, bolstered by Western support and a peace deal with Azerbaijan, that will ultimately save him, though it is not out of the realm of possibility that Pashinyan might resort to administrative resources and even a crackdown to guarantee victory as a last resort. It is widely believed that Pashinyan will face retribution from any opposition force that replaces him.

Yet, as recent history shows, uncertainty prevails both regionally and globally. The 10 November 2020 ceasefire should have set the stage for a peace agreement by late 2022, but geopolitical tensions, particularly following the restart of the Russia-Ukraine conflict, undermined this effort. While some key issues, like the return of occupied territories, have seen resolution, the failure to implement critical aspects of the ceasefire document—such as restoring regional transport links—remains a significant concern for Armenia's economic diversification.

The escalation of the Iran-Israel conflict into direct military engagement starting in 2023 has further complicated the geopolitical landscape of the South Caucasus. Stability in Georgia is also uncertain, and Western policy has shifted against a government contentiously reelected in that country's 5 November 2024 parliamentary election. Whether (and how) this will affect the peace process between two of its neighbors is a question that is unlikely to be answered before this book goes to press.

At this point, numerous unknowns complicate the situation. From the standpoint of late 2024, negotiations between Armenia and Azerbaijan appear to be increasingly oscillating between progress and setback.

Once again, it seems that momentum for peace could be lost, though without the possible resumption of war that was instead inevitable prior to 2020. While some Armenian analysts warn of a possible resurgence of armed conflict in 2025, this currently appears unlikely given significant investments by Baku in the previously occupied territories that could be targeted in any military escalation. Moreover, Baku has always refrained from extending its military operations deep into Armenian territory—when its troops did cross into territory controlled by Armenia in several instances since the 2020 war, it did so on an unclearly defined periphery (Armenia claims these territories as its own). Nonetheless, without a major breakthrough in Armenia-Azerbaijan relations soon, substantial peace negotiations may not resume until late 2026 or 2027, by which time Pashinyan's options will be even fewer.

A further unknown is the outcome of Pashinyan's quest to reduce Armenia's dependence on Russia for economic and energy needs. In light of potential punitive actions from Moscow—such as obstructing imports and exports—he must count on massive concrete support from the EU and the United States. This has not yet happened.

Regardless of whether Armenia can forge a new post-war future with or without Russia, there is no escaping the likelihood that failure to normalize relations with Azerbaijan and Türkiye will not guarantee stability or economic prosperity either way. Pashinyan might understand this—if only for his own survival. Even before the Second Karabakh War, he anyway had wanted to change the constitution in a departure and as an attempt to distance his post-revolution government from the Kocharyan and Sargsyan regimes. Following the 2020 war, however, that has become even more of a necessity: it represents a way to distance himself from any blame for the disastrous defeat.[362] Coincidentally, this distinction between the pre-2020 and post-2020 Armenia is anyway necessary for the country to advance.[363] It is not a surprise to many that he increasingly talks about a "historical Armenia" and the "new Armenia"[364] that will finally allow the country to move forward. This also includes coming to terms with Azerbaijan and Türkiye,[365] the two main issues that have arguably held Armenia back for so long.

Whether the country can succeed or not remains unclear, but the potential is there. But not if the peace (or normalization) process drags on for much longer. The next parliamentary elections, scheduled for no later than mid-2026, will be key. But the geopolitical stakes could prove even more influential, both positively and negatively, depending on how 2025 shapes up—especially with regards to the situation in Ukraine and Russia's position depending on that outcome.

---

362 Onnik James Krikorian, "Pashinyan Reignites Constitutional Reform Debate Amid Declining Ratings,' *Eurasia Daily Monitor*, January 31, 2024.

363 Onnik James Krikorian, "Historical versus real Armenia - Pashinyan's push for a new narrative," *Commonspace*, April 11, 2024.

364 For more on this topic, see Damjan Krnjevic-Miskovic, "The Two Armenias Debate and the Quest for Peace with Azerbaijan," T*he National Interest*, May 11, 2024,

365 Onnik James Krikorian, "Pashinyan Emphasizes Potential in Normalizing Relations With Türkiye," *Eurasia Daily Monitor*, May 6, 2024.

NO MORE WAR, NOT YET PEACE

On the Second Karabakh War and Its Aftermath

Fariz Ismailzade

To properly assess the conflict between Armenia and Azerbaijan—which can be characterized presently as 'no more war, not yet peace'—close attention needs to be paid to how the Azerbaijani side perceived both its immediate origins and the Karabakh occupation period that lasted nearly three decades. This will help us better understand the reasons why the Second Karabakh War erupted and brought about such an unexpected set of results, which in turn has produced myriad geopolitical consequences for the South Caucasus and, indeed, farther afield.

How Azerbaijanis Saw the Conflict

Azerbaijanis were deeply traumatized by the results of Armenian aggression in the First Karabakh War: they viewed it as a stab in the back from a neighbor during the turbulent times of the collapse of the USSR and the (re)emergence of independent states in the post-Soviet space. Since the Nagorno-Karabakh Autonomous Oblast (NKAO) was a part of the Azerbaijani Soviet Socialist Republic (SSR),[366] Azerbaijanis saw the Armenian demand to transfer it to the Armenian SSR (made in the midst of the collapse of the Soviet Union) as a betrayal of decades-long peaceful coexistence and as the result of a well-prepared conspiracy led by the Armenian lobby operating chiefly in the West (especially in France and the United States) and Russia, which was coordinated with local political forces seeking to advance a maximalist irredentist agenda by stirring up historical grievances that had been thought to have been long overcome.

Many Azerbaijanis recall with fondness their personal friendships with Armenians, retelling stories of them sharing meals in their respective homes and other enjoyable moments of living convivially together. These ties of friendship were suddenly broken, with feelings of betrayal increasing by the day. Azerbaijanis were understandably shocked that—in the July 1993 celebratory words of Levon Ter-Petrosyan—"Armenia and Artsakh have been completely cleansed of other ethnicities," and that the country's leaders believed that had this unconscionable war crime not happened, "then today we would not have a state."[367] From the Azerbaijani perspective, the First Karabakh War was about the pursuit of a territorial claim through armed aggression and the subsequent military occupation of land that resulted directly in the ethnic cleansing of more than 900,000 Azerbai-

---

366 On the legal background to the status of the former NKAO, see Javid Gadirov, "International Law and the Karabakh Question," *Liberated Karabakh: Policy Perspectives by the ADA University Community*, eds. Fariz Ismailzade and Damjan Krnjević Mišković, Baku: ADA University Press, 2021, pp. 33-49.

367 Levon Ter-Petrosyan, Address at the Inaugural Yerkrapah Congress, July 12, 1993, https://www.aniarc.am/2024/11/28/ltp-1993-erkrapah-congress-address, at 12:15-12:25 and 12:40-12:55.

jani civilians from their homes in Armenia as well as the former NKAO and other parts of Azerbaijan. It was thus also seen as a blatant violation of a cornerstone, sacrosanct principle of international law: that of the territorial integrity of sovereign states (i.e., UN member states). Four UN Security Council resolutions were passed in the early 1990s that demanded the immediate and unconditional withdrawal of Armenian military forces from Azerbaijani lands; but the "international community," led by the United States at a time of uncontested unipolarity, did virtually nothing to implement them and instead allowed Russia to serve as a prime mover in a peace process that amounted to the perpetuation of a status quo that was both unjust and illegal.[368] This translated into Azerbaijan's territorial integrity and sovereignty remaining unrestored. Naturally, this produced a major Azerbaijani disappointment with the Western conception and advocacy of values and principles like democracy, justice, and international law. The much-vaunted "rules-based" order somehow seemed not to apply to Azerbaijan. In many ways, this also affected the foreign policy orientation of the reemerging country, as in the early years of its renewed independence Baku mainly favored the pursuit of policies meant to lead to Euro-Atlantic integration.

Unfortunately, the conflict over Karabakh brought much human suffering and psychological trauma as well. For ordinary Azerbaijanis, the Armenian occupation of the former NKAO and the seven surrounding districts was associated not only with the violation of international law, the UN Charter, and the afore-

---

368 The Russian posture during this period has been well-defined by Vladimir Kazimirov, the country's first mediator in the conflict over Karabakh (1992-1996): "in early 1992 […] we were instructed not to view the conflict as 'our own': both Azerbaijan and Armenia had already proclaimed their independence. But it was impossible to treat it as a foreign affair either." See his *Peace to Karabakh: Russia's Mediation in the Settlement of the Nagorno-Karabakh Conflict*, Moscow: VES MIR Publishers, 2014, p. 25.

mentioned UN Security Council resolutions, but also with the mass murder of women and children in the village of Khojaly during a cold February night in 1992—the single-largest atrocity committed by either side during the First Karabakh War. Azerbaijanis also associated the Armenian aggression with the loss of Shusha, the nation's cultural capital; the wholesale looting of cities like Aghdam; and the tragedy of hundreds of thousands of ethnically cleansed Azerbaijani families living in makeshift IDP and refugee camps hastily built throughout the country (including in the capital, Baku). Such and similar images of horror, violence, and desperation had a deep, traumatic impact on the Azerbaijani population, which could not and did not accept the outcome of the First Karabakh War and dreamed of the day when these lands would be liberated.

Three decades of occupation were devoted to planning for one overarching goal: to modernize the country, strengthen its economy, improve its diplomatic capacity, and yes, rebuild its military—which was effectually non-existent in the early 1990s—so as to be ready to fight and win a war of liberation in the event of a manifest failure of diplomatic negotiations. Azerbaijan's post-Soviet nation- and state-building process was centered around this grand vision. It was the Armenian unwillingness to foresee the success of Azerbaijan's holistic strategy that led Yerevan and its supporters to perpetuate an uncompromising approach that ultimately led to the onset of the Second Karabakh War and the military, diplomatic, and psychological debacle that was its result.

Failed Diplomacy

Relatedly, Azerbaijanis view the onset of the Second Karabakh War as a result of a failed process of diplomatic negotiations. Although ordinary Azerbaijanis and perhaps, for that matter, ordinary Armenians, had put much hope in reputable intergovernmental organizations like the UN, the OSCE, and the Council of Europe to mediate effectively between the warring sides and bring lasting closure to the conflict, in reality all these aspirations went nowhere. Gradually, trust in foreign negotiators declined and the OSCE's Minsk Group Co-Chairs (France, Russia, and the United States) came to be seen as ineffective mediators, incapable of achieving anything. In fact, one of the people who served as the U.S. Co-Chair, Richard Hoagland, wrote candidly about the uselessness of the trips to Baku and Yerevan taken by the Minsk Group.[369]

On many occasions, both before and after the war, President Ilham Aliyev criticized the major powers, particularly the Minsk Group mechanism, for maintaining a very soft approach to the occupation and failing to put strict demands on Armenia to end its military aggression.[370] This is especially true when comparing the conflict over Karabakh to Georgia's and Ukraine's territorial problems and occupations following the conflicts in 2008 and 2014, respectively (and, of course, now starting in 2022 with respect to the latter). In those cases, the West seemed to show a much more unified and uncompromising stance, applying sanctions and using diplomatic channels to pressure Russia (and,

---

369 Richard Hoagland, "Does the Minsk Group Still Have a Role?", International Conflict Resolution Center, March 26, 2021.
370 "Aliyev says OSCE Minsk Group played no part in Karabakh settlement," TASS, December 12, 2020.

again in the context of 2022, providing comprehensive support to Kyiv's response to the Kremlin's aggression and occupation). For Azerbaijanis, this contrast in approach represented the epitome of double standards. Even the case of Libya in 2011—where Western powers mobilized their military resources within several hours to implement their interpretation of the relevant UN Security Council resolution—was touted as an example of Western power and its ability to engage forcefully in trying to resolve a conflict and enforce its interpretation of UN Security Council resolutions, since they saw doing so as being in their interest.

Although all UN member states (save Armenia) and intergovernmental organizations (including the UN, the OSCE, the Council of Europe, the Commonwealth of Independent States, and so on), as well as the EU, continued to recognize the territorial integrity of Azerbaijan, in practical terms they did very little to enforce it—that is to say, to incentivize, persuade, or force Armenia to reach a compromise in accordance with the cornerstone tenets of international law. At best, the Minsk Group busied itself either with putting forward unrealistic proposals, which were rejected by one or both parties to the conflict, or with trying to manage the status quo and prevent a large-scale escalation. It is not unreasonable to conclude that the Minsk Group Co-Chairs shared a hidden agenda, if only implicitly: to legitimize the Armenian occupation through the passage of time and convince Azerbaijan to "accept reality."

Why did foreign mediation fail so miserably prior to the onset of the Second Karabakh War? One explanation revolves around the 'competing interests of the Co-Chairs' argument. It is no secret that geopolitical competition has characterized the

South Caucasus and the broader Silk Road region since the early 1990s and that control over the region's energy resources pushed various outside powers to seek a more pronounced diplomatic presence and increased political leverage. This, of course, often brought competing and mutually exclusive perspectives on the conflict resolution process. Two examples will suffice to illustrate the point: the shooting in the Armenian parliament in 1999 when U.S. Deputy Secretary of State Strobe Talbot was about to finalize a peace deal during his trip to the region,[371] and the emergence of the "Lavrov plan" at the Kazan trilateral summit in Russia.[372] It was widely rumored that Russia had been involved in the shooting in the Armenian capital in order to prevent the U.S.-led peace process from coming to fruition. At the same time, U.S. policymakers were often suspicious of Russian Foreign Minister Sergey Lavrov's efforts to insert Russian peacekeepers into any form of final peace agreement. One can firmly state that both powers viewed each other through a "zero-sum" lens.

In any case, geopolitical competition eventually resulted in the mediators turning into passive travelers and ineffective diplomats. Everyone except Azerbaijanis seemed to be happy with entrenching the status quo, with the mediators being seen as often trying to firm it up instead of changing it. In this regard, the influence of Armenian lobby and diaspora organizations in Moscow, Paris, and Washington also played a crucial role in the 'status quo mediation.'

Successive representatives of the Minsk Group Co-Chairs themselves did not necessarily reject such criticism, but in return

---

371 Steven Mufson, "Leader Had Just Met with State's Talbott," *Washington Post*, October 28, 1999.
372 Richard Solash, "Kazan Summit: Time For Breakthrough In Nagorno-Karabakh Peace Process?", *RFE/RL*, June 23, 2011.

passed blame on the maximalist positions of the conflicting sides, which hindered and prevented the ability of both Baku and Yerevan to make any meaningful concessions; this also allowed the Co-Chairs to refer to themselves (and their collective mandate) as mere facilitators and not as conflict resolvers. Eventual choices on hard compromises and the terms of a final peace deal would rest on the shoulders of the leaders of Armenia and Azerbaijan themselves, the argument was made. The Co-Chairs thus absolved themselves of any responsibility, which effectually favored the status quo that, again, had as its principal effect the perpetuation of the Armenian occupation of Karabakh.

What also made the work of the mediators harder was the severe and angry nationalistic rhetoric coming from both sides, fueled by media, the internet, local intelligentsia, and a gradually growing hatred of each side toward the other one. Both sides seemed to focus on articulating their respective maximalist positions, ignoring the concerns and needs of the other side, and leaving very little room for both the foreign mediators and the leaderships of the two countries to make compromises and come up with creative win-win solutions. Decades of one-sided agitation via national media outlets, the lack of access to the views of the other side, and the absence of credible and broadly accepted platforms for dialogue between civil society, media, academia, and youth further contributed to this problem. One should also specifically note that, by and large, the Azerbaijani perspective on such a potential dialogue prioritized the return of the lands under Armenian occupation rather than engaging in Track Two diplomacy per se: it was widely believed in Baku that close contacts between representatives of the civil societies of the two sides would serve only to empower Armenia and further cement the occupation; outside mediators, especially those from the West, believed that Track Two confidence-building measures could (perhaps decisively) advance the peace process—notwithstanding the total lack of evidence of success in doing so anywhere in the OSCE space.

One can thus conclude that three decades of failed negotiations and the resulting loss of trust in the possibility of peacefully resolving the conflict over Karabakh eventually became one of the main factors for the start of the Second Karabakh War. Had the various foreign-led initiatives taken more consistent and focused steps to end the occupation, many lives could have been saved in 2020.

Reasons Why the War Started in 2020

Despite the failure of the negotiations process to produce concrete results—a failure that went back decades—the Azerbaijani side long seemed committed to staying on this path: the numerous rounds of negotiations since the ceasefire ending the First Karabakh War was signed in Bishkek in May 1994 speak to this point. These rounds focused on a litany of proposals and peace packages from the foreign mediators, which were known under various names including "step by step," "common state," "land swap," and "interim status." Summits at the highest level were held at various times and in the presence of assorted intermediaries, including Key West (April 2001), Astana (September 2004), Kazan (August 2005), Rambouillet (February 2006), Bucharest (June 2006), Madrid (November 2007), St. Petersburg (June

2008), Moscow (November 2008), Moscow (July 2009), Chisinau (October 2009), Munich (November 2009), Sochi (January 2010), Kazan (June 2011), Vienna (November 2013), Sochi (August 2013), Paris (October 2014), Bern (December 2015), Vienna (May 2016), St. Petersburg (June 2016), Dushanbe (September 2018), St. Petersburg (December 2018), Davos (January 2019), Vienna (March 2019), Ashgabat (November 2019), and Munich (February 2020). The cumulation of these meetings was complete deadlock, with Armenia refusing to vacate an inch of occupied land and Azerbaijan continuing to refuse to "accept the reality" of the occupation.

Meanwhile, sporadic violations of the ceasefire and small-scale military activities took place at regular intervals, leading to loss of life on both sides. The first serious bout of fighting post-First Karabakh War took place in April 2016, and by that time it was clear that the negotiations process was bearing no fruit, with Armenia refusing even to depart from the territories surrounding the former NKAO, to say nothing of the NKAO itself. At that time, the warfare that had been going on for four days was halted at the insistence of the Kremlin, but only after some not merely symbolically important changes happened along the 1994 ceasefire line. The Azerbaijani army was able to break through Armenian fortifications in the Fuzuli district and liberate a small portion of land, including strategic heights, something that allowed Azerbaijan to rebuild the formerly occupied Jojug Marjanly village and effectuate the return of IDPs to that location. Even though this was a small victory, it served as a demonstration to the Azerbaijani side how fragile and vulnerable the Armenian defense line was (it had been portrayed by the Armenian side as being impossible to breach). It should be also noted that in April 2016 the Kremlin insisted on a ceasefire in part because of its strong support for Armenia's then-president, Serzh Sargsyan, whose regime was known for its particularly tight political and military alliance with Russia.

The outcome of Armenia's 2018 "velvet revolution" brought different dynamics to the Karabakh peace process. While the previous regimes, led by Robert Kocharyan and Sargsyan, favored close relations with Moscow and the perpetuation of the status quo at the negotiating table, the populist Nikol Pashinyan—having come to power on a wave of street protests in Spring 2018 (its outcome was confirmed by the Armenian parliament in May 2018 and in a subsequent election in December 2018)—advocated for a more pro-Western foreign policy. This had the effect of weakening Russia's support for Armenia, as the Kremlin did not like the politics of the country's new leader. At the same time, because Pashinyan was, unlike Kocharyan and Sargsyan, not from Karabakh, he appears to have perceived an additional need to make populist statements in support of the continuing occupation of Azerbaijani territories. Thus, his first trip outside Armenia was to occupied Karabakh (this took place literally on the day after his parliamentary confirmation as prime minister, in May 2018).

Pashinyan's infamous August 2019 phrase "Karabakh is Armenia, period"[373] effectually signaled the end of the formal (even if inefficient) mediation process, because it made clear that Yerevan saw the future of Karabakh only within Armenia. A few months earlier, in March 2019, Pashinyan's Defense Minister,

---

373 Joshua Kucera, "Pashinyan calls for unification between Armenia and Karabakh," Eurasianet, August 6, 2019.

David Tonoyan, had gone even further by threatening Azerbaijan and using the phrase "new war for new territories."[374] Pashinyan's provocative visits to Karabakh, one of which (May 2019) included attending a party and dancing (perhaps in an inebriated state) in occupied Shusha, was considered by Azerbaijanis to be a purposefully provocative insult. A few months later, Pashinyan endorsed the planned move of the "parliament" of the separatist regime in Karabakh (unrecognized even by Armenia) from Khankendi to Shusha, a city established in 1752 by Panah Ali Khan, the founder of the Karabakh Khanate. This endorsement took place about a fortnight before the start of the Second Karabakh War and represented the final nail in the coffin of the peace process. It was clear that Armenia was telegraphing its position that Yerevan and Baku had nothing left to discuss after this series of unprecedented provocations. Azerbaijan received the message loud and clear.

Some analysts believe that Pashinyan's predecessors pushed him to engage in such provocations and make use of nationalistic rhetoric—that he was merely rhetorically pushing back against their accusations that he was being soft on the Karabakh issue.[375] Indeed, Pashinyan represented a new generation of politicians in Armenia, coming mainly from a largely non-governmental background and having never experienced war firsthand. Sargsyan and Kocharyan immediately put a fear in the minds of Armenians that Pashinyan would "sell out" Karabakh, leading the inexperienced Pashinyan to make a series of mistakes regarding the Karabakh issue, as detailed above.

---

374   "David Tonoyan. 'Territories for Security' Format Will No Longer Exist," March 30, 2019.
375   Kucera, op. cit. See also Onnik James Krikorian, "The Pashinyan Conundrum: Predictably Unpredictable, Consistently Inconsistent," *Baku Dialogues* 6, no. 3, Spring 2023, pp. 156-173.

The July 2020 attack by Armenians on Tovuz was a particularly poor decision. This region, located in the northwestern part of mainland Azerbaijan, is the location through which pass all the country's most important post-Soviet oil and gas pipelines (Baku-Tbilisi-Ceyhan and the first part of the Southern Gas Corridor, respectively), a new strategic railway line (Baku-Tbilisi-Kars), and other important transport and connectivity projects that connect Azerbaijan with Georgia, Türkiye, and the European Union. More broadly, this area—also known as the "Ganja bottleneck" or the "Ganja gap"—is the sole all-weather transit route in the South Caucasus that binds Asia to Europe.

For Azerbaijan, losing any sort of secure control over that particular part of the country would not only have meant losing control over strategic energy assets but also the loss of its chief connectivity corridor to the West via the Black Sea and Anatolia. For EU candidate and NATO aspirant Georgia, this would have meant geopolitical isolation; for NATO member state Türkiye, this would have meant the loss of its strategic contact point with the Silk Road region; for both NATO and the European Union, this would have meant the shutdown of its strategic outreach efforts to all the landlocked states between its eastern borders and the Chinese frontier and ignoring the geopolitical and geo-economic fact that Azerbaijan is the "cork in the bottle containing the riches of the Caspian Sea basin and Central Asia."[376] And it would, of course, have caused economic devastation for Azerbaijan, Georgia, and others. All in all, the attack on Tovuz, coupled with the first-ever killing of an Azerbaijani general by Armenian forces in this same period, resulted in much insecurity and anger not only

---

376   Zbigniew Brzezinski, *The Grand Chessboard: American Primacy and Its Geostrategic Imperatives*, New York: Basic Books, 1997, p. 46.

in Baku but also in Tbilisi, Ankara, Brussels, and Washington. Lastly, Armenia's attack on Tovuz finally mobilized the Azerbaijani public and political leadership for full-scale war. In reality, the Second Karabakh War "started as a result of Armenian military attacks in the Tovuz region."[377]

Reasons for Military Success

Azerbaijan managed to achieve an impressive victory in the 44-day Second Karabakh War thanks to three factors. First, Armenia had significantly underestimated the military capabilities of its archrival. Azerbaijan, in the past decade or two, had managed to modernize its army with the help of sophisticated Russian, Turkish, and Israeli equipment and through advanced training, mostly conducted by Türkiye. This military buildup and the consequent widening gap between the defense capabilities of Armenia and Azerbaijan began as soon as oil revenues started flowing into Azerbaijan, yet official Yerevan did not take seriously the implications of this trend, preferring instead to keep living in a comfortable bubble and in the expectation that Azerbaijan would never be able to effectively exercise the military option. A 1998 statement by Kocharyan illustrates this way of thinking, which in the subsequent period was never truly revised: "Are you sure the rich man fights better?"[378] Thus, during the Second Karabakh War, the Azerbaijani army was surprised to see how weak and overinflated the Armenian defensive line was. Often,

---

[377] Fariz Ismailzade, "Strategic Implications of the Liberation of Karabakh," *Liberated Karabakh: Policy Perspectives by the ADA University Community*, eds. Fariz Ismailzade and Damjan Krnjević Mišković, Baku: ADA University Press, 2021, p. 118.

[378] Stephen Kinzer, "Ethnic Conflict in Caucasus Shows Its First Glimmer of Hope," *New York Times*, September 14, 1998.

well-trained Azerbaijani battalions faced ill-equipped and very poorly trained Armenian military formations, which were either composed of young and inexperienced conscripts from Armenia or local Karabakh Armenian villagers. Even though a vocal segment of Armenian society continues to argue that the war was won by Türkiye (some go so far as to allege that jihadists from the Middle East were involved in the fighting),[379] the truth is that the Azerbaijani military, armed with modern equipment sourced from regional countries, established battlefield superiority over the Armenian army. Some foreign analysts even defined the Second Karabakh War as the first twenty-first-century war (in the sense of battlefield innovation), considering the number of drones and next-generation equipment used on the battlefield in a tactically coordinated fashion with more conventional arms.[380]

Second, the 2020 war showed the consequences of Armenia's growing diplomatic isolation, notwithstanding the avowed influence of the notoriously influential Armenian lobby and various diaspora groups in countries like France, Russia, and the United States. Azerbaijan in the past decades managed to form regional alliances and participate in the establishment of new organizations such as the Organization of Turkic States and GUAM, increased its influence in global networks such as the Non-Aligned Movement, and effectively neutralized Armenia's key allies in the Collective Security Treaty Organization (CSTO)—e.g., Belarus, Kazakhstan, and Russia itself—through increased bilateral trade and cooperation. It is not a coincidence

---

[379] Joshua Kucera, "Armenians accuse Turkey of involvement in conflict with Azerbaijan," Eurasianet, September 28, 2020.

[380] Paul Iddon, "The Last Azerbaijan-Armenia War Changed How Small Nations Fight Modern Battles," *Forbes*, March 25, 2021.

that in June 2021 Kocharyan complained that Azerbaijan had better relations with CSTO members than did Armenia itself.[381]

Armenia's diplomatic isolation was also a result of an irrational foreign policy conception that ignored regional and global trends; placed too much faith in the relevance of its partnership with allies Russia and Iran; dismissed the economic, political, and military rise of Türkiye; and ignored Azerbaijan's rising international clout and strengthened relations with such actors as the EU, the U.S., China, various Arab states, and Israel. The resulting diplomatic isolation ensured Armenia's inability to overcome its regional economic and energy marginalization, much of which resulted from its choice not to take measures that would result in the reopening of borders with its major neighbors.

Finally, the Second Karabakh War was won because of the strong national will in Azerbaijan—an unprecedented social unity coupled with the full consolidation of the country's resources—in contrast to the deep divisions and fragmentation in Armenian society in the wake of the 2018 "velvet revolution" that brought Pashinyan to power. Virtually all Azerbaijanis, irrespective of ethnicity, religion, economic standing, and political background, were inspired and mobilized to achieve a historical undertaking that had been clearly identified as the national mission for the past three decades. This national commitment has been also significantly backed by the fact that Azerbaijani society has, in the last 30 years, drastically increased popular awareness of the legacy of the Karabakh Khanate, which was the sovereign Muslim-Turkic state that governed the area before the Russian occupation of the South Caucasus began in 1828. By contrast, Armenians appeared

---

381 "Armenia former President Kocharyan on applying to CSTO: Why give 'air' to each other in vain?" news.am, June 15, 2021.

demoralized, seemingly betrayed by their politicians and major powers, on top of lacking resources to successfully wage a modern war against Azerbaijan.

Opportunities for Peace and Cooperation

The Second Karabakh War brought many positive changes to regional dynamics. Apart from the fact that Azerbaijan was able to liberate its formerly occupied lands and, in its wake, commence a massive reconstruction effort there (including demining, rebuilding of infrastructure, and the resettlement of IDPs), the war also resulted in a shift of mentality on the part of the Armenian political establishment. Perhaps for the first time since the collapse of the Soviet Union, there is a real chance now to set up a durable peace in the region on the basis of mutually beneficial cooperation arrangements between Armenia and Azerbaijan.

Despite much progress in the peace process, Armenian society still remains divided between those who refuse to accept the new reality (revanchists) and those who argue that Armenia should draw lessons from its defeat and build a different foreign policy, aimed at cooperation and peaceful coexistence with neighbors (primarily Azerbaijan, but also Türkiye) as opposed to the perpetuation of hatred, animosity, and historical revenge-seeking. Pashinyan's reelection in the June 2021 parliamentary elections marginalized revanchist voices to a great extent and, in turn, showed to both domestic and international audiences that the majority of Armenian citizens want peace and stability. Seemingly, this continues to be the case today.

The resumption of a full-scale war is unlikely in the foreseeable future due to the weak military power of Armenia and a growing realization that the country's foreign policy had been going in the wrong direction. Nevertheless, despite the loss that voters inflicted on the revanchist political forces in the most recent national elections, the peace process had more than once hit serious deadlocks and the resumption of hostilities still cannot be fully ruled out. The reasons have been numerous. They include the influence of often powerful and disruptive opposition rallies in Yerevan, the inability and unwillingness of the Pashinyan government to sign a peace treaty along the lines offered by Azerbaijan, the refusal to recognize in a written, binding agreement the territorial integrity of Azerbaijan,[382] including a constitutional amendment that would remove all doubt that Armenia has pretensions on or claims against sovereign Azerbaijani (and Turkish) territory, the unwillingness to support the abolition of the OSCE Minsk Group, and a failure to seize the strategic opportunities provided by the prospect of integrating Armenia into the growing number of regional connectivity and infrastructure projects that would come in the wake of normalized relations with, sequentially, Azerbaijan and Türkiye.

The 10 November 2020 tripartite statement agreed by the leaders of Armenia, Azerbaijan, and Russia that ended the Second Karabakh War includes stipulations about opening new and reopening old regional transportation routes, corridors, and closed borders, and engaging in the construction and reconstruction of road and rail links that would reconnect Armenia and

---

382 This would be categorically different from, e.g., stating publicly the number of square kilometers belonging to Armenia and Azerbaijan or consenting to language in a press release issued by the Office of the President of the European Council that says Armenia "confirmed [its] commitment to the Charter of the United Nations and the Alma Ata 1991 Declaration through which both recognize each other's territorial integrity and sovereignty."

Azerbaijan and bind them more fully to outside markets. Its full implementation would constitute a win-win scenario for all parties: its actualization would represent a significant turn of events from previous decades in which Armenia and Azerbaijan refused to cooperate and maintained closed borders. In such a scenario, Armenia would also become more connected to Russia, while Türkiye and Azerbaijan would gain easier railway access to each other and Iran. At the same time, Russian and Turkish railway systems would be connected, something that would be beneficial for East-West and South-North transport corridors in the Silk Road region. On the issue of the opening of transport routes, Armenia and Azerbaijan have also drifted apart, citing significant differences of views on the scale, scope, and jurisdiction of the Zangezur Corridor, which is intended to connect "mainland" Azerbaijan with its Nakhichevan exclave and Türkiye, in accordance with terms contained in the aforementioned tripartite statement.

Azerbaijan is keen not only to turn Karabakh into a well-functioning and important transport and connectivity hub, but also to bring in much economic investment by focusing on the potential of the region in agriculture, tourism, light industry, mining, and the instauration of large-scale sustainable development projects like green-tech parks, smart cities, and renewable energy hubs. By the end of 2024, Azerbaijan spent the equivalent of over $11 billion in public funds for reconstruction and development efforts in our liberated lands, with an additional $2.35 billion equivalent allocated in the 2025 state budget. Under these conditions, Karabakh Armenians who have stayed or wish to return could also benefit greatly from an economically booming

Karabakh region whilst enjoying better economic conditions than before. This would, in turn, produce mutual interdependence, peaceful coexistence, and, ultimately, reciprocal respect.

Russia and Türkiye—the guarantors of peace in the region—appeared to share the same overall vision and encouraged both Baku and Yerevan towards mutual compromise, especially on the issues of demining, humanitarian aid, local infrastructure, and the opening of trade routes, which could bolster commerce between these powers as well. (This congruence of the Ankara-Moscow vision has more or less continued, despite an escalation in the conflict over Ukraine.) Azerbaijan began sending positive signals to Armenia almost immediately after the end of the war, as shown by its decision to permit gas transit as well as transit of other humanitarian aid through its territory. The Kapan-Goris road, which leads to the sole bridge on Armenian territory that crosses into Iran at Agarak, now passes through liberated Azerbaijani lands and functioned normally (even during the period of heightened tensions between Azerbaijan and Iran right after the end of the 2020 war). Both sides have cooperated intensively to search for the bodies of fallen soldiers. And a process to delimitate the Armenia-Azerbaijan international border has begun, too (this included the return by Armenia of four Azerbaijani villages in the Gazakh district, which is located away from the former Karabakh conflict area).

Aside from Russia and Türkiye, other geopolitical actors have also actively participated in the peace process since 2020. Some, like the EU and the United States, acted more constructively in comparison to others like India, Iran, and France. Regretfully, more than a few of these hurt the peace process by supporting *inter alia* (1) the unrealistic ambitions of Karabakh Armenian "leaders" right up until our antiterrorist measure in mid-September 2023 (including their refusal to acknowledge Azerbaijani sovereignty over the areas they inhabited and accept Azerbaijani citizenship), (2) the Armenian weapons and armaments buildup (France has taken the lead on this front), and (3) policies that provided Yerevan with pretexts to evade fulfilling undertaken commitments. For instance, France's President Emmanuel Macron effectively undermined the EU-led thread of the peace process in various ways, including pushing for the EU to extend (more than once) the scale, scope, and duration of the mandate of its monitoring mission in Armenia along the border with Azerbaijan without an agreement with Azerbaijan. Iran, for its part, acted against the execution of the Zangezur Corridor, fearing the loss of the geopolitical and geo-economic significance of its northern border with Armenia.

Progress has not been linear, and more than a few setbacks have arisen. Still, the two countries have a unique opportunity to achieve sustainable peace, and President Aliyev has repeatedly called on Armenian politicians not to miss the opportunity on offer. But it is understood that this will require a further shift in the thinking and mentality of the Armenian public and political elite to switch into a cooperation mode with its two Turkic neighbors.

From the Azerbaijani perspective, the strategic benchmark can be put in the form of a question: is Armenia willing to do what it takes to adhere fully and unambiguously consistent with five key principles outlined publicly by Foreign Minister Jeyhun Bayramov on 14 March 2022 in a speech at the Antalya Diplomacy Forum?

These terms of peace are important enough to be reproduced in full: *one*, the mutual recognition of respect for the sovereignty, territorial integrity, and inviolability of internationally recognized borders and political independence of each other; *two*, the mutual confirmation of the absence of territorial claims against each other and the acceptance of legally binding obligations not to raise such a claim in future; *three*, the obligation to refrain in their inter-state relations from undermining the security of each other, from threat or use of force both against political independence and territorial integrity, and in any other manner inconsistent with the Purposes of the UN Charter; *four*, the delimitation and demarcation of the state border and the establishment of diplomatic relations; and *five*, the unblocking of transportation and other communications, building other communications as appropriate, and the establishment of cooperation in other fields of mutual interest.[383]

Future Scenarios

In the time ahead, Azerbaijan will face three different potential scenarios in the context of the Armenian question.

The most positive scenario envisions the end of military confrontation, a gradual peaceful delimitation of the border between Armenia and Azerbaijan, and the eventual signing and ratification of a peace agreement. This agreement would include the mutual recognition of territorial integrity and put a definitive end to Armenian territorial claims on Karabakh, which would require amending the Armenian constitution. Trade and

---
[383] Ministry of Foreign Affairs of the Republic of Azerbaijan, Press Service, no. 117/22.

communication linkages would resume, anyone belonging to the Karabakh Armenian minority who remains or wishes to return there would receive Azerbaijani security guarantees, and Karabakh Armenians would be integrated into the economic life of the South Caucasus for the first time in the twenty-first century. Luckily, a good precedent for this exists from the Soviet period. Demining and full reconstruction of formerly occupied lands would take place rapidly. This scenario also envisions harmonious relations between foreign powers, who would accept the new status quo and avoid geopolitical confrontation that could harm the peace process and undermine the region's development.

A second scenario involves continued Armenian contestation, with revanchist factions in Yerevan gaining ground and using military support from abroad as well as diaspora support in Western capitals to mount a political, diplomatic, and, potentially, military attack on Azerbaijan. Considering the fact that many Armenian political circles both inside the country as well as abroad still do not accept the new reality resulting from the outcome of the Second Karabakh War and continue to work hard in lobbying efforts directed towards Western politicians to gain support for territorial claims, this scenario is also plausible. Under such conditions, Azerbaijan would push back with heavy-handed policies against Armenia, further building up its own military capabilities and preparing for an eventual Third Karabakh War. Such a war could spill over into the Zangezur region and bring new territorial changes to the map of the South Caucasus, with very dangerous consequences for the sovereignty and independence of both Azerbaijan and Armenia.

A third scenario involves opportunistic external stakeholders like France, Iran, and Russia seeking to push for new geopolitical rivalry and confrontation in the South Caucasus, even against the will and interests of Azerbaijan and Armenia—in other words, external stakeholders would opt to continue regarding the region as primarily one in which spheres of clashing geopolitical and geostrategic interests could be played out. Despite the fact that the two warring sides might be interested in relative peace and stability, geopolitical actors might push Armenia into an arms race (that it cannot win) with Azerbaijan and stir up a new cycle of violence in the region in order to better defend their own perceived interests and push away "undesired" external rivals from the strategically important South Caucasus, understood as the gateway to the entire Silk Road region. Turbulent global events, tectonic changes in the Eurasian political landscape, East-West rivalry, and the fate of the Iranian nuclear program could also affect this scenario.

As of this writing, the first signs of the geopolitical rivalry characteristic of this third scenario are, regretfully, already in place. Baku will need to keep playing a very careful balancing game with its powerful neighbors and perhaps with major external powers in order not only to fully secure its military gains but also to pave the way for the establishment of a sustainable peace settlement with Armenia. Although the balance of power and security arrangements remain fragile, vulnerable, and incomplete, the South Caucasus has a genuine opportunity to delve into a peaceful model of coexistence, mutual respect, cooperation, and interdependence for the first time since the collapse of the Soviet Union. Integral to such a vision is Armenia making a historic decision to agree on the terms of peace, first with Azerbaijan and then with Türkiye.

MILITARY LESSONS FROM THE SECOND KARABAKH WAR

Niklas Nilsson

The Second Karabakh War had long been in the making. Since Azerbaijan's defeat in the First Karabakh War, as enshrined in the May 1994 ceasefire agreement that produced a cessation of large-scale hostilities, the country steadily built up its military capability, fueled by its hydrocarbon wealth. Baku did so for two interrelated reasons: first, to provide additional leverage in the peace negotiation process; and second, as a reserve option in the event of a failure to produce a negotiated settlement along terms acceptable to Baku's desires through Minsk Group-brokered (or other) talks. In the 2010s, the Azerbaijani leadership became increasingly disillusioned with the prospect of ever peacefully regaining control over its lost territories, which in turn meant that this reserve option gradually emerged as the most realistic one. Recurring skirmishes along the line of contact between Armenia and Azerbaijan became increasingly more violent and larger in scale, and most prominently escalated into a very brief four-day war between the two sides in early April 2016. The outbreak of the Second Karabakh War on 27 September 2020 thus followed a logic that appears quite clear in retrospect yet nevertheless failed to attract appropriate international interest or attention prior to its onset.

The war is indeed a significant event in the history of modern conflict. The Second Karabakh War is the third interstate war to erupt in Europe or its immediate periphery since the conclusion of the Yugoslav civil wars and the 1999 NATO air war against Serbia. The two previous wars in Georgia and Ukraine both involved Russia as a party, whereas the Second Karabakh War was a territorial conflict between two small states (albeit with significant support from external actors). Moreover, that war featured the extensive use of new technologies, of which unmanned aerial vehicles (UAVs) and loitering munitions have received by far the most attention. Whereas Russia had since 2014 put similar systems to frequent use in Ukraine, the Second Karabakh War demonstrated that they are also accessible, affordable, and manageable to use for far smaller actors. Indeed, these capabilities have played a prominent role in Ukraine's defense against Russia's full-scale invasion since February 2022. Yet whereas new technologies may provide a temporal edge to warfighting capabilities, the Second Karabakh War primarily demonstrated that established wisdoms regarding the preconditions for success in military operations still hold. In the end, it was Azerbaijan's ability to financially outspend, operationally outplan, and tactically outsmart its opponent that eventually led the country to a battlefield victory, which in turn was both expanded and consolidated at the negotiating table (and is almost certainly going to be enshrined in any future bilateral peace agreement, as is being contemplated at the time of writing).

This chapter demonstrates the foregoing point in three sections, beginning with a brief overview of Azerbaijan's military operations during the Second Karabakh War. It then discusses key aspects of the factors preconditioning the fighting that proved instrumental in Azerbaijan's victory. Finally, it draws on these experiences to extrapolate some general conclusions regarding military operations in a contemporary setting, as well as potential implications of the experiences of both Armenia and Azerbaijan in the Second Karabakh War for other conflicts.

Brief Overview of Military Operations

When Azerbaijan launched its offensive on Armenian-held positions in and around Karabakh on 27 September 2020, it did so with considerable advantages in terms of manpower, equipment, military organization, and external support. At the start of hostilities, Azerbaijan's defense budget amounted to $2.27 billion compared to Armenia's $621 million. Force ratios amounted to 66,950 to 44,800 active military personnel; 437 to 108 main battle tanks; 883 to 373 other armored fighting vehicles; 630 to 231 artillery pieces, with a substantial Azerbaijani advantage in self-propelled and rocket artillery; and 36 to 17 combat capable aircraft. Adding to the available resources on the Armenian side was the equipment operated by the Artsakh Defence Army, which was in 2019 estimated to consist of 200-300 main battle tanks, similar numbers of other armored fighting vehicles and artillery pieces, and 18,000-20,000 military personnel.[384] While these figures clearly speak to Azerbaijan's favor, they were not overwhelmingly asymmetric. Nevertheless, Armenia's stockpile to a large extent consisted of dated Russian equipment, whereas the Azerbaijani side had allocated considerable resources to purchase state-of-the-art equipment from a diverse number of suppliers. Significantly, over the ten years preceding the conflict Azerbaijan had made a substantial investment in large numbers of modern UAVs, loitering munitions, as well as high-precision ballistic missiles from Israel, Türkiye, and elsewhere.

At the onset of the Second Karabakh War, Azerbaijan attacked Armenian-held positions in the occupied areas from three directions: southwest into the Araz valley and into both the north and northwest of Karabakh. In the first days of fighting, the Azerbaijani side targeted Armenian air defenses, and suffered heavy casualties when assaulting heavily fortified Armenian defensive positions that could make use of antitank missiles and artillery. Mutual heavy artillery exchanges targeted towns and cities on both sides. Meanwhile, the Azerbaijani side proved able to utilize UAVs and ballistic missiles to attack command posts, lines of communications, supply depots, and infrastructure deep inside Armenian-held territory. After several days of heavy fighting, Azerbaijani forces were able to advance into the Araz valley. They took control of Jabrayil on 10 October, thus breaching the Armenian line of defense, and reached the outskirts of Hadrut on 13 October, placing them in a position to advance in the direc-

---

[384] International Institute for Strategic Studies, "Chapter Five: Russia and Eurasia," *The Military Balance* 121, no. 1, 2021; International Institute for Strategic Studies, "Chapter Five: Russia and Eurasia," *The Military Balance* 120, no. 1, 2020. The figures do not include equipment operated by Armenian and Azerbaijani border services and interior ministry troops (e.g., specialized police units).

tion of the Lachin road, the main artery connecting the former Nagorno-Karabakh Autonomous Oblast (NKAO) with Armenia. At that point, further advances on Lachin nevertheless failed in the face of heavy resistance from Armenian units. By 23 October, Azerbaijani forces had secured the entirety of the Araz valley along its border with Iran. Azerbaijan's offensive now turned northward—i.e., toward the road connecting the former NKAO capital of Stepanakert/Khankendi and Lachin, and towards Shusha, a strategically located city on high ground overlooking the road. Indeed, controlling Shusha would result in a decisive advantage to the Azerbaijani side, since this would allow for isolating the entire Stepanakert/Khankendi area and effectively conclude the war. In an operation spearheaded by special forces units, Azerbaijani forces launched their assault on Shusha on 4 November, announcing control of the city a few days later. The loss of Shusha constituted a final devastating blow to the Armenian forces, triggering a collapse of the defense. At midnight on 9-10 November, President Ilham Aliyev, Prime Minister Nikol Pashinyan, and President Vladimir Putin signed an agreement to end hostilities, almost entirely on Azerbaijan's terms.[385]

Losses on both sides during the conflict were heavy. The Armenian side has announced that 3,773 of its servicemen were killed in the fighting.[386] Azerbaijan has stated its number of servicemen killed to 2,908.[387] In terms of military equipment, actual losses are harder to state with certainty, since both sides tend to

---

385 Edward J. Erickson, "The 44-Day War in Nagorno-Karabakh: Turkish Drone Success or Operational Art?," *Military Review*, August 2021.
386 RFE/RL, "Armenian PM Says Almost 3,800 Soldiers Killed in War with Azerbaijan," August 24, 2021.
387 Ministry of Defense of the Republic of Azerbaijan, "List of the Servicemen Fallen Shehids in the Patriotic War," October 21, 2021.

exaggerate the damage inflicted on the opponent and understate own casualties. Nevertheless, evidence of documented losses provided by analyzing open sources by Stijn Mitzer and Joost Oliemans reveals a distinct pattern.[388] On the Azerbaijani side, the vast majority of destroyed equipment consisted of armored fighting vehicles that were apparently destroyed by direct fire, antitank missiles, and artillery. The Armenian side took heavy losses in armored fighting vehicles, but also in air defense systems, artillery pieces, radars, and trucks. Of the equipment that was destroyed in combat, an overwhelming share was destroyed by UAVs and loitering munitions. These figures are telling of the different modes of fighting employed by the two sides. Whereas the Azerbaijani side took decidedly heavier casualties in direct battle—reconfirming the advantages conferred by defensive battle from fortified positions—the Armenian side proved incapable of shielding itself from the airpower dimension added by Azerbaijan's considerable fleet of UAVs and loitering munitions.

Significant Features of the Fighting

Much attention has been paid particularly to the utilization of UAVs during the Second Karabakh War. Live-streamed imagery of Azerbaijani UAV strikes against Armenian positions were indeed the main communicated feature of this war, fueling analysis and debate about the significance of UAV capabilities and countermeasures against them on the modern battlefield. However, the success of Azerbaijan's military campaign did not rely on the introduction of any single technology or capability to

---

388 Stijn Mitzer and Joost Oliemans, "The Fight for Nagorno-Karabakh: Documenting Losses on the Sides of Armenia and Azerbaijan," *Oryx*, September 27, 2020.

the battlefield. Rather, what tipped the balance in Azerbaijan's favor was its ability to conduct a coordinated operation to retake Karabakh.

This operation involved multiple avenues of attack, with the main effort focused on the open terrain in the Araz valley along the Iranian border, and supporting attacks in the north of the former NKAO. This tied up defending Armenian forces in these areas. Having identified control over, or capability to interdict, the Lachin road as the key operational objective, Azerbaijani forces focused their efforts first in the south-eastern direction, then northward to conclude the war by taking Shusha and severing lines of communications between the former NKAO and Armenia. Crucially, Azerbaijan's selective investments into three main capabilities—UAVs and loitering munitions, long-range ballistic missile systems, and special operations forces—allowed its military to conduct "deep battle" across the operational area, engaging Armenian reinforcements, logistics, infrastructure, and high-value targets throughout the area of operations. Indeed, it became evident in the course of fighting that prioritization of these capabilities had come at the expense of investment into regular maneuver units, which (reportedly) frequently displayed deficiencies in tactical skill. Thus, while much of the fighting along the frontline appears to have been attritional, inflicting heavy casualties on the advancing Azerbaijani forces, the added dimension of airpower enabled a combination of close and deep strike capabilities that allowed Azerbaijani forces to isolate the battlefield, which proved crucial in overcoming the well-entrenched Armenian defensive positions. Overall, it was Azerbaijan's combined utilization of the land and air domains that imposed multiple and unmanageable dilemmas on the Armenian defenders.[389] Thus, rather than merely adding new capabilities to its existing land forces, the advantage granted by UAVs consisted in their successful *integration* with Azerbaijan's operational concept.

Yet while integration is key to evaluating the efficiency of Azerbaijan's utilization of UAVs in the war, there are also specific aspects of these capabilities that warrant particular attention. Over several years preceding the war, Azerbaijan had invested heavily in several unmanned systems provided particularly by Türkiye (Bayraktar TB2) and Israel (Harop, Orbiter, SkyStriker, Hermes, Heron, Aerostar, and Searcher).[390]

The Turkish TB2 is a large UAV that can be airborne for up to 27 hours, has a range of over 300 kilometers, and has a high operational altitude of over 5,000 meters. Aside from being utilized for reconnaissance to direct artillery or missile fire, it is a potent weapons platform in itself and can be armed with four laser guided munitions of various types.[391] The Israeli Harop loitering munition can fly for up to 9 hours, is designed to suppress enemy air defense (SEAD) operations, and was notably used to destroy several of Armenia's long-range S-300 batteries.[392] The SkyStriker and Orbiter are smaller loitering munitions with a shorter range and a lighter payload.[393] The small size of these

---

389 Edward J. Erickson, "The 44-Day War in Nagorno-Karabakh: Turkish Drone Success or Operational Art?."

390 Shaan Shaikh and Wes Rumbaugh, "The Air and Missile War in Nagorno-Karabakh: Lessons for the Future of Strike and Defense," *Center for Strategic & International Studies*, December 8, 2020.

391 Baykar Technology, "Bayraktar TB2".

392 Israel Aerospace industries, "HAROP Loitering Munition System," *Airforce Technology*, "Harop Loitering Munitions UCAV System," July 2, 2015; Uzi Rubin, "The Second Nagorno-Karabakh War: A Milestone in Military Affairs," *Mideast Security and Policy Studies*, no. 184, 2020.

393 Elbit Systems, "SkyStriker: Tactical Loitering Munitions for Covert and Precise Strikes"; Seth J. Frantzman, "Israeli Drones in Azerbaijan Raise Questions on Use in the Battlefield," *The Jerusalem Post*, October 1, 2020.

loitering munitions make them difficult to detect and destroy by radars and air defense systems, and can be automated to seek out targets with particular signatures. Moreover, they can be launched off mobile platforms and are therefore easy to move and hide.

These and other UAVs employed by Azerbaijan proved capable of performing many of the tasks normally assigned to reconnaissance and attack aircraft, yet at a fraction of the cost and at much lower risk, given the air defense systems at the Armenian side's disposal. Thus, Azerbaijan's fleet of manned aircraft only came to marginal use in the conflict; in addition, Türkiye's six F-16s based at Azerbaijan's Gabala airbase functioned as a deterrent against Armenia's air force (although Armenia claimed that a Turkish F-16 downed an Armenian SU-25).[394] Although Armenia had received four modern Sukhoi 30SM from Russia shortly before the beginning of the war, these were not utilized during the fighting. According to later statements from the Armenian leadership, the air force had not yet acquired missiles for these aircraft at the outbreak of the war.[395]

Azerbaijani forces also displayed innovative use of decoy UAVs: they remote-controlled old Soviet-era Antonov AN-2 biplanes, which were then targeted by Armenian air defenses. This in turn revealed the Armenian positions, which thereby allowed them to be targeted by Azerbaijani UAVs. In sum, Azerbaijan's UAV capability had a devastating effect on Armenian forces during the war. They directly or indirectly (by directing artillery fire) destroyed a staggering number of Armenian armored fighting vehicles and supply trucks, and drastically

---

[394] BBC, "Armenia Says Its Fighter Jet 'Shot down by Turkey'," September 29, 2020.
[395] Naira Nalbandian, "Armenian PM Denies Contradictions in Comments About Fighter Jets Purchased from Russia," *RFE/RL*, March 25, 2021.

reduced the advantages granted the Armenian defenders by the mountainous terrain they occupied.[396] Another capability offered by these systems is the provision of livestreaming the fighting. The Azerbaijani side took considerable advantage of this capability during the war, providing a steady stream of videos of exploding Armenian equipment for propaganda purposes.[397]

Azerbaijan had also purchased a large number of high-precision ballistic missiles of various origins, of which the most notable is the Israeli LORA, which has a range of 280 kilometers and is capable of hitting a target area within 10 meters. This allows for very precise targeting of military assets and infrastructure and was utilized by Azerbaijan to target, for example, a bridge across the Hakari river (a tributary of the Aras in southwestern Azerbaijan occupied at the time by Armenian forces). Compared to Armenia's utilization of Scud and Iskander missiles to target the cities of Ganja and Mingachevir in Azerbaijan (i.e., outside the area of operations), the LORA system enabled radically more precise targeting.[398] Nevertheless, the use of long-distance ballistic missiles was limited on both sides, most likely due to the risk of escalating the conflict beyond the area of operations and the two actors immediately concerned.[399]

The use of special operations forces for deep penetration behind enemy lines was another important component of Azerbaijan's deep battle. Teams of special forces units advanced

---

396 Ridvan Bari Urcosta, "Drones in the Nagorno-Karabakh," *Small Wars Journal*, October 23, 2020.

397 Heiko Borchert, Torben Schütz, Joseph Verbovszky, *Beware the Hype: What Military Conflicts in Ukraine, Syria, Libya, and Nagorno-Karabakh (Don't) Tell Us About the Future of War*, Hamburg: Defense AI Observatory, 2021.

398 Jack Watling and Sidharth Kaushal, "The Democratisation of Precision Strike in the Nagorno-Karabakh Conflict," *RUSI Commentary*, October 22, 2020.

399 Shaan Shaikh and Wes Rumbaugh, "The Air and Missile War in Nagorno-Karabakh: Lessons for the Future of Strike and Defense," *CSIS Critical Questions*, December 8, 2020.

ahead of the main force, securing key terrain along the route of advance, and were able to provide target locations for indirect artillery strikes. They were also capable of closing or disturbing supply routes to several Armenian defensive positions in the occupied lands, which were sometimes abandoned without the need for heavy and costly ground assaults. Special forces also played a crucial role in the assault on Shusha, utilizing unguarded and seemingly impassable mountainous terrain around the city in their advance.[400]

Azerbaijan's operational success has frequently been attributed to the very substantial support offered by its principal ally, Türkiye (a NATO member state with a formidable and battle-hardened military apparatus). Indeed, the tactics and utilization of capabilities displayed by Azerbaijan during the war were in some ways similar to those employed by Türkiye in its operations in Syria and Libya. Prior to the onset of the Second Karabakh War, Türkiye and Azerbaijan had conducted a large number of joint military exercises. Türkiye supplied Azerbaijan with many of the key technological capabilities employed during the war and engaged considerably with Azerbaijani forces through advisors and training. It seems likely that Turkish officers provided active operational and tactical advice to Azerbaijani forces before and perhaps during the war.[401] Owing in large part to Turkish training, Azerbaijan had built a military in 2020 that was orders of

---

[400] Ron Synovitz, "Technology, Tactics, and Turkish Advice Lead Azerbaijan to Victory in Nagorno-Karabakh," *RFE/RL*, November 13, 2020; John Spencer and Harshana Ghoorhoo, "The Battle of Shusha City and the Missed Lessons of the 2020 Nagorno-Karabah War," *Modern War Institute*, July 14, 2021.

[401] Edward J. Erickson, "The 44-Day War in Nagorno-Karabakh: Turkish Drone Success or Operational Art?."

magnitude improved compared to the disorganized forces it had sent to battle in the First Karabakh War.

However, the successes of the Azerbaijani side in this conflict cannot only be attributed to the considerable modernization, reorganization, and external support to the Azerbaijani military. Equally important is that the Armenian side lacked the means to counter the decisive advantages of Azerbaijan's deep battle. In large part, this reflects a failure or an inability to address the military imbalance, which had increasingly tilted toward Azerbaijan ever since the conclusion of the First Karabakh War in 1994. Some have attributed this failure to Armenian complacency following Yerevan's victory in the First Karabakh War, which in turn provided a disincentive to adapt to new realities by modernizing Armenia's armed forces.[402] However, it is simultaneously difficult to see how Armenia could have kept an equal pace with Azerbaijan even had it been motivated to do so, given the enormous discrepancy in resources between the two countries. With the benefit of hindsight, it could be argued that Armenia's only realistic option for avoiding military defeat in 2020 would have been to genuinely seek a political solution to the conflict in the interim, which would have required it to compromise more than Azerbaijan but could have perhaps avoided the losses it ended up incurring on both the battlefield and at the negotiating table.

In particular, the 2016 four-day war featured a foreboding utilization of new technologies and tactics by the Azerbaijani side, which ought to have rang alarm bells in Yerevan.[403] Instead, the

---

402 Alexander Stronell, "Learning the Lessons of Nagorno-Karabakh the Russian Way," *International Institute of Strategic Studies*, March 10, 2021.

403 Michael A. Reynolds, "Confidence and Catastrophe: Armenia and the Second Nagorno-Karabakh War," *War on the Rocks*, January 11, 2021.

Armenian side seems to have trusted the weaponry delivered from Russia, its well-entrenched defensive positions across Karabakh, the region's mountainous terrain, as well as its own investments into Russian long-range missile and rocket systems (including Iskander, Scud, and Smerch) capable of striking Azerbaijani territory, to function as a sufficient deterrent against Azerbaijani attempts to retake the region. The perhaps most glaring technological disadvantage was Armenia's air defense capabilities. Whereas Armenian forces possessed advanced air defense systems in the form of Russian S-300, Pantsir 1, and Buk-M1, the ease with which these systems were overcome has been attributed to the failure to upgrade the radars on these systems, making them apt at detecting and targeting fast-moving aircraft but not small, slow-flying UAVs. Moreover, they lacked the capacity for plot-fusion (i.e., the integration of data from various radars) to detect small objects such as modern UAVs—a capability lacking in export versions of these systems.[404] The apparent inability of, particularly, the Armenian Pantsirs to detect UAVs has been attributed to the possible use of the Turkish KORAL electronic warfare (EW) system to jam Armenian air defense systems, allowing them to be destroyed with little risk of detection.[405] Although the Armenian side possessed Russian Repellent EW systems, which should have been capable of disabling UAVs, these were not put to effect or did not function and were destroyed.[406] Towards the end of the war, Russia nevertheless may have applied the more powerful

---

[404] Gustav Gressel, "Military Lessons from Nagorno-Karabakh: Reason for Europe to Worry," *European Council on Foreign Relations*, November 24, 2020.

[405] John Antal, *7 Seconds to Die: A Military Analysis of the Second Nagorno-Karabakh War and the Future of Warfighting*, Havertown & Oxford: Casemate Publishers, 2022; Uzi Rubin, "The Second Nagorno-Karabakh War: A Milestone in Military Affairs."

[406] Uzi Rubin, "The Second Nagorno-Karabakh War: A Milestone in Military Affairs."

Krasukha EW system, based at the Gyumri military base, to down several TB2s dispatched deep into the territory of Armenia.[407]

Thus, the Armenian side had no efficient means for countering the Azerbaijani UAVs and loitering munitions. This includes EW capabilities used for this purpose, which is otherwise considered the most efficient countermeasure against UAVs.[408] Moreover, Armenian forces were scattered, with only two of its five army corps deployed facing what was then the line of contact with Azerbaijan; two facing the Azerbaijani exclave of Nakhchivan, and the final one facing Türkiye—a clear disadvantage when it came to organizing a coordinated defense against the Azerbaijani advances.[409]

General Lessons

Several analysts have pointed to general military lessons that can be extrapolated from the Second Karabakh War. In light of the particular advantages gained by the Azerbaijani side through its use of UAVs, loitering munitions, and high-precision ballistic missiles, the war epitomizes the "democratization of precision strike."[410] This refers to the fact that a state like Azerbaijan—which regardless of the wealth accrued through the export of hydrocarbons is still a small country with limited financial resources—proved capable of acquiring and exercising precision

---

407 Gustav Gressel, "Military Lessons from Nagorno-Karabakh: Reason for Europe to Worry."

408 Zachary Kallenborn, "Drones Are Proving to Have a Destabilizing Effect, Which Is Why Counter-Drone Systems Should Be a Key Part of US Military Aid to Partners," *Modern War Institute*, December 9, 2020.

409 Edward J. Erickson, "The 44-Day War in Nagorno-Karabakh: Turkish Drone Success or Operational Art?."

410 Jack Watling and Sidharth Kaushal, "The Democratisation of Precision Strike in the Nagorno-Karabakh Conflict."

strike capability across the operational area, thus employing a deep battle operational concept. This is telling of the fact that advanced precision strike capabilities are both relatively cheap and accessible in the contemporary conflict environment and are thus not reserved for major powers. Indeed, simpler capabilities of this kind are not even exclusive to states, demonstrated by the fact that non-state actors such as ISIS did utilize cheap, off-the-shelf UAVs to carry explosives—a simple loitering munition. We can thus expect these capabilities to come into play across a range of future conflicts that will take place both between and within states.

However, as discussed above, technological capabilities count for little on their own. The real advantages of the Azerbaijani side came not from utilizing their technological edge, but from their ability to combine various capabilities at their disposal—armor, artillery, air superiority, and precision strikes—to produce several multiple dilemmas for the Armenian side. This enabled the isolation of defensive positions denying them supplies and fire support, suppression of air defenses, and eventually the collapse of the defending forces.[411] This is far from a new practice of warfare; rather, it is an example of the advantage accrued through a higher accessibility and proficiency in combined arms warfare relative to the opponent. However, the Second Karabakh War does underline the possibilities offered by new technologies to integrate sensors and precise fire.

Yet, the Second Karabakh War should not be considered an overly generalizable example of the advantages of UAVs. Their efficiency in this war hinged to a very large extent on deficien-

---

411   Gustav Gressel, "Military Lessons from Nagorno-Karabakh: Reason for Europe to Worry."

cies in Armenia's air defenses. Although saturated attacks with UAVs and loitering munitions indeed pose a difficult challenge, the picture would potentially be different against an opponent possessing a more robust network of air defense and EW systems, such as Russia or China.[412] As a case in point, although Russia initially suffered significant losses due to Ukraine's employment of UAVs during the full-scale invasion in 2022, the situation has changed as Russia has improved its employment of countermeasures along the frontline. Indeed, UAVs have become a highly disposable resource in the war—according to one estimate, equipment losses on the Ukrainian side could amount to 10,000 UAVs per month.[413]

Reverberations

International attention to the Second Karabakh War and its aftermath was quickly overshadowed by Russia's buildup for and execution of its "special military operation" in February 2022. As of mid-2025, that war had already gone through several phases of maneuver and static attrition and had produced very substantial losses on both sides. Russia's war in Ukraine will undoubtedly be the defining geopolitical event for Western security and military analysis in decades to come, and the primary example from which to draw lessons and experiences on contemporary and future warfare. In this perspective, and in retrospect, the relatively short Second Karabakh War can be considered a foreboding demon-

---

412 Michael Kofman, "A Look at the Military Lessons of the Nagorno-Karabakh Conflict," *Russia Matters, Belfer Center for Science and International Affairs*, December 14, 2020.
413 Jack Watling and Nick Reynolds, "Meatgrinder: Russian Tactics in the Second Year of Its Invasion of Ukraine," *RUSI*, May 19, 2023.

stration of the real possibility of large-scale interstate war in Europe and its periphery. Moreover, several observations from the Second Karabakh War are valid for, and likely in part inspired, Ukraine's successful defensive operation, particularly during the first months of the renewed conflict.[414] As part of its preparations, Ukraine had purchased and manufactured a wide range of UAVs, from Turkish TB2s to small and cheap systems. Integrated with the overall operational concept, these systems performed both reconnaissance and strike roles, providing precisely the airpower dimension and battlefield situational awareness that helped Ukraine cripple Russia's stymied advance on Kyiv, induce serious attrition to Russian logistics, and sink the Moskva missile cruiser. Both Ukraine and Russia have made extensive use of UAVs throughout the war.

The Second Karabakh War also has potential effects on other unresolved conflicts in the post-Soviet space and beyond. Particularly Abkhazia and South Ossetia in Georgia share a background and composition that is at least comparable to the conflict over Karabakh. Azerbaijan's victory could be taken to demonstrate that military solutions to these conflicts—as risky and costly as they may be—should not be ruled out since they provide an additional point of leverage in dealings with separatist regions and their external patrons, in this case Russia, in addition to other political and economic means. Yet Georgia's extremely exposed geographical location became particularly salient during the Second Karabakh War. The country directly borders both Azerbaijan and Armenia, as well as the two main external players in the conflict, Türkiye and Russia. Especially since Geor-

---

[414] Yuri Lapaiev, "Ukraine Looks for Applicable Lessons in Latest Karabakh War," *Eurasia Daily Monitor*, November 9, 2020.

gian territory constitutes the only land route connecting Russia with Armenia, a Russian decision to more directly intervene in support of Armenia could have drawn Georgia into the conflict. The deployment of a peacekeeping contingent in parts of the former NKAO as part of the tripartite agreement that ended the war contributed even further to the vital Russian military interests encircling Georgia until it was withdrawn in the first half of 2024. Russia's war in Ukraine has further exacerbated Georgia's predicament, and the country's government has sought to keep a very low profile in relation to condemning the Kremlin's actions, the issue of (not) imposing sanctions, and the question of military support for Ukraine mobilized by its Western partners, much to the resentment of Georgia's political opposition.

For the separatist regions located in Georgia and Moldova, as well as those in Ukraine, the Second Karabakh War serves as a stark reminder that they are expendable from the Russian perspective. Although Armenia is in a nominally close alliance with Russia as a strategic partner and a member of the Russia-led Collective Security Treaty Organization (CSTO), Russia did not come to Armenia's defense against Azerbaijan on the grounds that Armenia was not defending its sovereign territory and thus Moscow had no cause to come to Yerevan's aid. Judging from Russia's conduct during the Second Karabakh War as well as the terms of the tripartite agreement that ended it, Moscow was prepared to accept Azerbaijan's regaining of control over Karabakh, provided that the war did not spill over into Armenian territory and Russia could retain a substantial element of control and influence over the subsequent settlement process, which actually allowed the deployment of Russian troops ("peacekeepers") in the Lachin corridor and Armenian-controlled parts of the former NKAO (until, that is, it didn't). The key lesson for other separatist authorities is, therefore, that Russia will support them only as long as this support is perceived in Moscow as being politically expedient. This is another factor that could potentially affect dynamics in other conflicts, since it could incentivize separatist authorities to raise the stakes for Moscow under particular circumstances, for example through provocative actions in Georgia.

Finally, Russia's preoccupation with its war in Ukraine has served to alter the dynamics also between Azerbaijan and Armenia in the aftermath of the Second Karabakh War. Yerevan's disappointment with the lack of support from its CSTO ally is palpable, with Armenia taking steps to move away from the Russian orbit by reaching out to the EU (via France) and the United States (an early indication of Armenia's shift was its refusal to host CSTO exercises in January 2023). Long before Russia's April 2024 agreement with Azerbaijan to withdraw its "peacekeeping" contingent operating in parts of the former NKAO, Russian troops had proven incapable of fulfilling their duties and had come under increasing criticism from both Armenia and Azerbaijan. Thus, what initially appeared to be a Russian success in securing continued influence over both states and their interactions increasingly proved to be a liability. Azerbaijan, emboldened by its victory in 2020 and Russia's degraded capability to project power in the South Caucasus, has employed aggressive means to pressure Armenia to fully implement the tripartite agreement and agree to border delimitations on Azerbaijan's terms. These have included several military incursions into Armenia, which have led to hundreds of casualties. Thus, the aftermath of the

Second Karabakh War is still very much ongoing. While negotiations facilitated by Russia, the U.S., and the EU have resulted in some promising progress, renewed hostilities between the parties remains a distinct possibility.

Conclusions

One of the main military takeaways from the Second Karabakh War is the technology-enabled lethality of the modern battlefield. The experience reconfirms the well-known advantages of successfully combining arms and integrating effects, as well as the devastating consequences of failure to dimensionalize tactics, capabilities, and materiel relative to the opponent. In this case, the role of UAVs in Azerbaijan's victory has frequently been exaggerated or erroneously singled out as the key to its wartime success. Indeed, Azerbaijan's investment in these novel capabilities provided a significant advantage in the form of air power, thus adding an additional dimension to its tactical options. Nevertheless, the decisive factor was Azerbaijan's ability to integrate this dimension with maneuver and artillery elements, as well as special forces units, in frontal assaults as well as in depth.

Equally important is the gap that was present in Armenian defenses, which allowed the full utilization of UAV capabilities. The single most important vulnerability in this regard was Armenia's air defenses, insufficiently adapted and integrated to counter the threat presented by UAVs. Neither did Armenian forces possess sufficient electronic warfare capabilities to counter the threat. Should Azerbaijan have relied on regular fighter aircraft to establish air superiority, the outcome might well have been different (to its credit, Azerbaijan realized this and found an innovative solution to overcome the risk). For these reasons, the experiences of the Second Karabakh War should be interpreted carefully. The evolution in UAVs and loitering munitions certainly present new opportunities and challenges for militaries by providing cheap and accessible access to airpower, which is simultaneously flexible in the sense that these systems can be directly integrated with land forces, even at lower tactical levels. However, they are no panacea in modern warfighting. Countermeasures in the form of air defenses, electronic warfare, and tactical solutions such as dispersion and passive defenses, are also under rapid development and employment.

Regarding broader military lessons of the Second Karabakh War, Azerbaijan's victory underlines that military options remain a potential solution to other unresolved conflicts. This reminder has potential implications for all actors involved, and will likely affect decisions on force structure, arms purchases, and military planning in the years to come—not just in the former Soviet space and other parts of Europe, but farther afield.

THE GEOPOLITICAL CAUSES AND CONSEQUENCES OF THE SECOND KARABAKH WAR

Armenian Tragedy, Azerbaijani Vindication, and Prospects for Peace

Damjan Krnjević Mišković

Through a sophisticated combination of strategic foresight, limited war objectives, operational artistry, active diplomacy, and impeccable geopolitical timing, Azerbaijan accomplished a feat that no other state anywhere in the world has been able to achieve since the end of the Cold War: the full restoration of its territorial integrity executed without the organized commission of grievous atrocities or similar defilements. Addressing his nation from liberated Shusha in August 2021, Azerbaijan's president called the Second Karabakh War a "victory is unique in our history."[415] In contrast, Armenia's prime minister has called the Second Karabakh War a "national tragedy" on several important

---
415   Ilham Aliyev, "Speech at the Opening of Vagif Poetry Days in Shusha," August 30, 2021.

public occasions, including during an Address to the Nation in December 2020.[416] Later in this chapter, we will have occasion to build upon these insightful self-reflections, with reference to Aristotle's writings on tragedy.

First, it seems important to acknowledge the point that in some decision-making and analytical circles, this war of restoration was portrayed as an act of aggression[417] that intruded against what its proponents call the "rules-based liberal international order." But the military actions of a state to retake what is universally acknowledged to be its own sovereign territories are undeserving of opprobrium. Nevertheless, fantastic interpretations were put forward that the war was somehow in violation of international law.[418] Yet given the official political position of every single sovereign state, including now Armenia itself (as indicated in several of Pashinyan's postwar public statements, including one reproduced later in this chapter), it is clear that the territories formerly occupied by Armenian forces are in fact indisputably Azerbaijani lands. It thus seems difficult to understand on what reasonable basis such claims continue to be made, much less taken seriously. Moreover, it should go without saying that the salience of the foregoing has only grown stronger since the onset of the

---

416 Nikol Pashinyan, "'The Tragedy Should Not Kill Us; Instead It Should Save Us,' PM Addresses the Nation," December 19, 2020.

417 Not only the 2020 war but also its two-part epilogue: the 19-20 September 2023 "antiterrorist measure" and the 15 October 2023 raising of the Azerbaijani flag in liberated Khankendi. Ilham Aliyev conducted this flag-raising ceremony in person, which took place on the 20th anniversary of his election as President of Azerbaijan.

418 See Tom Ruys and Felipe Rodriguez Silvestre, "The Nagorno-Karabakh Conflict and the Exercise of 'Self-Defense' to Recover Occupied Land," *Just Security*, November 10, 2020. A convincing refutation of such farrago is provided by Dapo Akande and Antonios Tzanakopoulos, "Use of Force in Self-Defence to Recover Occupied Territory: When Is It Permissible?," *Blog of the European Journal of International Law*, November 18, 2020. Cf. *Chiragov and Others v. Armenia* [GC], no. 13216/05, ECHR 2015, paragraphs 96, 170, 180, 186, and so on. For a general primer, see, e.g., Heiko Kruger, *The Nagorno-Karabakh Conflict: A Legal Analysis*, Berlin: Springer, 2010, and Javid Gadirov, "International Law and the Karabakh Question," in Fariz Ismailzade and Damjan Krnjević Mišković, eds., *Liberated Karabakh: Policy Perspectives by the ADA University Community*, ADA University Press, 2021, pp. 33-49.

present stage in the conflict over Ukraine, when the supremacy of the cornerstone concepts of sovereignty and territorial integrity was reasserted, in both speech and deed, by people belonging to the very same circles. Perhaps it is this fact that explains, at least in part, the more active role played by Western interests in facilitating and supporting the ongoing peace process between Armenia and Azerbaijan on the basis of the five key principles as outlined publicly by Azerbaijan's foreign minister, Jeyhun Bayramov, in March 2022 during a speech at the Antalya Diplomacy Forum.[419]

The foregoing leads us to ask the question that lies at the heart of the present inquiry: what caused the Second Karabakh War to start and end as it did? In other words, what were the proximate affronts and provocations, as well as the immediate grounds, that led to the effective cessation of a negotiation process, and how did this bear upon Azerbaijan's victory and Armenia's defeat?[420] The foregoing can be reformulated in a more generalized manner thusly: why did the flow of the particular political events at issue, as experienced by both belligerents and onlookers, happen as it did and not otherwise? What judgments and miscalculations informed the thoughts and actions of decisionmakers and does an examination of these help us determine what Thucydides called the "truest" reason or cause (*prophasis*) of the war (Thuc. I.22.4)?

To delve fruitfully into such and similar questions requires that we begin with a brief, preliminary examination of the nature of geopolitics. From this will emerge a consideration of the pres-

---

[419] The five principles were made public by Azerbaijan's Ministry of Foreign Affairs (Press Service, no. 117/22): https://www.mfa.gov.az/en/news/no11722.

[420] Azerbaijan also chose its moment of execution impeccably: our companion chapter to this book examines in more detail the "perfect timing" of the Second Karabakh War by providing a survey of contemporaneous external developments and the postures and preoccupations of relevant foreign actors.

ent and novel state of international relations, which in turn will enable us to uncover both the contours of an emerging order in the Silk Road region[421] and the leverage held by one of the states most responsible for its advent, namely Azerbaijan. Thus equipped, we shall be in a better position to examine more directly what sorts of considerations animated the speeches and deeds of the Second Karabakh War's protagonists, how these relate to its outcome, and what boons and dangers lie ahead now that the guns have fallen silent.

A Keystone State Emerges in a G-Zero World

Geopolitics consists of more or less prudential exercises in acceptable exceptions by major powers conducive to the continued operation of an international system. If a given international system precludes or disallows such exercises of acceptable exception—defined as a succession of power maneuvers understood in the context of the need to maintain equilibrium and legitimacy, operating according to a logic of restraint and proportioned reciprocity—it is either too rigid and hence ripe for renovation, or too amorphous and thus not really a system.

Our current global condition is such that, paradoxically,

---

[421] The area of the Silk Road region is defined "loosely" in "Editorial Statement," *Baku Dialogues* 4, no. 1, Fall 2020, p. 7 in the following manner: "the geographic space looking west past Anatolia to the warm seas beyond; north across the Caspian towards the Great Plain and the Great Steppe; east to the peaks of the Altai and the arid sands of the Taklamakan; and south towards the Hindu Kush and the Indus valley, looping down around in the direction of the Persian Gulf and across the Fertile Crescent." We have argued in favor of this term and examined the deficiencies of alternative terms, including "Greater Central Asia," "Inner Asia," "Middle Asia," "Caspian Basin," "Caspian Sea Region," "South Caucasus and Central Asia," and, of course, "Central" or "Core Eurasia" (or, simply, "Eurasia") in Damjan Krnjević Mišković, "On Some Conceptual Advantages of the Term 'Silk Road Region': Heralding Geopolitical and Geo-Economic Emancipation," *Baku Dialogues* 6, no. 4, Summer 2023, pp. 20-27 and Damjan Krnjević Mišković, "The Rise of the Silk Road Region," *Orbis* 67, no. 3, Summer 2023, pp. 332-337.

aspects of both are present. A generation or so ago, Thomas M. Franck wrote that "in the international system, rules are not enforced and yet they are mostly obeyed."[422] Today, it would be more accurate to say that rules are not enforced and increasingly disobeyed—or, to put it in terms more familiar to international legal scholars: the applicable scope of *jus cogens*, out of which follow the *obligato erga omnes*, is narrowing in practice.

The gravity of the present condition is further compounded by the ironic fact that connectivity is becoming a catalyst for further dividing our world: the specter of technological bifurcation hangs precariously over a transforming international system—whether this is called "decoupling" or "de-risking" or "friend-shoring" is not of paramount importance: what needs to be understood is that all these are shorthand for policies designed to enshrine politically-motivated trade blocs (including increasing tariff rates), which in turn speaks to the re-politicization of economic decision making and the increase in frequency of the use of economic coercion tools (e.g., sanctions). This helps to explain the conceptual onset of a process of de-globalization due, *inter alia*, to the rapid escalation of Sino-American tensions, which to a great extent is predicated on a disagreement not only about the rules of the game, but also on a more fundamental question: who gets to set and enforce the rules (and who doesn't)? All this has become a recipe for skyrocketing unpredictability and increased instability in a world characterized, in part, by the absence of sufficiently acknowledged leadership.

The foregoing description of our present global predicament confirms the observation made by Ian Bremmer and Nouriel

---

[422] Thomas M. Franck, *The Power of Legitimacy Among Nations*, Oxford: Oxford University Press, 1990, p. 3.

Roubini that "we are now living in a G-Zero world," which they define as "one in which no single country or bloc of countries has the political and economic leverage—or the will—to drive a truly international agenda."[423]

A telling illustration of the veracity of the G-Zero world paradigm is what Vasif Huseynov has called the "geopolitical heterogeneity"[424] of the contemporary Silk Road region. Nikolas Gvosdev has described "this strategic area" in the following manner: it "interlinks not only the world's two most critically important regions (the Euro-Atlantic and Indo-Pacific basins), but also directly interconnects South Asia, the Middle East, and the Eurasian space with each other. […] In geostrategic terms, this region is the geopolitical hinge where the North Atlantic Treaty Organization meets the Shanghai Cooperation Organization, and where the Belt and Road Initiative connects with the wider European neighborhood and the European Union itself."[425] The predominant reality in that part of the world today consists of a combination of formal treaties and informal understandings in which no single power dominates, equilibrium (but not necessarily equidistance) is maintained, and a general balance is kept.

At some point between the launch of the Belt and Road

---

423 Ian Bremmer and Nouriel Roubini, "A G-Zero World," *Foreign Affairs* 90, no. 2, March/April 2011, p. 2. Note that, more or less contemporaneously, Nader Mousavizadeh popularized his "archipelago world" concept in various publications, which is effectually synonymous with the G-Zero world one. His first attempt was made in 2008: "a world of parts is emerging—of states drifting farther away from each other into a global archipelago of interests and values; and that in an archipelago world, appeals to freedom, democracy and human rights must compete with aims of stability, resource security and the projection of national power." See Nader Mousavizadeh, "How to Navigate the New Global Archipelago," *The Times*, August 29, 2008. In 2023, the Foreign Editor of the *Financial Times* coined the term the "*à la carte* world," contrasting it to its predecessor, the "*prix fixe* world." This, too, is a variant on the concept of a G-Zero world. See Alec Russell, "The À La Carte World: Our New Geopolitical Order," *Financial Times*, August 21, 2023.

424 Vasif Huseynov, "Vicious Circle of the South Caucasus: Intra-Regional Conflicts and Geopolitical Heterogeneity," *Caucasus Strategic Perspectives* 1 no. 1, Summer 2020, p. 128.

425 Nikolas K. Gvosdev, "Geopolitical Keystone: Azerbaijan and the Global Position of the Silk Road Region," *Baku Dialogues* 4, no. 1, Fall 2020, pp. 26, 27.

Initiative in September 2013 and the onset of the Second Karabakh War, the Silk Road region began to be seen increasingly as being located at a significant political and economic crossroads between various geographies, an important intercessor between major powers, and a hard-to-avoid "gateway between different blocks of states, regional associations, and civilizational groupings."[426] The resulting vision can be described thusly: regionally-driven economic connectivity priorities is on the way in; outside power agenda-setting is on the way out. Some outsider powers are seeing their relative power decline whilst others are seeing an increase. In the aggregate, the power of outsiders is being reduced overall. This, in turn, suggests that the Silk Road region is now on the cusp to come into its own as a distinct, autonomous, and emancipated subject of international relations (as opposed to remaining an object of great power competition—a geography to be won and lost by others) as it continues to move cogently and deliberately in the direction of establishing sturdier contours of a fledgling regional order by building upon classical balance-of-power principles applied toward major outside powers.

An important prerequisite for the development of such a regional order is the presence of a number of states of substantially equal strength, which can enable the Silk Road region to maintain and possibly deepen its own balance of power system, notwithstanding the G-Zero world paradigm. This seems to be well on its way to being successfully executed, for at least five reasons. *First*, the unique complexities involved in realizing the potential of connectivity—for example, of transporting hydrocarbons and other natural resources to market, as well as the

---

[426] Nikolas K. Gvosdev, "Keystone States: A New Category of Power," *Horizons* no. 5, Autumn 2015, p. 105.

infrastructure provisions necessary to facilitate trade—require a region-specific type of cooperation and compromise. *Second*, no state belonging to the region is strong enough to dominate the others, economically or otherwise, which encourages equilibrium. *Third*, no state in the region is weak enough to succumb to crude attempts at all-out domination without others aligning to significantly limit the depth and scope of said attempt. *Fourth*, no major outside power truly behaves hegemonically, notwithstanding latent (or not so latent) desires or ambitions.

The *fifth* reason is perhaps the most interesting: the burgeoning set of arrangements characterizing the Silk Road region appear on their way to being anchored by what Giovanni Botero was the first to call "middle powers." In his 1589 work titled *The Reason of State*, he defined these as states that have "sufficient force [or strength, *forze*] and authority to stand on [their] own without the need of help [or rescue, *soccorso*] from others."[427] In Botero's telling, leaders of middle powers tend to be acutely aware of the dexterity required to maintain security and project influence in a prudential manner beyond their immediate borders; and, *because* of that, middle powers are apt to have facility in promoting trade and connectivity with their neighbors and their neighbors' neighbors.

Unquestionably, Azerbaijan is one such middle power: a "strategic hub by virtue of being situated at a critical geographical fulcrum point of rapidly expanding transport and communi-

---

[427] Giovanni Botero, Della Ragion di Stato I:2. Cf. Carlsten Holbraad, Middle Powers in International Politics, London: Macmillan Press, 1984, pp. 10-44; see also Gabriele Abbondanza, "Middle Powers and Great Powers through History: The Concept from Ancient Times to the Present Day." History of Political Thought 41, no. 3, 2020, pp. 397-418.

cation infrastructure."[428] This echoes Zbigniew Brzezinski's 1997 description of Azerbaijan as the "cork in the bottle containing the riches of the Caspian Sea basin and Central Asia."[429] After its victory in the Second Karabakh War and the onset of the present stage in the conflict over Ukraine, Azerbaijan even became an indispensable country for the advancement of the strategic energy and connectivity ambitions of all the major powers that surround the Silk Road region—Western and non-Western alike. This speaks to the point that Azerbaijan is a rare contemporary example of successful national statecraft: of leadership and success, foresight and perseverance, modernization and the consolidation of power; it is all the more impressive given that just thirty years ago the country was widely considered to be a failing or even failed state.[430]

The Silk Road region boasts at least two other such middle powers: Kazakhstan and Uzbekistan. Gvosdev and others have identified these sorts of Boteran middle powers as "keystone states" to denote the significant (and growing) strategic leverage they hold in giving coherence to, as well as orienting the direction

---

428 Gregory Gleason, "Grand Strategy Along the Silk Road: The Pivotal Role of Keystone States," *Baku Dialogues* 4, no. 2, Winter 2020-2021, p. 160.

429 Zbigniew Brzezinski, *The Grand Chessboard: American Primacy and Its Geostrategic Imperatives*, New York: Basic Books, 1997, p. 46. His next sentence reinforces the point: "the independence of the Central Asian states can be rendered nearly meaningless if Azerbaijan becomes fully subordinated to Moscow's control"—or that of any other great or major power, for that matter.

430 There are several excellent book-length accounts of Azerbaijan's time as a failing state, which corresponds roughly to the period that immediately followed the forced retirement of Heydar Aliyev from the posts of Full Member of the Politburo of the Communist Party of the Soviet Union and First Deputy Premier of the Soviet Union in October 1987 and his return to power in Azerbaijan in June 1993. These include Tadeusz Swietochowski, *Russia and Azerbaijan: A Borderland in Transition*, New York: Columbia University Press, 1995; Thomas Goltz, *Azerbaijan Diary*, Armonk, NY: M.E. Sharpe, 1998; Svante E. Cornell, *Azerbaijan Since Independence*, Armonk, NY: M.E. Sharpe, 2011; and Tadeusz Swietochowski, *Azerbaijan: Legacies of the Past and the Trials of Independence*, London: Routledge, 2015.

of, a regional order.[431] Unsurprisingly, no scholar or practitioner has suggested anything similar with regards to Armenia. Indeed, we would be hard-pressed to dispute the applicability of Botero's definition of a small state to Armenia (that is, one that "cannot be maintained by itself, but needs the protection and support of others"[432]). In the case of Yerevan, those "others" are Moscow and Tehran: Armenia is at once an entrenched 'satellite (or vassal) of Russia and ally of Iran' (this is Michael Doran's phrase) and, it now seems, an object of major power rivalry that, ironically, has no realistic way of not remaining firmly within the Russian sphere of influence—notwithstanding recent indications of its present government's desire to do so and the entreaties of Western powers like France and the United States.

Keystone States and the Weight of 2008

Thus equipped, we may now add the following codicil to the definition of geopolitics provided earlier in this chapter: Regional orders that build upon classic geopolitical balance-of-power prin-

---

431 The term "keystone states" was introduced in Nikolas K. Gvosdev, "Keystone States," pp. 104-120. However, in his 1998 U.S. Independence Day address at the U.S. Embassy in Baku, then-U.S. Ambassador to Azerbaijan Stanley Escudero called Azerbaijan the "keystone country" and reportedly used the term frequently. This later evolved into the term "Caspian keystone." See Elin Suleymanov, "Azerbaijan: The Wider Black Sea's Caspian Keystone," in Ronald D. Asmus (ed), *Next Steps in Forging a Euroatlantic Strategy for the Wider Black Sea*, Washington, DC: The German Marshall Fund of the United States, 2006, pp. 175-183. The reference to Escudero's speech is on p. 179. Two years later, it was appropriated, seemingly without attribution, by Elkhan Nuriyev, the founding director of the now-defunct Center for Strategic Studies (SAM), who used it on several occasions. See Elkhan Nuriyev, "Azerbaijan and the New Geopolitics of Eurasia: Foreign Policy Strategies, Caspian Energy Security, and Great Power Politics," lecture delivered to the Kennan Institute at the Woodrow Wilson International Center for Scholars, October 14, 2008, https://www.wilsoncenter.org/event/azerbaijan-and-the-new-geopolitics-eurasia-foreign-policy-strategies-caspian-energy-security. For a discussion of the contemporary scholarly understanding of "middle power" and its inapplicability to the three keystone states of the Silk Road region, see Damjan Krnjević Mišković, "Superseding Middle Power Theory with the Keystone Concept: The Persuasive Case of Azerbaijan and the Silk Road Region," *Caucasus Strategic Perspectives*, Special issue no. 1 (February 2024), pp. 31-65.

432 Botero, *Della Ragion di Stato* I:2.

ciples can gain a foothold in a G-Zero world in the event they can be held together by keystone states. This suggests that keystone states are coming to serve as trusted interlocutors, reliable intermediaries, and "critical mediators" between what Western scholars call "status quo powers and revisionists."[433] This integrative power is supplemented by the fact that "an effective keystone state can serve as a pressure-release valve in the international system, particularly as the transition to conditions of non-polarity continues, by acting as a buffer and reducing the potential for conflict between major power centers."[434] Non-polarity, here, is to be understood as an active approach in which constant engagement with all the major stakeholders is a *sine qua non*. Non-polarity recognizes that in conditions of a G-Zero world no one power can establish and guarantee absolute security or impose a uniform set of preferences—and that to align exclusively with one major power increases, rather than reduces, insecurity by incentivizing other powers to then take action detrimental to one's national interests.[435]

The onset of the G-Zero world is traceable back to the political decision by a number of Western countries to recognize (and champion) the unilateral declaration of independence of the ethnic-Albanian secessionist authorities of the Serbian province of Kosovo and Metohija on 17 February 2008. Serbia's then-foreign minister, Vuk Jeremić, characterized what was at stake succinctly in the *New York Times*:

---

[433] Gleason, "Grand Strategy," pp. 148, 156.
[434] Gvosdev, "Keystone States," p. 120.
[435] Gvosdev, "Geopolitical Keystone," p. 31.

Recognizing the unilateral declaration of Kosovo's independence from Serbia legitimizes the doctrine of [outsiders] imposing solutions to ethnic conflicts. It legitimizes the act of unilateral secession by a provincial or other non-state actor. It transforms the right to self-determination into an avowed right to independence. It legitimizes the forced partition of internationally recognized, sovereign states. It violates the commitment to the peaceful and consensual resolution of disputes in Europe. It supplies any ethnic or religious group that has a grievance against its capital with a playbook on how to achieve its ends. It even resurrects the discredited cold-war doctrine of limited sovereignty. [...] Recognizing Kosovo means saying, in effect, that Serbian democracy must be punished because a tyrant—one who committed heinous deeds against the Kosovo Albanians in the 1990s—was left unpunished. Such misplaced revenge may make some feel better, but it will make the international system feel much worse. [...] The legitimacy of the international system hangs in the balance.[436]

The onset of the G-Zero world was further made manifest over a period of only forty days that began in August 2008 with the Russo-Georgian conflict and the Kremlin's correct judgment that the West could not make a credible attempt to prevent or

---

[436] Vuk Jeremic, "One Nation, Indivisible," *New York Times*, February 27, 2008. At the time of writing, I was serving as Senior Adviser and Chief Speechwriter to the Foreign Minister of Serbia and had a hand in writing this op-ed.

reverse it, as that would mean going directly to war with Russia;[437] the second and last stage of the onset of the G-Zero world came not even two months later, when Lehman Brothers went into bankruptcy. This last rapidly cascaded into a collapse of Western stock markets and the onset of a global financial recession. This forty-day period in 2008 thus represents the moment in which the credibility of the West cracked on two critical fronts: great power politics and international economics. This, in turn, triggered the serious calling into question of the West's claim to primacy in global leadership—what Jeremić had termed the "legitimacy of the international system"—which rested not insignificantly on predictability, prosperity, and a "monopoly on patronage."[438]

At least two facts serve to illustrate the weight of the 2008 moment. *First*, remedial efforts to overcome the effect of the economic crash could not have succeeded without significant non-Western participation—an unprecedented turn of events. *Second*, the criteria for membership in the new institutional arrangements that were hastily arranged at the time in response to the West's financial collapse—most notably the establishment of the G20—did not involve having Western-style liberal democracy as a form of government. What mattered most was having cash in one's state coffers, coupled with the willingness to spend it liberally. It

---

[437] This was clearly understood in the White House. See Condoleezza Rice, *No Higher Honor: A Memoir of My Years in Washington*, New York: Crown Publishers, 2011, pp. 668-669: "The session [of the National Security Council] was a bit unruly, with a fair amount of chest beating about the Russians. At one point [National Security Adviser] Steve Hadley intervened, something he rarely did. There was all kind of loose talk about what threats the United States might make. 'I want to ask a question,' he said in his low-key way. 'Are we prepared to go to war with Russia over Georgia?' That quieted the room, and we settled into a more productive conversation of what we could do."

[438] This case is made in Damjan Krnjević Mišković, "Back with a Vengeance: The Return of Rough and Tumble Geopolitics," *Orbis* 65, no. 1, Winter 2021, pp. 118-135. See also Nikolas K. Gvosdev and Damjan Krnjević Mišković, "Great Power Populism," *The National Interest* no. 167, May/June 2020, pp. 39-48. This section draws freely from parts of both essays. Cf. Charles William Maynes, "Squandering Triumph: The West Botched the Post-Cold War World," *Foreign Affairs* 78, no. 1 (Jan/Feb 1999), pp. 15-22.

so happens that there is a sempiternal correlation between a state having readily available funds and the ambitions of its leaders to play an active and influential geopolitical role in geopolitics. After the events of 2008, the field for autonomous, even independent action notwithstanding of Western liberal preferences opened up owing to the lessening of the aforementioned constraints.

From this came to be derived the following strategic takeaway for much of the rest of the world: the West cannot solve international problems by itself anymore—even problems primarily of its own making. At the time, most Western decisionmakers did not grasp the scope of the paradigm shift this triggered, although most everyone else did (including Azerbaijan, Türkiye, and of course Russia, but tragically, as it turns out, not Armenia)—namely, the return of geopolitics.

Entanglement

The Second Karabakh War that began on 27 September 2020 marked the start of what Aristotle famously called the tragic unravelling (*lusis*) or dénouement (Arist. *Poet.* 1455b25-ff and 1460b6-ff) of the conflict between Armenia and Azerbaijan that originated in February 1988.[439] In the intervening decades, the one constant had been the Armenian occupation of about 20 percent of the internationally recognized territory of Azerbaijan: the former Nagorno-Karabakh Autonomous Oblast (NKAO) and its seven surrounding districts (i.e., Kelbajar, Lachin, Gubaldi, Zangilan, Jabrayil, Fuzuli, Agdam). This all changed by

---

[439] "The first bullet released by me in February 1988 was released for the security of the Armenian people." Vitaly Balasanyan, "Dear Compatriots, The First Bullet...," Facebook post, December 1, 2020. (www.facebook.com/412749769529573/posts/874138043390741/?d=n.)

war's end, with Yerevan's effective capitulation being enshrined in the 10 November 2020 tripartite statement signed by President Ilham Aliyev of Azerbaijan, Prime Minister Nikol Pashinyan of Armenia, and President Vladimir Putin of Russia.[440]

We must underline that at no time since it regained its independence did Armenia fully admit to its occupation, in the dual sense that it neither formally recognized the ethnic-Armenian secessionist regime installed in Khankendi,[441] nor did it formally annex any part of the territory in question (although Yerevan did clearly and, for much of the period of occupation, unconditionally provide political, budgetary, military, and other forms of support to the entity its supporters call 'Artsakh'). Thus, it can be credibly said that effectually no one fundamentally disputed that these lands were occupied illegally; and that effectually no one disputed that they needed to be returned: four UN Security Council resolutions and various OSCE documents directly related to the conflict made this clear,[442] as did the formal positions of all the major powers, not to mention the rest of the world. The undeniable fact that Armenia had totally cleansed its own country as well as the then-occupied lands of its pre-war ethnic-

---

[440] The full text is available at: en.kremlin.ru/events/president/news/64384.

[441] Most Armenians and some of their supporters continue to call the city of Khankendi by its Soviet-era name, "Stepanakert." This term was imposed in 1923 by the Soviet authorities in homage to the Bolshevik revolutionary Stepan Shaumian, an ethnic-Armenian born in Tbilisi and nicknamed by his supporters the "Caucasian Lenin." Shaumian is best known for leading the short-lived Baku Commune (April-July 1918) whose most notorious act involved the massacre of thousands of Azerbaijanis: a 19 October 1919 article in the *New York Times* put the figure at 12,000 (see https://www.nytimes.com/1919/10/19/archives/land-of-eternal-fires-so-the-little-republic-of-azerbaidjan-is.html). At the time, Shaumian's Bolshevik faction was in a tactical alliance with the Armenian Revolutionary Federation (ARF). It almost goes without saying that neither was known for its commitment to pluralism, tolerance, the rule of law, and democracy. Some scholars claim that the massacre was initiated by the ARF and not the Bolsheviks. However, none have made a persuasive case that Shaumian took decisive action to prevent the violence, much less bring it to an end.

[442] Almost all the relevant UN and OSCE documents are available at: www.mfa.gov.az/files/shares/Documents%20of%20international%20organizations.pdf. The integral text of the original Madrid Principles (29 November 2007) is available at: www.aniarc.am/2016/04/11/madrid-principles-full-text.

Azerbaijani population[443] had obviously not helped advance its claim of victimhood or demand for remedial justice, either. (It may also be relevant to note that Armenia is itself now the most ethnically homogeneous country in both the Silk Road region and the OSCE space, a state of affairs without precedent for that territory.[444])

The bottom line was this: irrespective of ancient grievances, a convoluted historical record, and whatever other vagarious claims have been put forward, the situation was unambiguous: Yerevan's military occupation of those foreign lands had to come

---

443 During the First Karabakh War, Armenia's first head of state spoke of this during a closed meeting that was video recorded. See Levon Ter-Petrosyan, Address at the Inaugural Yerkrapah Congress, July 23, 1993, https://www.aniarc.am/2024/11/28/ltp-1993-erkrapah-congress-address, 12:05-14:08: "Armenia and Nagorno-Karabakh solved a problem that the Armenian people had not been able to solve for 600 years: Armenia and Artsakh have been completely cleansed of other ethnicities. I say again, this was a 600 year-old problem, and its significance will be felt by the Armenian people for another 600 years. Imagine if today there were those 180,000 non-Armenians in Armenia who lived here until 1988, then today we would not have a state. We would not be able to protect Zangezur, safeguard our northeastern regions, or preserve the shores of Lake Sevan. We would have had several new autonomies here. Let us recall that Azerbaijanis were the majority in three regions: Vardenis, Masis, and Amasia—and they were numerous throughout the Zangezur zone. This problem has been resolved—not as a gift from Heaven, but through the efforts of our movement, [through] the national liberation struggle of our people [led by] the Armenian National Movement [HHS] and its military wing, our units of self-defense, the units of [the] Yerkrapah [Volunteer Union (YMU)]. [And the problem has been resolved] also in Artsakh: today, all the territory of Artsakh, plus much more, is in the hands of Armenians." With regard to "all the territory of Artsakh, plus much more,"—i.e., the Azerbaijani territories occupied by Armenian forces between the two Karabakh Wars—the census data presented by the occupation authorities in 2005 indicates that 6 individuals were identified as Azerbaijani (and 125 as "other"), out of an indicated total of 137,737 (the numbers are taken from *2005 Census of the Nagorno-Karabakh Republic*, "Table 5.1 De Jure Population (Urban, Rural) by Age and Ethnicity," p. 197); the census data presented by the 'Artsakh' authorities in 2015 indicates that 0 individuals were identified as Azerbaijani (and 50 as "other"), out of an indicated total of 145,053 (the numbers are taken from *Population Census of the Republic of Nagorno-Karabakh-2015*, "Table 5.1 Population (urban, rural) by Ethnicity, Sex, and Age," p. 174).

444 Evidence of the extreme ethnic homogeneity of Armenia is extrapolated from the "Historical Index of Ethnic Fractionalization (HIEF) version 2.0 dataset for the year 2013" (the latest year contained in the dataset) compiled by Lenka Dražanová and archived in the Harvard Dataverse (available at: dataverse.harvard.edu). The HIEF is an ethnic fractionalization index for 165 countries across all continents. The ethnic fractionalization index corresponds to the probability that two randomly drawn individuals within a country are not from the same ethnic group. Armenia's ethnic fractionalization score (EFindex) for 2013 is 0.045. Only six other countries ranked lower in 2013: Japan (0.019), North Korea (0.02), Bangladesh (0.025), Tunisia (0.03), Egypt (0.041), and Jordan (0.044). The HIEF dataset does not include the following OSCE participating States: Andorra, Holy See, Iceland, Liechtenstein, Luxembourg, Monaco, and Montenegro. For an overview of the dataset, see Lenka Dražanová, "Introducing the Historical Index of Ethnic Fractionalization (HIEF) Dataset: Accounting for Longitudinal Changes in Ethnic Diversity," *Journal of Open Humanities Data*, vol. 6 no. 1, 2020.

to an end, and the hundreds of thousands of Azerbaijani civilians forcibly expelled from those same lands had to be allowed to return.

The Armenian irredentist claim to the former NKAO (but not the seven surrounding districts, which were conquered outright out of a combination of desiring to establish a security buffer and precipitating an Armenian colonization effort that did not, in fact, materialize in substantial numbers) was based on falsely equating the concept of national self-determination with the avowed right of secession: the former falls qualifiedly within the scope of international law whereas the latter does not. And the reason is simple: the avowed right of secession directly infringes on the right of sovereignty and territorial integrity. Moreover, by construction, self-determination is subordinate to sovereignty and its corollary, territorial integrity. In the geopolitical rough-and-tumble, there are three basic ways to counter this subordination: by treaty (when the aggrieved state signs away its legal territory), by a decision of the UN Security Council (essentially, by mandating the appropriation of sovereign state lands, a highly theoretical possibility), or by force and conquest (maintenance of occupation). Armenia knew full well that the first and second options were effectually impossible; thus, it had opted, from around the time of the breakup of the Soviet Union, for the third. Now this last, too, has run its course.

There seem to have been at least two immediate causes that resulted in the onset of the dénouement of the conflict between Armenia and Azerbaijan. *First*, Yerevan's increasingly agitated advocacy of the false equation of self-determination and secession, as discussed above. One saw this in terms of statements coming out of Armenia in the years before the Second Karabakh War that made it clear that Yerevan was no longer interested in participating in good-faith negotiations that would have as their strategic objective the end of the military occupation of the sovereign lands of Azerbaijan (this will be discussed below). *Second*, this rhetoric was matched, increasingly, in terms of actions on the ground: incremental increases in the bellicosity of ceasefire violations and provocations. The attack at dawn on 27 September 2020 perpetrated by Armenian forces that resulted in a number of Azerbaijani deaths in Azerbaijani territory unclaimed by Armenians was judged by Baku to have been a step too far: the strategic patience of Azerbaijan was brought to an end after decades of fruitless talks led by the 'international community' aimed at peacefully and multilaterally reversing a military occupation.[445]

Obviously, Azerbaijan had been preparing for this eventuality: Baku's counterstrike was not a spur-of-the-moment reaction.

---

445 The use of the term "international community" is an example of what social scientists call "false universalism," namely the tendency to present as global in scale and scope something that is in fact predominantly Western or Western-led (the OSCE Minsk Group Co-Chairs was composed of two Western states and a non-Western one; the Minsk Group as a whole was also predominantly composed of Western states, as can be ascertained by the composition of its permanent membership: Belarus, Finland, France, Germany, Italy, Russia, Sweden, Türkiye, and the United States, as well as Armenia and Azerbaijan; on a rotating basis, the OSCE Chairmanship-in-Office Troika was also a permanent member). Hence, the political and scholarly rhetoric in the West gives the impression that the term "international community" is synonymous with "the world"—that its use intimates (1) a set of normative convictions universally held in common; (2) the existence of a shared global approach to policy questions; and (3) a worldwide acceptance of burden-sharing in the name of solidarity. This is simply ludicrous and becomes rather obviously so once Amitai Etzioni's definition of 'community' is brought forth: "a shared moral culture and bonds of affection." See Amitai Etzioni, *From Empire to Community: A New Approach to International Relations*, New York: Palgrave Macmillan, 2004, p. 49. At best, we could say, the "international community" can be understood as the "arena for minimizing conflict and maximizing common interests in deference to the minimum common denominator." See Ernst B. Haas, "International Integration," *International Organization* 15, no. 3, Summer 1961, p. 392. Cynics, of course, would add that "the idea of international community, though it presents itself as the general interest of all its constituent parts, is in fact the preoccupation of a subset of international actors whose claim to speak for all is highly dubious. [...] The international community is [...] the voice of classically liberal normative aspiration: what the world should be like. [...] This comes in many guises, from various forms of cosmopolitanism and universalism on one side to various particular iterations such as American exceptionalism or Western civilization on the other." See Tod Lindberg, "Making Sense of the 'International Community'," *Working Paper of the International Institutions and Global Governance Program of the Council on Foreign Relations*, January 2014, pp. 11, 15-16.

But there was nothing politically, legally, or morally wrong with its chosen course of action: the country acted well within its right of "inherent" self-defense under Article 51 of the UN Charter, which unambiguously includes the use of force. Clearly, Azerbaijan took pains to ensure the steady improvement of its military capabilities and worked diligently to lock in the strong, effectually unconditional support of Türkiye that made it harder for other major outside powers to exert undue pressure on Azerbaijan to stick to evidently fruitless negotiations or renew its subscription to sterile agendas set by others, and so on. Azerbaijan also chose its moment of execution impeccably: our companion chapter to this book examines in more detail the "perfect timing" of the Second Karabakh War by providing a survey of contemporaneous external developments and the postures and preoccupations of relevant foreign actors.

But again, the emphasis needs to be put on Yerevan's evident and categorical unwillingness, prior to the onset of the Second Karabakh War, to bring the occupation to an end peacefully, through good-faith negotiations. This is the fundamental point. Thus, Yerevan's words and its resulting actions led directly to the Azerbaijani counterattack. Yerevan did not think Baku would respond decisively to what amounted to a war of attrition, in part because it overestimated the extent of its own external backing. This was obviously a failure of Armenian statecraft.

We can be justified in delivering such a harsh judgment on the basis of even a cursory examination of the reactions to the July 2020 military flare up at the uncontested (albeit undelimited and non-demarcated) state border between the two countries, which took place near critical energy and transportation infrastructure nodes. During this intense period, Armenia was very publicly told by Russia and others that it could not invoke the protections under Article IV of the Collective Security Treaty Organization (CSTO).[446] Instead of understanding this to mean that it could not rely on the unconditional support of its main treaty ally and should therefore return in earnest to the negotiating table, Yerevan threatened to attack the network of oil and gas pipelines that run from Azerbaijan through Georgia into Türkiye and from there onto the territory of EU member states like Greece and Italy.[447] This was understandably interpreted by Azerbaijan—but also by Georgia, Türkiye, and Azerbaijan's Western strategic energy partners—as representing a clear and present danger to their respective core national interests and to regional energy security arrangements designed to ensure a diversification of supply from Russia originating in the landmark 1994 "Contract

---

446 On 14 July 2020 Armenia's permanent representative to the CSTO Permanent Council Viktor Biyagov stated, "The existing situation is a cause of attention and concern for the entire Organization and for each of its member states, since it's an attempt of direct aggression against one of the members of the Organization in the zone of responsibility of the Organization. We call on our allies to demonstrate solidarity and support in line with the nature of the CSTO Charter. This unprecedented situation becomes a serious test for each of us and for the entire Organization." The call went unheeded. This statement should be read in light of the refusal of the CSTO to even hold an emergency meeting to address the July 2020 clashes. The CSTO took the same position during the Second Karabakh War, as of course did Russia itself. During the war, (on 7 October 2020), Putin stated on the Rossiya24 television network, that "we have certain obligations as part of the [CSTO] treaty. Russia has always honoured and will continue to honour its commitments. [...] It is deeply regrettable that the hostilities continue, but they are not taking place on Armenian territory." Kremlin spokesman Dmitry Peskov was even more explicit, saying Russia's obligations under the CSTO "do not extend to Karabakh." For the Putin and Peskov quotes, see "Russia's Security Guarantees for Armenia Don't Extend to Karabakh, Putin Says," *Moscow Times*, October 7, 2020.

447 During the Second Karabakh War, Armenia followed through on its threats to take aim at Azerbaijan's infrastructure network. For a partial chronology of these attacks, see Hikmet Hajiyev, "Attacks by Armenia against Azerbaijani Civilians and Critical Infrastructure Should Not Be Overlooked," *Euractiv*, October 16, 2020.

of the Century."⁴⁴⁸ It stands to reason that Moscow took unkindly to such threats for the simple reason that their execution would have set a dangerous precedent for Russia's own pipeline network in places like Ukraine as well as to the then-ongoing Nord Stream project connecting the country directly with Germany.

But this is far from the whole story: it is not enough to point the finger at Armenia. The principal outside mediators—the Co-Chairs of the Minsk Group (France, Russia, and the United States)—are also at fault: there was a formal negotiation process, launched in 1992, that had essentially produced no concrete results on the ground since the May 1994 ceasefire mediated by Russia, in the sense that the occupation of the former NKAO and the seven surrounding districts had not come to an end, Azerbaijani refugees and internally displaced persons (IDPs) had been prevented from exercising their right of return, and so on. In other words, for nearly three decades—including more than a decade since the onset of the G-Zero world—the Minsk Group led negotiations the objectives of which were clearly and unambiguously set down on paper. The 'international community,' in the form of the Co-Chairs, gave themselves the responsibility of leading a defined process to achieve a defined result, and yet the conflict remained unresolved: prior to the onset of the Second Karabakh War, *none* of the Minsk Group's defined objectives had

---

448 During an interview with Turkish broadcaster Habertürk on 14 October 2020, Aliyev stated, "Armenia is trying to attack and take control of our pipelines. [...] If Armenia tries to take control of the pipelines there, I can say that the outcome will be severe for them." Had Armenia's attacks been successful, it seems a near certainty that Türkiye would have intervened directly in the war. Although no evidence has emerged in public, it seems likely that what almost certainly amounted to a 'red line' was communicated by Ankara to Moscow at the highest level; if so, it is equally likely that the Kremlin would have communicated this to the Armenian leadership. The fact that Armenia ceased trying to target Azerbaijan's energy and transport infrastructure around this time lends credence to this speculation. Corroboration of a sort on the foregoing can be found here: "Pashinyan expressly forbade usage of Iskander on two strategic sites of Azerbaijan – Russian reporter reveals details of conversation with Onik Gasparyan," Aysor.am, February 24, 2021.

been achieved—not even close. Thus, their actions or inaction—whether by design or circumstance—resulted in the perpetuation of a status quo that was the opposite of the agreed objectives. So, this is why it is not enough to just point the finger at Yerevan.

Unravelling

And so, we come to the start of the dénouement of the war. Objectively, the solution to the conflict was predicated upon the return of the aforementioned occupied lands by Armenia to Azerbaijan: that is what the various documents of the 'international community' indicated, particularly those of the UN Security Council and OSCE. This result could have been achieved through diplomacy—through negotiations—or through war. It is a truism of contemporary political science to affirm that the former is preferable to the latter, of course. And this was indeed the option that had been pursued by Azerbaijan in good faith for decades. The problem was that this good faith was not only unreciprocated by Armenia, but it was instrumentalized and abused throughout much of the interbellum period, particularly after the onset of the G-Zero world. Yerevan simply believed that it could stall indefinitely, all the while entrenching its occupation. All appearances that a breakthrough was approaching turned out to be illusory or duplicitous. And instead of heeding the rather commonsensical lesson *quieta non movere*, Armenia continued to provoke Azerbaijan and violate the ceasefire (of course, Azerbaijan did so too).

This took place in parallel to various incendiary remarks by Armenia's leadership that Azerbaijan rightly interpreted as constituting the abandonment of the pursuit of a peaceful, negotiated solution to the conflict within the previously agreed framework. Five examples will suffice to make this point. *One*, in late October 2018, Pashinyan told then-U.S. National Security Adviser John Bolton that "those who determine whether to resolve the Karabakh conflict or not are the people of Armenia, the people of Artsakh, and the diaspora because this is a pan-Armenian issue."[449] *Two*, in late March 2019, Armenia's then-defense minister David Tonoyan called on the country to prepare for the pursuit of a "new war for new territories" hours after Pashinyan had held his first official meeting with Aliyev in Vienna.[450] *Three*, in mid-May 2019, Pashinyan effectually repudiated the Madrid Principles, thereby rejecting the existence of a documentary basis for resolving the conflict.[451] *Four*, in early August 2019, Pashinyan declared, in occupied Khankendi no less, that 'Artsakh' is a part of Armenia,[452] which Baku interpreted as being tantamount to a political declaration of Yerevan's intent to formally annex Azerbaijan's sovereign territories. And *five*, right after the July 2020 military flare up at the state border between the two countries, Pashinyan stated that the "Azerbaijani myth that their army can defeat the Armenian Army" in order to force Armenia to "make concessions has vanished. [...] Azerbaijan's position that the negotiations are the continuation of war and they should help to address military objectives at the negotiation table undermines the meaning of the

---

449 Vladimir Socor, "How Yerevan Walked Away From the 'Basic Principles' of Karabakh Conflict Settlement," *Eurasia Daily Monitor*, November 25, 2020.
450 "David Tonoyan. 'Territories for Security' format will no longer exist" (translated from Armenian), Aravot.am, March 30, 2019.
451 "Armenia's Pashinyan rejects Madrid Principles for resolving Karabakh conflict?" News.am, May 10, 2019.
452 Pashinyan's exact words were "Artsakh is Armenia, period." See "'Artsakh is Armenia,' Says Pashinyan during Stepanakert Rally," Asbarez, August 5, 2019.

whole peace process."[453] In short, the occupier kept aggressively pushing the aggrieved party (according to international law) and the foreign mediators did nothing in response. No wonder that Azerbaijan judged the situation to no longer be tenable. Frankly, by the start of the Second Karabakh War, Armenia no longer had a solid leg to stand on—no just cause to complain.

Thus, both on the field of battle and at the negotiating table, Armenia overplayed its hand; Yerevan lost, in part, because the "Pashinyan government became a hostage of its own nationalist rhetoric"[454] while failing to adopt what a South Korean political scientist may have been the first to term a "porcupine defense."[455] Perfect timing aside, Azerbaijan won for two other basic reasons. *First*, because it had patiently built up its military prowess (a topic that is beyond the scope of this article[456]); and *second*, because its leadership fully understood the transformed geopolitical circumstances in play as a result of the onset of the G-Zero world characterized, as noted above, by the fact that no single country or durable alliance of states can proffer a coherent, uncontested set of ideas or policies that amount to a credible and confident claim to international leadership. The resulting global power

---

453   "July victories took us to new level of resilience: PM Pashinyan," Lragir.am, July 23, 2020.

454   "Glen E. Howard: Fighting in Nagorno Karabakh Going Quite Badly for Pashinyan," Azernews, October 2, 2020.

455   Chae-Ha Pak, "A Grand Strategy for Korea's Defense," *The Korean Journal of Defense Analysis* 1, no. 2, 1989, pp. 192-193, defines this posture thusly: "the basic concept must be that since we would obviously be the loser should they invade us (because of their enormous size and military might), we have to do everything within our power to deter such an invasion. While we could not overcome an invasion [...], we have to sharpen our military expertise and systems mainly in terms of accuracy, so that they are as effective as the poisonous quills of a porcupine. If we are perceived not to be such an easy pushover, they will be less likely to attack us, just like the little porcupine which most larger and better-equipped hunters usually avoid." Cf. William S. Murray, "Revisiting Taiwan's Defense Strategy," *Naval War College Review* 61, no. 3, Summer 2008, pp. 2-27.

456   A good short summary of Russian sources on this point is made by Alexander Stronell, "Learning the Lessons of Nagorno-Karabakh the Russian Way," IISS Online Analysis, March 10, 2021.

vacuum, characterized by centrifugal geopolitics at the level of the major powers, was starting to be filled by nascent efforts to establish a centripetal regional order in the Silk Road region and held together by, *inter alia*, an Azerbaijan that increasingly conducted itself in accord with the precepts of a keystone state (as explained earlier in this chapter). And this gave Azerbaijan a strategic advantage the significance of which Armenia simply did not fathom.

But this simply should not have been the case. Aliyev made no secret of his thinking or his conduct. Consider, for example, the following words pronounced in February 2019:

> I have always said that the force factor is coming to the fore in the world. Look at how international law is flagrantly violated in various parts of the world. Whereas earlier attempts were made to somehow conceal that, today they don't even see the need for that. Today, the 'might is right' principle prevails in the world. This is a new reality. We must be ready for it. The world is changing, and we must be prepared for these changes. Fortunately, we have been building up our economic and military power for many years. We were somewhat preparing ourselves for the current situation and are now ready for it. Therefore, the force factor has always been and will remain on the agenda. We see this in the example of not only our conflict but also in many other conflicts around the world. Therefore, we will use various opportunities, and the restoration of the territorial integrity of Azerbaijan is our main goal. The people of Azerbaijan should know that this is the main task of every citizen and

the main task of the state. We will continue our policy in this direction.[457]

By war's end, Aliyev had been able to secure recognition from those that matter most that Azerbaijan has been geopolitically lifted up, as it were, to the level of an autonomous actor—a keystone state that is now indisputably a direct and level participant in regional affairs that is poised to take on the role of an autochthonous guarantor of peace, security, and prosperity in the Silk Road region. There is undoubtedly a certain irony that Azerbaijan achieved this by tactically consenting to the presence of Russian and Turkish troops on its own soil. To wit: the 10 November 2020 tripartite statement provides for a "peacekeeping contingent of the Russian Federation" composed of 1,960 regular Armed Forces personnel (and equipment), whose presence was guaranteed to last five years. In this context, we should note, however, that the Russian military has maintained a continuous presence in the South Caucasus from around the time of the French Revolution, with the exception of a few short years following the Bolshevik Revolution. The weight of this fact should be measured against another clause of the tripartite statement and what came afterwards. The clause reads thusly: "In order to increase the effectiveness of control over the implementation of the agreements by the Parties to the conflict, a peacekeeping center shall be deployed to exercise control over the ceasefire." We note that there is no mention of Türkiye. However, one day later (on 11 November 2020), the defense ministers of Russia and Türkiye signed a memorandum to "establish a Joint [Monitoring]

---

457   Ilham Aliyev, "Interview to Real TV," February 12, 2019.

Centre to control the ceasefire and all hostilities in the zone of the Nagorno-Karabakh conflict."[458] Shortly thereafter (on 17 November 2020), the Turkish parliament authorized the deployment of Turkish Armed Forces personnel as well as civilians to this center. We can make two observations on the basis of the above events. *First*, their arrival in Azerbaijan at the very end of 2020 represents the first time in a century that Turkish troops are durably deployed in the South Caucasus. *Second*, this represents the first time *tout court* that non-Russian troops are deployed in the South Caucasus with the perspicuous consent of Russia, which had for two centuries held a monopoly on this matter in this part of what Moscow used to call its "near-abroad."

We are now in a better position to affirm that the 10 November 2020 tripartite statement represented the beginning of the final stage in the geopolitical emancipation of Azerbaijan (its end is represented by the complete withdrawal of Russian peacekeeping troops and Turkish military personnel from the country in April-June 2024, precipitated by the 19-20 September 2023 "antiterrorist measure" that led to the formal extinction of "Artsakh" on 1 January 2024). More broadly, it represents a paradigm shift in the Silk Road region: certainly, Putin achieved important tactical gains for his country; yet, ironically, he appears to have been unable to prevent a country whose name is most conspicuously absent from the document in question from emerging as a principal strategic beneficiary (alongside the victor, of course) of the region's now evident geopolitical heterogeneity.

One indication of this is that plenipotentiary and commercial discourse in the Silk Road region is now being conducted

---
458 "Russia, Turkey Sign Memorandum on Creation of Joint Centre to Control Ceasefire in Karabakh," *Sputnik Globe*, November 11, 2020.

in various Turkic locutions to a greater extent than it has been in many centuries. Another is the manner in which the ongoing peace process between Armenia and Azerbaijan is being managed. The first stage consisted of a lot of moving parts, with aspects of the endeavor being concomitantly *mediated* by the President of Russia, *facilitated* by the President of the European Council, and *supported* by the U.S. Secretary of State and U.S. National Security Advisor (and, to some extent, the presidents of France and Türkiye as well as the EU High Representative for Foreign Affairs and Security Policy) and their respective staffs. The start of the second stage is traceable back to October 2023 and has been increasingly characterized by direct bilateral talks between the two parties taking place at agreed venues provided by trusted third parties, including Kazakhstan. Confirmation came in April 2024 thanks to two events: *one*, the diplomatic fallout of a high-level meeting involving senior U.S. and EU officials and the Armenian prime minister on 5 April 2024, the outcome of which Baku interpreted as a new trilateral cooperation platform (including a military component) the result of which disqualified Washington and Brussels to continue acting in a fair or neutral manner (this also explains Baku's dismissal of a last ditch, remedial effort by the lame duck Biden Administration to organize a trilateral meeting in December 2024); and *two*, the onset of a series of concrete results beginning in mid-April 2025 stemming from direct agreements between the two parties in the context of their border demarcation process. Success in the Armenia-Azerbaijan peace process is still not a foregone conclusion, however: a derailment is still possible, notwithstanding the fact that each of these foreign players portray themselves as honest brokers and both

Baku and Yerevan—at least in the first stage, as defined above—seemed to trust sufficiently their various approaches, albeit to varying degrees. Although Moscow and the Western actors do not trust each other's intentions, initiatives, and actions in almost all other geopolitical theaters, some evidence—perhaps even a preponderance of the evidence—indicate that the main foreign players did not (and perhaps still do not) seek to systematically and decisively undermine each other's efforts in the Armenia-Azerbaijan theater.[459]

Meanwhile, the heretofore central role of the Minsk Group has disappeared, which confirmed the redundancy of the Madrid Principles that the 'international community' long championed through ultimately ineffective diplomacy.[460] Namely, for the first time in decades, the operative document accepted by the two belligerents to the conflict is silent on the self-determination question—what the Madrid document called the "final legal status of Nagorno-Karabakh."[461] The 10 November 2020 document also stipulates the construction of "new transport links [...] to connect [Azerbaijan's] Nakhchivan Autonomous Republic and the western regions of Azerbaijan" so as to provide for the *"unobstructed movement of persons, vehicles, and cargo in both directions"* (surely it is significant that the term "unobstructed" is used *only* in the context of this route).

---

459 The revelation that American, EU, and Russian officials met secretly in Istanbul on 17 September 2023 to discuss the Armenia-Azerbaijan peace process speaks to this point. See Gabriel Gavin, Nahal Toose, and Eric Bazail-Eimil, "EU, Russia, and US Held Secret Talks Days Before Nagorno-Karabakh Blitz," *Politico*, October 4, 2023.

460 For more on this, see Robert M. Cutler, "The Minsk Group is Meaningless," *Foreign Policy*, July 23, 2021.

461 The status issue was a cornerstone of the Minsk Group negotiation parameters. Cf. Thomas de Waal, "Unfinished Business in the Armenia-Azerbaijan Conflict," *Carnegie Europe*, February 11, 2021: "The OSCE's Basic Principles framework document, which was the basis for negotiations since 2006, looks even less viable than before. The Armenian side did not embrace it strongly before the conflict and the Azerbaijani side has disavowed it as a result of the conflict."

To repeat: this new postwar reality was set in motion primarily by Armenia in the runup to the Second Karabakh War and as a consequence of its outcome—although, we now add, obviously the result turned out to be the opposite of what Yerevan presumably had in mind.

In writing about tragedy, Aristotle speaks of the moment of reversal: the inflection point (*eschaton*) of misfortune, as it were, that marks the onset of the tragic unravelling (*lusis*) or dénouement, as noted earlier. When those textual references are closely examined in light of others (Arist. *Poet.* 1460b6, 1460b22, and 1461b24), we see that *lusis* (and the related *luein*) is also given the meaning of "solution" (or "solve") or "resolution" (or "resolve"). When all this is put together with yet another passage in the same text (Arist. *Poet.* 1454a37), whereby *lusis* connotes "interpretation" (or "analysis"), we understand the Aristotelian lesson that tragedies contain in themselves their own unmistakable interpretation, namely that the "inflection point" (*eschaton*) is foreshadowed by the "complication" (*desis*, literally "knotting") that becomes the *lusis*. Such an understanding is wholly consistent with the events that produced Armenian *hubris* in the period 1988-1994, the resultant complacency with the status quo established by the 1994 ceasefire, the blindness to subsequent geopolitical change brought on by the onset of a G-Zero world, the woeful underestimation of its chief adversary, and the fantastic hope in the temporal sempiternity of the frozenness of the conflict that prevailed in Armenian circles right up to the start of the Second Karabakh War. In this, one finds what Aristotle calls the "lesson of tragedy" (*pathei mathos*): the mistaken demand men make that their particular and thus partial understanding of justice must prevail in the world (see Arist. *Poet.* 1453a8-23).

On this basis, we can assess that Armenia failed to see that its maximalist position was no longer tenable, certainly not in September 2020—an inexcusable act of geopolitical malpractice on the part of the leadership in Yerevan that naturally produced the sort of response one would expect from the leadership of any serious, strategically conscious, and geopolitically literate keystone state such as Azerbaijan. Simply put, Armenia was outmatched, outgunned, and outmaneuvered. And it has only itself to blame for, in effect, having bluffed itself into a corner from which it could not extricate itself. This calls to mind the pitiful lamentation of Prometheus as he helplessly contemplated his *moira*: "To my friends, I am a spectacle of pity. [...] I stopped mortals from foreseeing doom [...] I drugged them with blind hopes" (Aesch., *PV* 248-252). This in turn calls to mind the characterization made by Soviet-era dissident and political prisoner Vardan Harutyunyan of Armenian leaders from 1998 onwards as "all speaking with the same [...] irresponsible heroism"[462] We thus agree with two assessments offered by Michael Reynolds in the aftermath of the end of the Second Karabakh War: "Armenian statecraft [...] revealed itself as a mix of delusional self-confidence and naive sentimentality" and "Armenia's example perhaps suggests that historical trauma coupled with limited experience of sovereignty can lead states voluntarily to pursue self-destructive policies."[463]

---

[462] Vardan Harutyunyan, "The Plagues," *Aravot*, October 4, 2023. I am indebted to Onnik James Krikorian for bringing this formulation to my attention.

[463] Michael A. Reynolds, "Confidence and Catastrophe: Armenia and the Second Nagorno-Karabakh War," *War on the Rocks*, January 11, 2021.

This accurate assessment is consistent with Aristotle's understanding of tragedy.

Conflicting Strategic Takeaways

At the end of the day, the consequences of the onset of the G-Zero world were tragically misunderstood by Armenia and understood by Azerbaijan.

For Yerevan, the strategic takeaway went something like this: as Artsakh is to Armenia, so South Ossetia (or Abkhazia—take your pick) is to Russia. In other words, geopolitics in the South Caucasus will remain primarily within the referential purview of the traditional suzerain, who will remain on the side of Armenia. The country's national interest consists in entrenching a posture of clientelism and supplication towards the sole arbiter that truly matters, which will engender its leadership to demonstrate solidarity and support for a state dedicated to the expression of nearly unconditional loyalty. Thus, Yerevan must continue to rely on its great power ally to maintain the status quo of occupation while feverishly encouraging its diaspora to convince rival great powers that genuine outreach on the part of Armenia to each of them will be forthcoming shortly. This is evidently not the way it was put in any written form or public forum. But the point is that the above formulations are wholly consistent with the discursive logic informing Yerevan's official foreign policy posture right up until the start of the Second Karabakh War.

For Baku, in contrast, the strategic takeaway went something like this: in continuing to reach out to major external powers, Azerbaijan will not allow itself to become dependent on any single line of access to the outside world. The country will strategically harness the fact that most of the world's major powers look at the Silk Road region—specifically, the South Caucasus—and conclude that they have variously important national security and economic interests. And it will take advantage of the fact that there is tension between those same major powers in terms of how they each define their respective interests in that part of the world by managing relations between them in such a way as to ensure that Azerbaijan becomes a subject of the international system instead of a mere object of major power rivalry—indeed, that it positions itself (as noted above) as an indispensable country for the advancement of the strategic energy and ambitions of all the major powers that surround the Silk Road region—Western and non-Western alike. This strategic takeaway has been aptly translated into contemporary scholarly terminology by Ilgar Gurbanov, "conceptually classif[ying]" Azerbaijan's foreign policy posture in the following manner: careful bandwagoning, pragmatic balancing, strategic hedging, finding a balance of interests, predictability, and strategic patience.[464] From such considerations emerged a bedrock principle of Azerbaijan's national strategy: to ensure it becomes sovereign and strong enough so that it—and it alone—may determine the time and manner of the restoration of its territorial integrity (given the fruitlessness of negotiations). Niccolò Machiavelli had written pretty much the same thing more succinctly more than five centuries ago: "one should never fall in the belief you can find someone to pick you up." (NM, *P.* 24). As it appears from the perspective of Baku, the result of this line of reasoning is the coming-into-being of an exonerated state and its

---

[464] Ilgar Gurbanov, "Relevance of Non-Alignment for Azerbaijan's Foreign and Security Policy," *Caucasus Strategic Perspectives* 1, no. 1, Summer 2020, p. 16.

vindicated statesman who has long been teaching a masterclass in statecraft—an accomplishment all the more impressive given that his classroom is located in one of the world's most unforgiving and unenviable neighborhoods.

And so came to pass the liberation of Karabakh, which took place in a rough-and-tumble G-Zero world and an emerging local reality in which keystone states like Azerbaijan could come together safely to build an order in the Silk Road region sturdy enough to counter major power aspirations without antagonizing or providing any of them with a reason to oppose such a development.

Turning the Page?

The scale and scope of the horrors and vandalism wrought by the Armenian occupation and uncovered by Azerbaijan in the postwar period is grievous. The catalogue of offences can be classified into two periods that correspond to two types of outrages. *First*, the ethnic cleansing campaign, which was absolute in its success, as our earlier reference to the census data published by the occupiers makes clear. Given that the commission of that crime had taken place almost entirely during the First Karabakh War, one could argue that, at least in some instances, those atrocities had taken place within the fog of war—certainly not as a justification, but perhaps as a mitigation. The crime may not have resulted in genocide in the strict sense, but it certainly produced a complete expulsion. *Second*, the demolition, desecration, and defilement of virtually everything built or cultivated by Azerbaijani and other non-Armenian hands. Almost all of this plunder occurred in the wake of the May 1994 ceasefire. This crime is in a way even more rotten: surely its perpetrators had acted with both method and malice of forethought. Some of this wanton conduct even continued right up until the hour of the withdrawal of occupying forces, as mandated in the 10 November 2020 tripartite statement. The resulting desolation, much of which I observed with my own eyes in the immediate aftermath of the 2020 war, reminded me like nothing else of the sowing of salt upon the soil of Shechem (Judg. IX:45). Thirty years of occupation had produced an archipelago of detritus, minefields, and mass graves.

More than four years after the end of the Second Karabakh War, it is still too early to speak of undertaking any sort of reconciliation in earnest, partly due to the unresolved yet often downplayed matter of reparations (Aliyev has stated that damage estimates "exceed $150 billion"). On the other hand, Aliyev has spoken of the "need to turn the page" and "win the peace."[465] This is reinforced by Azerbaijan's concerted efforts on making its liberated territories sustainably inhabitable.

It is also too early to speak in Yerevan of reconciliation in earnest: the Republic of Armenia as a political community—much less competing centers of influence in the Armenian world like the Armenian Apostolic Church, the ethnic-Armenian population of the former NKAO, and various Armenian diaspora organizations—has not indicated that it is prepared to take responsibility for the litany of crimes that were committed in the name of the titular nation during the occupation of Karabakh. This is both regrettable and understandable: since 10 November 2020, the Armenian state and the Armenian nation have entered

---

465 Ilham Aliyev, "Interview with *El Pais*," president.az, December 15, 2021.

into an even more profound crisis. The depth of this crisis has not been lessened by collective introspection (notwithstanding more recent attempts by Pashinyan and a few Armenian public intellectuals to initiate such a course of action); on the contrary, too many Armenians still associate their nation with victimhood—a condition reinforced by the effects of the September 2023 "antiterrorist measure." However, it serves no healthy purpose for either friend or foe to enable the Armenian world to present their suffering in other geographies and in generations past—a suffering that ought to be acknowledged without equivocation—as an extenuation for the aggression, carnage, and destruction that took place in Karabakh throughout the occupation. And yet there is a movement that seeks this sort of remedy; there is another that justifies this mayhem on the basis of a right of revenge or a doctrine akin to *Lebensraum*; there is yet another that simply denies anything nefarious happened. Adherents (and fellow-travelers) of all three aforementioned movements share a national starting point that equates autochthony with justice whilst pledging allegiance to a halcyon past that in truth fell to the wayside centuries, nay, millennia ago, and has no chance whatsoever of making a comeback.

There is thus still a distinct possibility that Armenia could opt to rebuff Azerbaijani overtures and the benefits these entail by choosing to pursue a strategy aiming to overturn the definitive result of the Second Karabakh War and the consequences deriving thereof, including the conduct of the "antiterrorist measure." This is both a futile and dangerous option, for even the possibility of its success would be predicated on the instauration of novel geopolitical circumstances that Armenia simply does not have the capability to engender, much less set in motion.

Yet there are Armenians in positions of power or influence who nonetheless believe the opposite and champion its pursuit. By way of conclusion, here is what, at a minimum, this sort of thinking would need to entail in practice. *First*, the sudden discovery of massive hydrocarbon and rare-earth mineral deposits (plus game-changing renewable energy sources) in Armenia or the country's rapid transformation into the Singapore of the Silk Road region. *Second*, the aptitude to safely and forever push Türkiye back out of the South Caucasus. *Third*, the ability to incentivize the "international community" to engage in the region on the side of Armenia more seriously, more consistently, and more durably than it ever has. And *fourth*, the wherewithal to entice Russia to support Armenia's maximalist position actively, unconditionally, and by any means necessary—up to and including a readiness to engage in an offensive military campaign against Azerbaijan (and almost certainly Türkiye) for the sake of land it has consistently recognized as being Azerbaijan's sovereign territory—and in political and economic conditions that are, shall we say, suboptimal for the Kremlin.

We cannot leave it unsaid that all the above would also need to take place more or less synchronously with the wholescale political isolation, economic constriction, and military disassembly of Azerbaijan. This is, of course, effectually impossible; frankly, it would require embracing a belief in the sort of divine intercession that so far has been limited primarily to the works and days of Moses and David: the founder and re-founder of a nation whose uniqueness is unbreakably tied to its covenantal status as *'am 'olam*—the eternal nation—or, as Leo Strauss once defined it, of having "one's roots deep in the oldest past and committed to a future beyond all futures."[466] The logical progression of such a truly heretical position would also require the categorical substitution of Jerusalem by Etchmiadzin—or, even more radically, of Christ by Gregory—as the eschatological focal point of humanity. That would indubitably constitute the paradigmatic definition of both theological absurdity and ethnophilic maximalism in the absence, of course, of a new divine revelation.

To this can be added the obvious, namely that there is no indication that Pashinyan is inclined to embark on a journey compatible with this or similar way of thinking. This is the hinge upon which agreement on the draft text of the peace treaty ultimately became possible, although the bottom-line appraisal of Pashinyan's approach—"predictably unpredictable, consistently inconsistent" [467]—made by a contributor to this volume who has followed the Armenian prime minister's career for decades, remains a cause for concern.

Gone Dreams, Harsh Realities

We can only hope that sagacity and common sense fully and enduringly prevail in Yerevan, for it would be truly foolhardy for Armenia to henceforth advocate, much less pursue, policies that would compound the effects of what amounts to a capitulation

---

466 Leo Strauss, "Memorial Remarks for Jason Aronson," in *Jewish Philosophy and the Crisis of Modernity*, ed. Kenneth Hart Green, Albany: SUNY Press, 1997, p. 475. It almost goes without saying that neither the classical version of political Zionism nor Israeli statecraft take much stock in the likelihood of miracles (cf. Ps. 137). The best response to the tendency in some Armenian circles to compare what their country ought to become with what Israel has been and remains is that of Jirair Libaridian, who quotes a phrase Saul Bellow wrote of Jean-Paul Sartre in *From Jerusalem and Back*: "a great deal of intelligence can be invested in ignorance when the need for illusion is deep." I was reminded of the existence of this sentence upon reading the missive written by Libaridian, which is referenced below.

467 Onnik James Krikorian, "The Pashinyan Conundrum: Predictably Unpredictable, Consistently Inconsistent," *Baku Dialogues* 6, no. 3, Spring 2023, pp. 156-173.

by burdening another generation of its citizens with the perpetuation of illusions and the realities of poverty and insecurity.

This includes refusing to come to terms with the reality that 'Artsakh' is finished. This is obviously difficult and painful for those who supported and may still latently or overtly support that secessionist project from the outside, much less for those who lived or still live within its self-proclaimed boundaries. But the Artsakh dream is gone for good, as is the dream of Greater Armenia. As Gerard Libaridian so aptly phrased it near the hundred-day mark of the end of the Second Karabakh War, "it takes a particular kind of impudence to prescribe again the cure to the disease that incapacitated the patient and brought him close to death."[468]

Armenia can be nursed back to health, or it can succumb to "disease." This is the binary choice faced by its citizens—and legitimately by no one else. With all the travails that the quest for peace has brought to Pashinyan's door, nevertheless it seems he would still rather enter into the annals of Armenian history as the man who crafted a peace than as one who lost a war. Perhaps the clearest public articulation of his peacemaking intention is contained in a statement he made in the Armenian parliament on 14 September 2022, which is worth reproducing here:

> We want to sign a document because of which many people will criticize us, scold us, call us traitors, they may even decide to remove us from power, but we will be grateful if as a result Armenia will have lasting peace and security in an area of 29,800 square kilometers. I clearly state that I will sign a document that will ensure that. I am not interested in

---

[468] Jirair Libaridian, "Response to Vahan Zanoyan," *The Armenian Mirror-Spectator*, February 7, 2021.

what will happen to me, I am interested in what will happen to Armenia. I am ready to make tough decisions for the sake of peace.

The prime minister's reference to "29,800 kilometers" is key, for this figure unmistakably excludes any territory claimed by 'Artsakh.' Such and similar statements represent Yerevan's acknowledgement that, as far as the Pashinyan government is concerned, the territorial conflict between Armenia and Azerbaijan over Karabakh has indeed come to an end.

The concluding assessment that flows from the cumulation of our present considerations is that Pashinyan does not want another war; and that he is fully aware of the paucity of realistic alternatives to forging a peace agreement, the pursuit of which he has committed himself and his government despite the opposition he faces from various quarters and the possibility that elements of Armenia's armed forces, police, and even security services are not under his full political control.

Aliyev, too, does not want another war; he is genuinely desirous of peace on terms he feels befit a country that, as he said in Lachin in September 2022, is "proud" to have "liberated our lands by force."[469] And it is precisely the sincere desire for such a peace that drives this statesman to strengthen preparations for martial deeds that may still be required to achieve it. However, pursuing a course of action that would require the commission of further deeds of this sort against Armenia is certainly not Azerbaijan's preference. Baku nonetheless elected to conduct an "antiterrorist measure" against Armenian military targets located *on its own ter-*

---

469 Ilham Aliyev, "Speech During a Trip to Lachin," president.az, September 21, 2022.

ritory (i.e., not in Armenia) in mid-September 2023. Although this undoubtedly resulted in another "lesson of tragedy," it resulted in "no recorded incidences of mistreatment" [470] and produced no "reports—neither from the local population interviewed nor from the interlocutors—of incidences of violence against [ethnic-Armenian] civilians"[471] that chose to depart the territory. Baku's reasons for taking this controversial step were several. *One* was a judgment that Yerevan was unwilling to make what Baku deemed to be necessary concessions on Karabakh-related issues within an optimal timeframe. A *second* was a determination that Armenia had not only not withdrawn its forces and military equipment from those parts of the former NKAO that fell within the Russian peacekeeping zone (as required by the terms of the 10 November 2020 tripartite statement) but that Armenia, with the assistance or at least complicity of the Russians, had in fact sent reinforcements in both men and arms to that part of Karabakh, which made it an intolerable "grey zone."[472] A *third* was the laying of untold numbers of new mines and, it seems, improvised explosive devices (IEDs) in the liberated areas by Armenians, which resulted in hundreds of Azerbaijani fatalities and injuries since the end of the Second Karabakh War, including six deaths in the hours preceding the "antiterrorist measure." A *fourth* was the unwillingness of representatives of Karabakh's ethnic-Armenian community to engage in timely and serious negotiations on the

---

470   Peter Kenny, "UN Refugee Agency Says It Has No Reports of Mistreatment of Armenians Fleeing Karabakh, Anadolu Agency, September 30, 2023.

471   Press Statement of the UN Office in Azerbaijan, October 2023, https://azerbaijan.un.org/en/248051-un-team-completes-mission-karabakh.

472   Putting a stop to the Armenian remilitarization of that part of Karabakh helps to explain Azerbaijan's decision to install a border checkpoint at the terminus of the Lachin Corridor, an act that cannot be considered to be in violation of the 10 November 2020 tripartite statement, which made no guarantee of *unimpeded* communication, nor did the installation of the checkpoint affect Russia's control of the Corridor itself.

terms of the dissolution of 'Artsakh' and the reintegration of that community into the constitutional fabric and legal framework of Azerbaijan.

Azerbaijan considered itself free to conduct its deliberations and undertake its resulting actions in this unforgiving manner because no aspect of the peace process can be said credibly to be taking place against the background of equal power dynamics. Both Pashinyan and Aliyev know who is stronger and who is weaker; and both know this will not change—in fact, both know the power disparity will grow further the longer the process drags on. Finally, both are fully cognizant of the fact that when their vital interests are in play, the leaders of responsible, strategically conscious, and geopolitically literate keystone states like Azerbaijan do not bluff; they keep their word, too. This is the "effectual truth" (NM, P. 15) that ought to drive the quest for peace to its successful conclusion.

Neither opponents of the peace dividend on offer nor foreign players sympathetic to the weaker party ought to be under the illusion that downplaying the harshness of the foregoing assessment would either serve their own interests in the long run or that of the object of their sympathy.

ABOUT THE CONTRIBUTORS

Svante E. Cornell is Research Director of the American Foreign Policy Council's Central Asia-Caucasus Institute and a co-founder of the Institute for Security and Development Policy (ISDP). He is also a member of the Royal Swedish Academy of War Sciences and Policy Advisor with the Jewish Institute for National Security of America (JINSA). Previously, he was Associate Professor of Government at Uppsala University and Associate Research Professor at Johns Hopkins University's Paul H. Nitze School of Advanced International Studies (SAIS).

Robert M. Cutler is Senior Research Fellow and Director of the Energy Security Program at the NATO Association of Canada and a practitioner member of the University of Waterloo's Institute for Complexity and Innovation. He is a retired Senior Research Fellow in the Institute of European, Russian and Eurasian Studies at Carleton University.

Michael Doran is Senior Fellow and Director of the Center for Peace and Security in the Middle East at Hudson Institute. Previously, he served as a Senior Director in the U.S. National Security Council, Senior Adviser in the U.S. State Department, and Deputy Assistant Secretary in the U.S. Defense Department.

Nikolas K. Gvosdev is Professor of National Security Affairs at the U.S. Naval War College. He is a 2024 Templeton Fellow and the Director of the National Security Program at the Foreign Policy Research Institute, where he is also a Senior Fellow in the Eurasia Program and Editor of *Orbis*. Previously, he served as Editor of The National Interest and Senior Fellow for the U.S. Global Engagement Initiative at Carnegie Council for Ethics in International Affairs.

Fariz Ismailzade is Vice Rector for Government and External Affairs and Professor of Practice at ADA University, where he serves concurrently as Director of the Institute for Development and Diplomacy and Editor-in-Chief of *Baku Dialogues. He is also* an independent Member of the Milli Majlis of Azerbaijan. He has been a Visiting Fulbright Scholar at Princeton University.

Onnik James Krikorian is a Tbilisi-based journalist and photojournalist from the UK who has covered the South Caucasus continuously since 1994. He regularly writes articles and analyses for a variety of regional and international publications, including *The Los Angeles Times, The Wall Street Journal, BBC, National Geographic, the Jamestown Foundation's Eurasia Daily Monitor, commonspace, the Independent,* and *The Economist*.

Damjan Krnjević Mišković is Professor of Practice at ADA University, where he serves concurrently as Director for Policy Research, Analysis, and Publications at the Institute for Development and Diplomacy and Co-Editor of *Baku Dialogues*. He is also a Fellow of the Agora Strategy Institute. Previously, he served as Senior Special Adviser to the President of the UN General Assembly, Senior Adviser and Chief Speechwriter to the Foreign Minister of Serbia, Director of Policy Planning and Analysis of the Presidential Administration of Serbia, Special Adviser to the President of Serbia, and Managing Editor of The National Interest.

Niklas Nilsson is a Senior Research Fellow with the Central Asia-Caucasus Institute and an Associate Professor in War Studies at the Swedish Defence University, where he also serves as co-convenor of the Hybrid Warfare Research Group (HWRG) and the Land Warfare Research Group (LWRG).

Michael A. Reynolds is Associate Professor of Near Eastern Studies at Princeton University, where he also serves as Director of the Program in History and the Practice of Diplomacy. He has been a visiting scholar at Harvard University and Moscow State Institute of International Relations (MGIMO).

Brenda Shaffer is a Research Faculty Member of the Energy Academic Group at the U.S. Naval Postgraduate School, a Non-resident Senior Fellow at the Atlantic Council Global Energy Center, and Senior Advisor for Energy at the Foundation for Defense of Democracies.

www.ingramcontent.com/pod-product-compliance
Lightning Source LLC
Chambersburg PA
CBHW031846220426
43663CB00006B/514